CHEROKEES OF THE OLD SOUTH

A People in Transition

CHEROKEES OF THE OLD SOUTH

A People in Transition

HENRY THOMPSON MALONE

THE UNIVERSITY OF GEORGIA PRESS
ATHENS

Paperback edition, 2010
© 1956 by the University of Georgia Press
Athens, Georgia 30602
www.ugapress.org
All rights reserved
Printed digitally in the United States of America

The Library of Congress has cataloged the hardcover edition of this book as follows:
Library of Congress Cataloging-in-Publication Data
LCCN Permalink: http://lccn.loc.gov/56013002

Malone, Henry Thompson, 1916–1977.
Cherokees of the Old South; a people in transition.
238 p. illus. 25 cm.
Includes bibliography.
1. Cherokee Indians. I. Title.
E99.C5 M3
970.3 56-13002

Paperback ISBN-13: 978-0-8203-3542-1

ISBN-10: 0-8203-3542-8

TO MY WIFE

PERRILLAH ATKINSON MALONE

CONTENTS

ILLUSTRATIONS

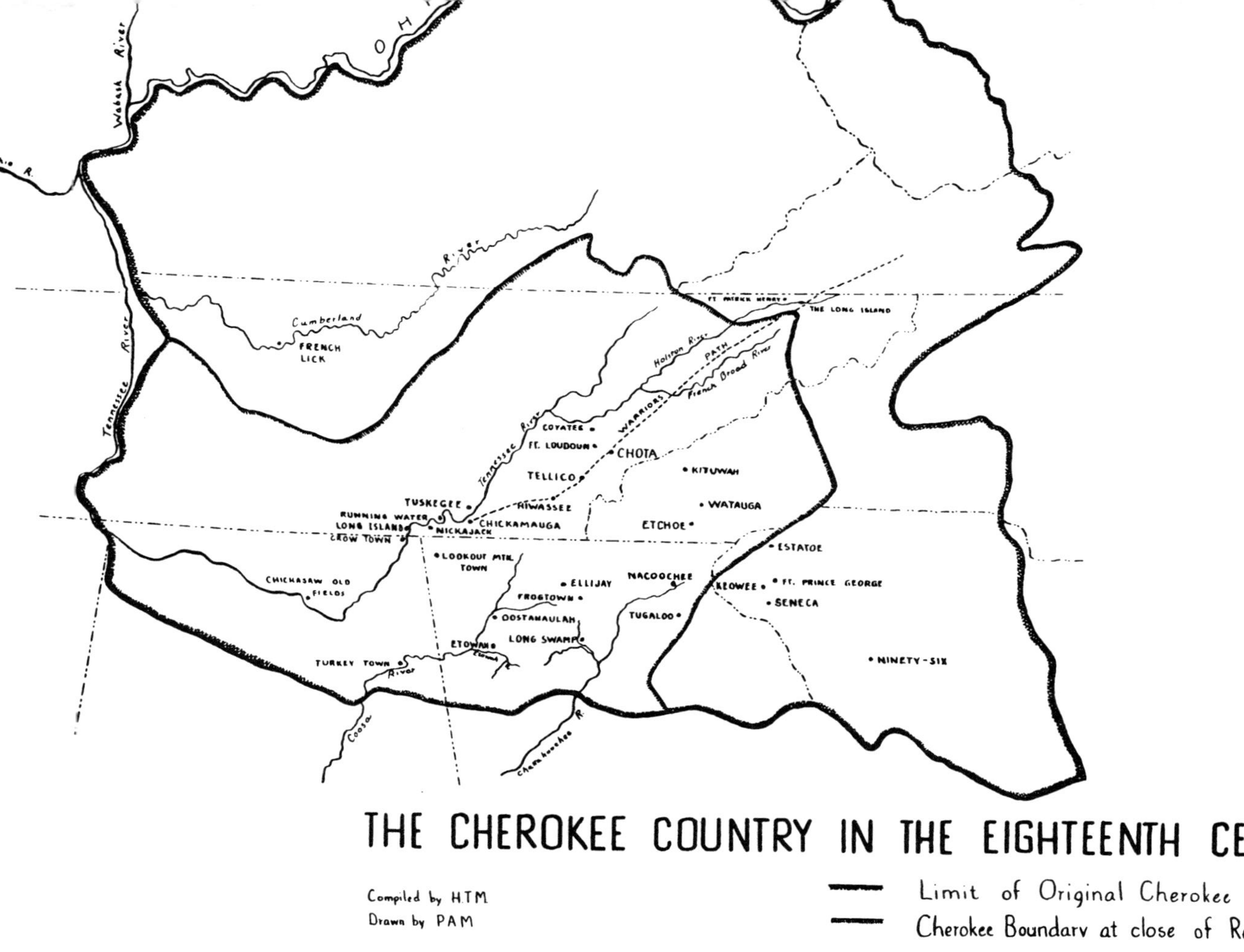
THE CHEROKEE COUNTRY IN THE EIGHTEENTH CENTURY
Compiled by H.T.M
Drawn by PAM
Limit of Original Cherokee Claims
Cherokee Boundarv at close of Revolution
OHIO
Wabash River
Ohio R.
Tennessee River
Cumberland River
FRENCH LICK
FT. PATRICK HENRY
THE LONG ISLAND
Holston River
PATH
French Broad River
WARRIORS
COYATEE
FT. LOUDOUN
CHOTA
TELLICO
KITUWAH
WATAUGA
ETCHOE
Tennessee River
TUSKEGEE
HIWASSEE
RUNNING WATER
LONG ISLAND
CHICKAMAUGA
NICKAJACK
CROW TOWN
ESTATOE
LOOKOUT MTN. TOWN
CHICKASAW OLD FIELDS
ELLIJAY
NACOOCHEE
KEOWEE
FT. PRINCE GEORGE
SENECA
FROGTOWN
OOSTANAULAH
TUGALOO
LONG SWAMP
ETOWAH
NINETY-SIX
TURKEY TOWN
Etowah R.
River
Coosa
Chattahoochee R.

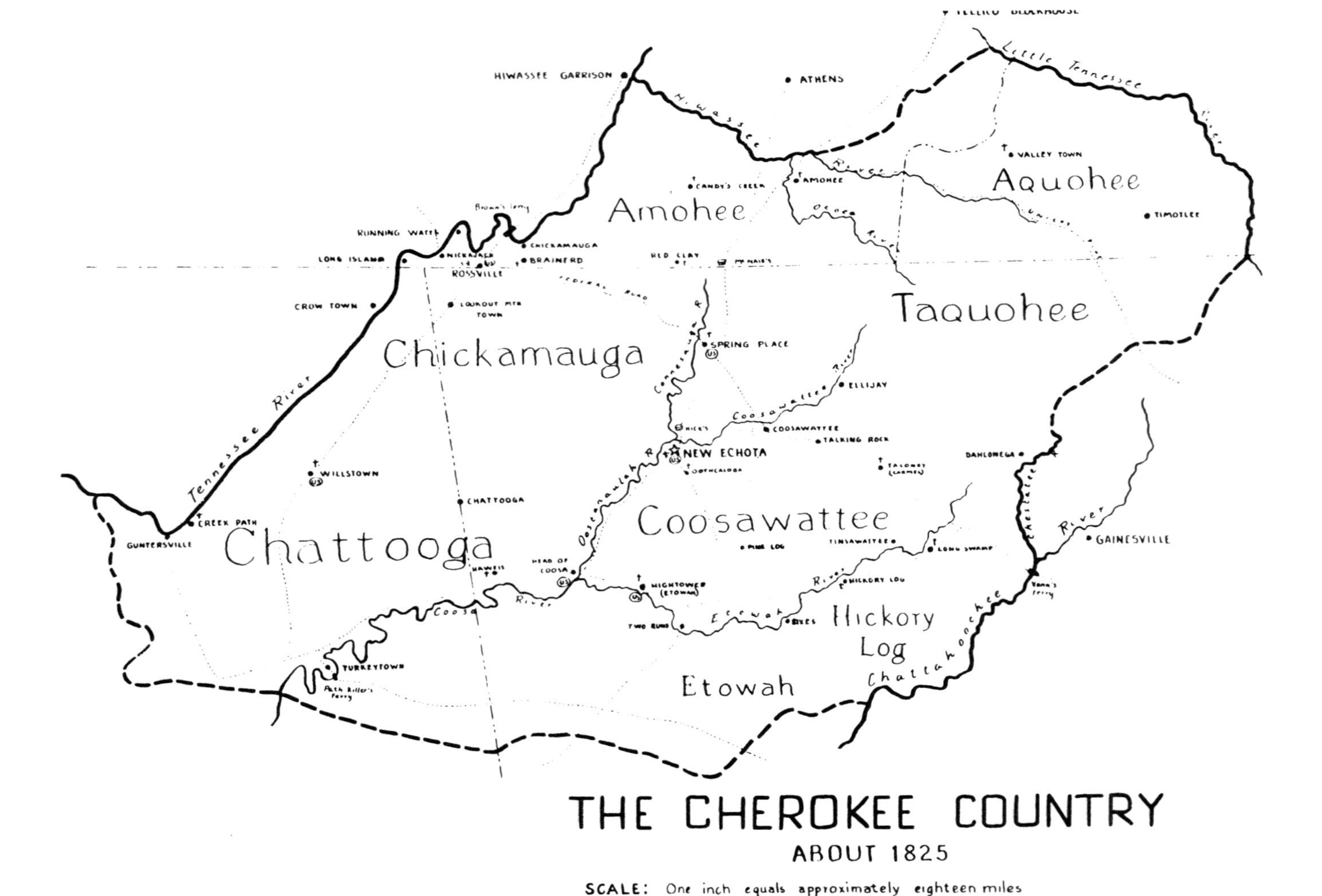

THE CHEROKEE COUNTRY

ABOUT 1825

SCALE: One inch equals approximately eighteen miles

PREFACE

A PLOW, a four-poster bed, and a crude sewing machine are stellar attractions at an Indian museum in Oklahoma. Inscriptions on these exhibits proclaim proudly that they were brought from Georgia in 1838 by emigrating Cherokees.

The virtue of these commonplace devices is that they represent graphically the remarkable social development of a nation of Indians more than a century ago. When land-seeking Americans forcibly ejected these people from their Southern Appalachian homelands during the 1830's, the Cherokees had attained a standard of living peculiarly similar to that of their white neighbors. They resided on farms and plantations in homes ranging from log cabins to palatial mansions; many of them wore the traditional frontier costume, while the dress of some resembled stylish fashion-plates. English was often spoken and occasionally written, but the majority of Cherokees used a conveniently developed native syllabary. Elected representatives carried on the affairs of a republican government; and a national bi-lingual newspaper kept the Cherokees informed, while proclaiming Indian progress to the world. Christian natives worked with white clergymen in mission stations and on circuits to bring religion and education to thousands.

These were remarkable developments for an Indian tribe of the early nineteenth century. In earlier times Cherokees were chiefly concerned with the problems of daily existence in a strife-torn land. Caught between the pressures of avaricious settlers and diplomatic intrigues, the Indians turned from fighting each other to protect their life and property. Their early social structure was picturesque, as many travellers attested; but it was basically primitive.

The forcible establishment of peace late in the 1790's, however, set the stage for a change in the social order of the Cherokees.

White men residing in Indian villages suggested new ideas for living, and gave the Cherokees mixed-breed descendants who led the others in the adoption of innovations. A suddenly benevolent Great White Father deliberately encouraged abandonment of primitive ways and gave utensils and instruction for mastering the white man's agrarian culture. Missionaries brought religious and educational advancement. Early in this curious metamorphosis, the tribe began a written code of laws, and shortly thereafter created a republic. As a dramatic acceleration in Cherokee development, a written native language was produced early in the 1820's, and the decade that followed witnessed what was probably the high tide in early nineteenth century Cherokee progress along the "white man's road." The literary climax was the emergence of a national newspaper dedicated to Indian welfare and justice, the *Cherokee Phoenix.*

Dreams of greater progress were rudely shattered in the 1830's. Impatient white men, brandishing long-held claims to Indian territory, stormed into the Cherokee lands. Within a few years the Cherokee Republic in the East had collapsed and its people had been driven into a strange western country.

The tragic history of the Cherokee people has been told and retold, but the emphasis has been on political aspects. The removal, treaty developments, and other phases of the Indian's relations with the white man have been minutely examined. A few anthropological studies have revealed various phases of tribal existence. Strangely neglected, however, has been the unique social transformation of the Cherokee Nation which resulted in an odd culture, a red-white amalgam, during the early nineteenth century. This is the story which is here attempted.

The sources for this study of early Cherokee social history are varied and widespread. Numerous original materials have been examined, the location and description of which are given in the bibliographical notes. The miracle of microfilm and photography has made available a pieced-together file of inestimable importance: a complete run of the *Cherokee Phoenix,* published in Cherokee and English from 1828 to 1834 at the height of early Cherokee social development. Numerous libraries have provided important items, notably the Library of Congress, the Emory University Library, and the Boston Public Library.

Portions of this work have appeared in the following magazines, whose editors have graciously permitted republication here:

Emory University Quarterly, Georgia Historical Quarterly, and *Tennessee Historical Quarterly.*

Grateful acknowledgement is offered to the following individuals who have made valuable contributions to this study: Mrs. Penelope J. Allen of Chattanooga, Tennessee, whose personal assistance has extended far beyond the use of her large collection of Cherokee materials; Mr. Gilbert Govan and Mr. Aubrey Folts, also of Chattanooga; Mr. William H. Gilbert, anthropologist and ethnologist, Library of Congress; the entire staff of the Bureau of Indian Affairs Records Unit, National Archives; Miss Mary Walker, Librarian of the American Board of Commissioners for Foreign Missions, Boston; Miss Carolyn Jakeman, Custodian of the American Board's voluminous manuscript file at the Houghton Library, Harvard University; Miss Rella Looney, Archivist of the Oklahoma Historical Commission; Dr. Edward E. Dale and Mr. Gaston Litton of the University of Oklahoma; Mrs. Mary Bryan, Archivist of the State of Georgia; and numerous members of the Emory University faculty and staff, notably Dr. Walter B. Posey, Dr. John H. Goff, Mr. L. L. Clegg, and Mr. Richard B. Harwell. The author owes a special debt of gratitude to Emory University and the Atlanta Division, University of Georgia, for financial assistance.

Particular acknowledgement is made to two persons whose understanding, encouragement, and technical assistance in the writing of this work cannot be over-stressed. They are Dr. Bell Irvin Wiley, Professor of History at Emory University, whose insistence on high standards of research and writing are a continual inspiration to his students; and the author's wife, Perrillah A. Malone, without whose suggestions, criticism, and hard work the study could not have been completed.

HENRY T. MALONE

ONE

PRIMITIVE FOREST CHILDREN

IN THE SUMMER of 1828 Joseph Vann was a successful candidate for the National Council, lower house of the Cherokee legislature. He may have conducted his campaign by travelling through his native District of Coosawattee, seeking the votes of his many agrarian countrymen. Undoubtedly he visited the Indian capital at nearby New Echota, but much of his contacts with fellow Cherokees must have been made right at home, for Joseph Vann lived in a spacious two-story brick mansion located near the cross-roads of two well-travelled thoroughfares, about two miles from present-day Chatsworth, Georgia.

It is not hard to imagine Vann in his home, seated in a comfortable chair near one of the large windows which overlooked the rolling countryside. He could watch some of his many Negro slaves toiling in the cotton and corn fields. Perhaps he read the latest Indian news and opinion in the bi-lingual pages of the *Cherokee Phoenix,* published at New Echota.

Like other progressive-minded Cherokees, Joseph Vann was the personification of the peculiar red-white culture which characterized his people in the early nineteenth century. He and other mixed-breeds were leaders in numerous and varied efforts to adapt the white man's ways to Indian life. A constitutional republican form of government, a national press, and a widespread agrarianism attested to this progress, which was also reflected in the Cherokee diet, dress, speech, commerce, and religion.

Far removed from such "civilized" customs were the ancestors of these Cherokees, whose primitive life was similar to that of other American Indians. A brief examination of the early developments and social structure of the Cherokees is a necessary prelude to a discussion of their subsequent cultural developments.

Who were the Cherokees? Originally, they were an Iroquoian tribe driven southward in successive groups during pre-Columbian times.[1] In the Southern Appalachians Cherokees settled among the highest portions of that great chain. Within these beautiful but isolated hills and valleys the Indians became a hardy folk. They were especially noted for their endurance and skill which served them well in hunting and warfare.[2]

Probably the first white men to see the Cherokees were Hernando De Soto's Spanish *conquistadores* in 1540. Their meager comments on Cherokee life generally depicted a primitive and occasionally an almost unbelievable backwardness among the first Indians encountered. By one account the Cherokees lived "on roots of herbs which they seek in the open field and on game killed with their arrows. The people are very domestic, go quite naked, and are very meek." Conditions farther west along the Tennessee River in present-day Tennessee and northern Alabama were described as more prosperous. Indians were observed eating corn, mulberries, pumpkins, cooked beans, and honey. Corn fields seemed bigger, villages better organized, and life more orderly. Some natives were found using oil produced from nuts, acorns, and bear fat, kept in large gourds called calabashes.[3]

Later Spanish exploring parties, notably that of Captain Juan Pardo in 1567, followed or crossed De Soto's trail in the Cherokee country. The prime object of these expeditions was to find gold and the chroniclers had little interest in recording social aspects of Cherokee life. More revealing are the remarks of a Spanish missionary who asserted that the Cherokees were superior to any Indians he had encountered. To this Jesuit they appeared "sedate and thoughtful, dwelling in peace in their native mountains; they cultivated their fields and lived in prosperity and plenty. Their morals were far superior to those Indians of lowlands: polygamy was unknown. . . ."[4]

After the Spanish discarded their inland search for gold, the Cherokees were left undisturbed by white invaders for about a century. If the French, who were actively trading among the Indians, ventured into the Cherokee country they seem to have left no record. As a result, almost nothing is known of Cherokee life during this era.

At the beginning of the eighteenth century, the "Cherokee country" included vast land (and hunting ground) claims covering a sprawling area. It stretched from the Ohio River to the southernmost reaches of the Tennessee River, westward and north along this river's valley, and eastward from the Great Kanawha to the headwaters of the Savannah.[5] Within this immense territory their villages tended to locate in four main regions: the Over Hill settlements, on the Tellico River below the Cumberland Mountains; the Middle Towns, on the Little Tennessee and Tuckasegee rivers; the Lower Settlements, on the headwaters of the Savannah; and the communities to the west of the Middle Towns near the Valley river, which became known as the Valley Towns.[6] The first Cherokee village may have been Kituwah, on the Tuckasegee River in the Middle Towns. A village on the Little Tennessee, Chota, rose in importance and by the eighteenth century had become the principal town (See Map A).[7]

The flora and fauna of the Cherokee country were varied and abundant. More than 800 species of plants were known and used by the Cherokees for food, medicine, and crafts. Most frequently cultivated were corn (maize) and beans, supplemented by peas, pumpkins, strawberries, tobacco, potatoes, squash, and gourds. The lush forests provided framework and covering for houses, as well as fuel, medicinal bark, and fibers for weaving and for twine. Animals were useful for food, clothing, shelter, and medicine.[8]

Cherokee expansion in the Southern Appalachians led to a lengthy series of wars with other Indians. The bitterest enemies of the Cherokees were the Creeks to the south and two tribes to the east and north, the Tuscaroras and the Iroquois. The Cherokees particularly dreaded the fierce raiding parties of their northern kinsmen, the Iroquois. When not engaged in defense of their lands the Cherokees utilized opportunities to launch quick raids against another enemy, the Algonquin tribe on the Ohio. These attacks and counter-attacks gave full meaning to the name applied to the North-South trail, the "Warrior's Trace." Enmity with the Creeks grew naturally out of the Cherokee usurpation of lands on the headwaters of the Coosa, the Chattahoochee, and the Savannah, and continued intermittently into the nineteenth century.[9] Rivalry and fighting also disturbed relations with the neighboring Shawnees, Savannahs, Congarees, Catawbas, Yemassees, Yuchi, Pedees, and Cheraws. Perhaps the most peaceful relations were those with the Chickasaws, traditional friends of the Cherokees, although some fighting between the two developed when the

Cherokees, under the pressure of white advances, attempted unsuccessfully to expand into the Chickasaw areas.[10]

Cherokee fighting prowess increased with experience, and by the eighteenth century all Indian intruders had been driven from Cherokee domains. The warriors had acquired particular skill with the more modern weapons, the gun and the knife.[11] In 1725 a British agent seemed certain that peace existed in a certain Cherokee town only because the men were "going out to Warr daily against the Creeks." Five years later several Cherokee leaders opposed an effort on the part of white men to bring about a truce between the Cherokees and their then current foes, the Tuscaroras, with the statement: "We cannot live without war: should we make peace with the Tuscaroras . . . we must immediately look out for some other with whom we can be engaged in our favorite occupation."[12]

One important result of frequent fighting and the development of a war economy was the gradual emergence of a group of well-known Cherokee leaders famous for military abilities or for skill in diplomacy. Perhaps the greatest of the eighteenth century leaders were Attakullakulla, Ostenaco, and Oconostota. Attakullakulla (or "The Little Carpenter"), "a man of remarkably small stature . . . but . . . of superior abilities," was probably the most outstanding Cherokee known to contemporary Europeans. Called "the Solon of his day," he was noted in his maturity for wisdom, oratory, and graciousness. Born around 1700, and known at first as Onkanacleah, he was taken to England at the age of thirty, and so developed a friendly attitude toward the English. This friendship remained fairly constant and was a valuable asset to the British during their struggles with France and their American colonies. Attakullakulla died just as the latter conflict ended.[13]

Oconostota occupied a higher position than Ostenaco but wielded less influence. Of powerful build and slow speech, Oconostota's fame lay in his war wisdom and resourcefulness. He and Attakullakulla gave the Cherokees an able leadership. Ostenaco, known as "Judd's Friend," led a delegation of chiefs who journeyed to England in 1761. Those accompanying him were Outacity (or "Man-killer") and Uschefeesy ("Great Hunter" or "Scalper").[14] Other Cherokee leaders of the century included Dangerous Man, Old Hopp, Caesar, Standing Turkey, Black Dog, Moytoy, and Dragging Canoe.[15]

Although inter-tribal strife was frequently a dangerous threat to the peace and security of frontier settlers, it was also an occasional boon to the European powers who could play one Indian nation off against another. The contemporary opinion on this practice was well expressed by a trader named James Adair, who observed that "one pack of wolves, was the best watch against another of the same kind."[16] The English used the consistent support given by the Cherokees to gain not only military and diplomatic advantage but profitable trading privileges as well. Probably the first Englishmen to visit the Cherokee country were James Needham and Gabriel Arthur, who led a small exploring party from the province of Virginia in April, 1673. The little group, sent by a trader named Abraham Wood, reached the Over Hill Cherokees in July and apparently were successful in establishing friendly relations and trading concessions for Wood. Arthur was left behind, "to learn ye language," while Needham attempted to return. Although he was killed on the journey, the party found its way back to Wood's trading house and reported success.[17]

The Cherokee lands interested not only commercial houses but governments as well. The English royal governors and colonial boards of trade spurred themselves to establish and maintain cordial relations with the redskins. In 1690 James Moore, Secretary of the Carolina colony, and Maurice Matthews went into Cherokee settlements in an effort to find gold and to make trading arrangements; but an unexpected attack upon Cherokees by frontiersmen thwarted the attempt.[18] In 1703 the Lords Proprietors of Carolina instructed Governor Johnson to

> take Great Care That the Indians be not abused and that all means may be used to Civilize them and that you Endeavour your utmost to Create a Firme Friendship with them & to bring them over to your part for yor better Protection & defense against ye Enemy the neighbouring French and spanyards against whome you are to Protect our sd Province. . . .

Similar instructions were issued to later governors, who made earnest efforts to carry out these intentions.[19]

Other colonies were also active in promoting better Indian relations. The Trustees of Georgia desired both to regulate and to improve trade and trading conditions, and as early as 1733 had laws enacted for that purpose. One of these edicts had the laudable purpose of seeking to end the practice of supplying liquor to the Indians. Others sought to establish friendly relations with Creeks and Cherokees and to set a rigid control on the important deerskin trade.[20] Virginia, of course, had been interested since the days of Abraham Wood. When Georgia began, much later, to assert a priority over the entire Cherokee trade, a prominent Virginian complained that "of late the new Colony of Georgia has made an act obliging us to go 400 miles to take out a license to traffick with those Cherokees, tho' many of their towns ly out of their Bounds, and we had carry'd on this Trade 80 years before that Colony was thought of."[21]

The techniques of the white man's commerce in the Cherokee country were probably exemplified in the activities of South Carolina traders. Charles Town was the hub center of this trade with the Cherokees, as with other Indian tribes. It was a common sight during the eighteenth century to see caravans loading up at the warehouses of Charles Town merchants for an Indian venture. The staple commodity which the Cherokees desired was coarse cloth; other items amongst the trader's stock with which he hoped to dazzle Indian eyes were blankets; hoes, axes, and other implements; and such miscellany as brass, kettles, salt, hatchets, guns, knives, powder and bullets, flints, tobacco, pipes, and rum. Especially appreciated were guns and ammunition, which, with the eagerly sought rum, were the most popular items by 1715.[22]

Perhaps the first trader to live in the Cherokee country was Eleazar Wiggan, whose presence there was noted as early as 1711. By 1716 he had so gained Cherokee confidence that he was given the affectionate title of "The Old Rabbit," and was serving as interpreter. In 1730 he accompanied Attakullakulla to London as official interpreter for the party. Outstanding among the later tradesmen was James Adair, of Scotch-Irish descent, who began an Indian trade with the Cherokees and Catawbas in 1735. A well-educated man, Adair attained much fame among the Indians, often giving advice and sometimes lending a hand with the fighting. Some traders were troublesome, of course. A visitor to the Cherokee country in 1776 noted somewhat sadly that "it is a fact, I am afraid too true, that the white traders . . . give great and frequent occasions of complaint of their dishonesty and violence: but yet there are a few exceptions."[23]

The effort of the English to maintain just trading practices was a major phase of their Indian diplomacy, which was generally successful. Courteous and generous treatment accorded to Cherokee leaders was a standard policy of the astute British officials. Such a procedure was exhibited in 1730 when Attakullakulla and other Cherokees were escorted to London by Sir Alexander Cuming for personal conferences with the King of England. A treaty highly favorable to the English resulted, although the agreement was somewhat unofficial since the Indian signers did not represent the entire Cherokee council. By the terms of the documents the Cherokees agreed to be allies of the English in the event of future war with outsiders, to "Keep the Trading Path Clean," to allow only British traders to enter Cherokee territory, and to return runaway slaves. Mutual friendship was pledged eternally, and the British promised that any English who killed Cherokees would be captured and punished.[24] Thirty years later the English in Virginia followed a similar policy when a Lieutenant Henry Timberlake escorted two successive delegations of chieftains from the Cherokee country to London. The value of Cherokee friendship with England's colonies was noted in 1760 by a London magazine in an item which described South Carolina Governor Lyttleton's recent successful invasion of Cherokee villages in the Lower Towns:

> The Cherokees are the most numerous nation of Indians adjoining to the British colonies on the continent; they . . . possess a country that extends from the frontiers of Virginia and Carolina, to the French settlements on the Mississippi. Hence their importance as allies to Britain is very evident.[25]

The treaty made in England in 1730 brought generally friendly and peaceful relations which lasted some thirty years. Traders consolidated their arrangements with the Cherokees, and individuals, companies, and colonial officials built up a thriving trade between Charles Town and the Indian country. Costly gifts to Cherokee leaders brought further guarantees of friendship.[26]

Important treaty conferences were held between representatives of Carolina and the Cherokee Nation. At the first meeting in 1753 and again in 1755 the Cherokees agreed to terminate their current war with the Creeks in return for a promise by the English to build forts within the Cherokee boundaries. This unusual request by the natives was probably due to the presence of French forts in the Creek country, the possible effect upon hostile Indians to the North and Northwest, and the desire to see unscrupulous traders curbed. The treaty of 1755 was settled at Saluda Old Towns, and resulted in a large cession of Cherokee claimed – but very sparsely occupied – land in upper South Carolina. British willingness to comply with treaty stipulations was evidenced to the Cherokees by the construction of three military posts: Fort Prince George, which was begun in 1753 near Keowee among the Lower Towns; Fort Loudoun, at the junction of the Tellico and Little Tennessee rivers, in the same year; and Fort Dobbs (near present-day Salisbury, North Carolina) in 1756.[27]

The peace so carefully established in the late 1750's was short-lived. Unfortunate misunderstandings, stupid management, and the machinations brought on by the diplomatic and military maneuvering of the French and Indian War resulted in a series of raids and counter-attacks between the Cherokees and English which in 1760-1761 finally led to a short but devastating war. One of the worst blows struck by the Cherokees was the massacre of the occupants of the recently established Fort Loudoun. In 1761 the whites crippled the Cherokees with the campaign led by Captain James Grant. So successful was Grant that he seems to have broken the Cherokee fighting spirit for several years. The Lower and Middle Towns were especially hard hit; fifteen settlements in the latter group were totally destroyed. Captain Grant's own estimate was that he "had destroyed fourteen hundred acres of corn, beans, and peas and driven five thousand Indians into the forest, where they were on the point of starvation."[28]

During the succeeding years the Cherokees slowly rebuilt their shattered towns and returned to their former relationship with the English; while the latter, fresh from triumph over the French, sought to consolidate control of newly won areas. One of the measures employed was the creation of two Indian districts, Northern and Southern. Appointed as His Majesty's Indian Agent for the Southern District was Edmund Atkin, who was given control of the Cherokees, Chickasaws, Creeks, and Choctaws. Atkin died shortly thereafter and was succeeded by John Stuart. The latter was well known to the Cherokees and demonstrated kindliness toward them even during the recent wars between Cherokees and English. On one occasion, when Stuart was captured and his life in danger, his liberty was bought by Attakullakulla who thereupon, by Cherokee custom, made Stuart his "eldest brother." The life-long friendship thus assured proved most profitable to the English.[29]

Mobile became Stuart's headquarters. From there he sent two representatives to reside in the Cherokee Nation, both of whom seem to have been well liked by the Indians. The first of these was Alexander Cameron, who lived at Keowee and later at Toquo in the Over Hill region. "Scotchie," as the Cherokees called him, married an Indian woman and founded a large estate named "Lochabor." The other deputy, John McDonald, settled at Chickamauga Creek and married a prominent Indian woman named Anne Shorey, halfbreed daughter of a white interpreter. Their grandson, John Ross, became a great Cherokee leader of the nineteenth century.[30]

Another British measure to control the newly won western country was the Proclamation of 1763 which forbade settlement beyond the Appalachian divide. Despite this prohibition, hundreds of migrants began to spill over into the Indian lands. The colonial Indian officials were not only forced to accept these migrations but to obtain a number of land grants from the Cherokees and other Indians. By the outbreak of the American Revolution, the Cherokees had lost thousands of acres.[31] Equally troublesome for John Stuart and his deputies were the actions of unscrupulous traders who seem to have taken advantage of the peace in 1763 to rush into Cherokee lands and capitalize on the rich trading opportunities there. Alexander Cameron wrote in 1766 concerning these men in the Cherokee country: "No Nation was ever so infested with such a set of villains, and horse thieves, they were enough to create disturbances among the most Civilized Nations." It was one of Stuart's regrets that he was not charged with authority over traders.[32]

From the Indian's viewpoint, activities of traders and diplomatic agents must have been far more tolerable than the continued pressure of the colonial frontiersmen and settlers. Evidence of this is found in the military assistance given the British. In 1766 at Stuart's request one hundred Cherokees went to the Ohio River and successfully attacked several villages of Illinois Indians whom it was believed the French were about to employ against the English.[33] A decade later Cherokees decided to aid England in the American Revolution.

The decision to help the British forces in this war was disastrous for the Indians. Already in 1775, just as the Revolution began, the Cherokees had sold the famous Henderson Purchase by which, for the consideration of £10,000 (paid in merchandise), Richard Henderson and associates acquired a huge tract comprising central and western Kentucky, southwestern Virginia, and part of northern and northwestern Tennessee.[34] If the Cherokees had joined the English in the Revolutionary War in the belief that they would be better protected by that alliance, they were dealt a heavy disappointment. In 1776 a force from South Carolina struck at towns on the Keowee and Tugaloo rivers. At the same time American troops from North Carolina and Virginia destroyed towns in the Over Hill region. As a result of these expeditions the Cherokees ceded in 1777 almost all of their lands in South Carolina and large tracts in North Carolina and Tennessee.[35]

Fighting continued on both sides until 1785, with the most stubborn resistance coming from a recalcitrant group of Cherokees who seceded after the Carolina cession in 1777 and established themselves first on Chickamauga Creek and later on the Lower Tennessee River. These die-hards became known as "The Chickamaugas of the Five Lower Towns" and were among the last of the Cherokees to lay down their arms.[36] For the majority of the Cherokee Nation the first real step toward peaceful relations with the new American republic came in 1785 with the Treaty of Hopewell; but a successful peace was not arranged until 1791, in the Treaty of Holston.[37]

For the Cherokees, then, the eighteenth century was largely one of fighting. The warfare often left their villages ravaged and the cream of their manhood dead. More than fifty towns were burned (some of them several times), hundreds of Cherokees were killed or put to flight, and tremendous property damage inflicted. Other disasters struck during that century: in 1739 and again in 1783 smallpox decimated the population.[38] Yet despite these calamities the Cherokees were able to adapt themselves to the situations which developed, making a living through whatever means available. Between wars and disease they built their huts, established their villages, and repopulated their land. The peak years of the century, as far as population and town growth were concerned, occurred in the era prior to the French and Indian War. A trader estimated in 1735 that Cherokee villages aggregated sixty-four, with a population of over sixteen thousand, including more than six thousand warriors. The estimates of numbers of fighting men, however, dropped successively to 2,590 in 1755, and 2,300 in 1760, while a survey of 1795 showed only 43 villages with a fighting strength of 2,500. Other estimates were even smaller.[39]

More than mere warriors and diplomatic pawns were the eighteenth century Cherokees. They were human beings who lived in cabins, obtained their food by hunting, fishing, and farming, and conducted their daily affairs as circumstances and tradition demanded or suggested. Aspects of their institutions and progress will be examined in detail in subsequent chapters.

TWO

THE EARLY CHEROKEES AT HOME

THE EIGHTEENTH CENTURY Cherokee village usually contained from twenty to sixty houses. The first known dwellings were rough lean-tos constructed of poles, but contact with white settlers led to adoption of log houses. By 1776 the log cabin was standard in the Cherokee country.[1] The manner of house-building was described by the naturalist-explorer William Bartram in 1776:

> The Cherokees construct their habitations on a different plan from the Creeks; that is, but one oblong four square building of one story high; the materials consisting of logs or trunks of trees, stripped of their bark, notched at their ends, fixed one upon another, and afterwards plaistered [*sic*] well, both inside and out, with clay well tempered with dry grass, and the whole covered or roofed with the bark of the chestnut tree or long broad shingles. This building is however partitioned transversely, forming three apartments, which communicate with each other by inside doors. . . .[2]

Several years later a Moravian missionary named Martin Schneider reported that the dwellings of Cherokees were "7 feet high to the Roof, 14 feet long & 10 feet broad. . . ." He further noted that windows were lacking and that the one door was usually very small.[3]

With the advent of cold weather Cherokee families took to the "hot houses" at night for greater sleeping comfort. These were small, dirt-covered, cone-shaped houses located close to the main dwelling, with openings so small that occupants could barely wriggle through. Use of these sleeping quarters was described by Schneider:

> After the Fire which is made in the Middle is burnt down, the coals

are covered with ashes. Their couches of Cane fixed round about are their Sleeping Places, which they scarce ever leave before 9 O'clock in the morning. Then they make again Fire for the whole Day & at night they make another. The Old People having but little & the Children, till they are 10 years old, no Clothes at all, they could not hold it out in cold weather without such houses.[4]

The largest building in the Cherokee village was the town-house, or council-house. Normally the local seat of government, it was also used for rituals and ceremonies. The town-house was a large building which could seat some five hundred persons on its circular "sophas," or benches. Walls of posts and tree-trunks supported a bark roof "neatly placed, . . . tight enough to exclude the rain." This in turn was covered with a thin layer of earth, the whole being supported by a tight network of rafters mounted upon a series of posts in concentric design.[5] Shells may have been used in ornamenting the town-houses. They and other furnishings were sometimes renewed, perhaps annually, in a special ceremony during which "seats, mats, dance rattles, drums and sticks, medicine blow-canes, &c," were burned.[6] When Henry Timberlake visited one of these council-houses, which appeared to him like "a small mountain at a little distance," he seemed struck by its gloomy interior:

It is . . . extremely dark, having, besides the door, which is so narrow that but one at a time can pass, and that after much winding and turning, but one small aperture to let the smoak [from the council fire] out, which is so ill contrived, that most of it settles in the roof of the house.

William Bartram noted, however, that owing to the custom of using "dry small wood divested of its bark" there was very little smoke in the council-houses. In warm weather the council met in an open pavilion often built upon a large oblong base.[7]

Of the four main areas of Cherokee habitation, the Over Hill country was the most powerful during the greater part of the eighteenth century. Two of the important towns, Chota and Tellico, were located in this isolated region. The earliest available description of Chota is that of the pioneer English trading entrepreneur Abraham Wood. Writing to a friend in London, Wood told of the town as seen by the exploring party which he had sent out in 1763 under James Needham:

This towne is seated on ye river side, haveing ye clefts of ye river on ye one side being very high for its defence, the other three sides trees of two foot over, pitched on end, twelve foot high, and on ye topps scafolds placed with parrapits to defend the walls and offend theire enemies which men stand on to fight. . . . This forte is foure square; 300: paces over and ye houses sett in streets. . . .[8]

About sixteen miles from Chota, on the "Tenase" (now Little Tennessee) River, was the town of Tellico, sometimes called Great Tellico, whose importance grew during the eighteenth century. Its size grew also, and apparently by 1725 it and the neighboring town of Chateauke had grown into each other's limits. In that year an English Commissioner named George Chicken noted that Tellico was "very Compact and thick Settled. . . . Here are two town Houses in this Town by reason they are the people of Two towns settled together . . . both Enforted and their houses which they live in all Muskett proof." In 1741 a Frenchman named Antoine Bonnefoy was captured by the "Cherakis" and taken to a village in the Over Hill country. According to his account the village was called "Chateauke and Talokoa [Tellico], which are two different councils, though the cabins are mingled together indistinguishable."[9]

Colonel Chicken was much interested in the military aspects of the Cherokee towns. His remarks on Old Estatoe, in the Lower Towns, emphasize these characteristics:

We . . . went to Old Estotoe a large Town & very well fortifyed all round with Punchins and also ditched on the Outside of the sd Punchins (wch Ditch) is Stuck full of light wood Spikes so that if the Enemy should ever happen to fall therein, they must without doubt receive a great deal of Damage by those Spikes – I also Observe that there are Sevl. New flankers made to the fortifications of the Town & that the Town House is also Enforted.

Perhaps the most detailed information about Cherokee villages in the eighteenth century comes from William Bartram, whose journal locates and describes some forty-three villages observed during an exploratory visit to the Cherokee country in 1776.[10]

A curiously important although foreign element in the larger Cherokee towns during the middle and late eighteenth century was the white traders. Many of them served the Indians in several capacities other than that of convenient salesman and buyer; some, like James Adair, became trusted advisers on military, diplomatic, and government affairs. Their homes and trading posts acquired considerable local prestige, and generally far surpassed the native houses in construction, appearance, and furnishings. The trader's house became a mecca for travellers and interested or admiring Indian leaders. Usually the merchantmen found one or more Indian women who served as cooks and housekeepers, and often as mothers of half-breed children. The example of these entrepreneurs was extremely important in molding the Cherokees to the white man's ways.

The Indian inhabitants of the Cherokee towns were almost universally average to tall in height, with slender bodies. These characteristics were true for both sexes. In comparison with the Creeks, Bartram found the Cherokees taller and more robust. He thought them "the largest race of men I have seen." As for the women, Bartram was charmed: "They are tall, slender, erect and of a delicate frame; their features formed with perfect symmetry, their countenance cheerful and friendly, and they move with a becoming grace and dignity."[11] Although the Cherokee hair was usually long, black, and coarse, complexions were often very light, more so than that of other Southern Indians. An ancient Cherokee tradition indicates that many had beards prior to the coming of the white man but discarded them thereafter in order to avoid being confused with the newcomers.[12]

The language spoken by Cherokees, which sounded "loud somewhat rough and very sonorous" to Bartram, more closely resembled Iroquois than that of any Southeastern tribe. The Cherokee tongue varied with the geography of the nation, producing three main dialects: the Elati, used in the Lower Towns; the Atili, spoken by Valley and Over Hill Indians; and the Kituwah, or Middle Towns variation. Absence of a Cherokee written language undoubtedly helped them along the white man's road, for they early began to utilize the convenience of the newcomer's writing. Martin Schneider reported that it was used for profanity. Generally speaking, political and economic trends in the eighteenth century tended to favor English as the predominant white language adopted.[13]

Despite Schneider's notice in 1783 that the very old and very young Cherokees seemed to have very few if any clothes, it is likely that most Cherokees kept themselves very well clad. Clothing, which was usually made by the women, included the following items: a shirt of buckskin, which hung to the knees, and became generally known as "the Cherokee hunting shirt"; robes of buffalo and other animal skins, or sometimes of a decorated textile; moccasins or boots of cloth; and, as an undergarment, a loincloth or "flap" of animal skin. Frequently the body was decorated with tattooing or paint; jewelry of many sorts was worn, usually earrings, neckpieces of strung clam shells, and bracelets. Generally, men's garb was gaudier than women's. In extremely cold weather gloves of animal skin may have been worn.[14] On ceremonial occasions costume varied from near nakedness to elaborate regalia. During the London visit of several Cherokee leaders in 1730, a press notice described thus the ceremonial attire of the Indians when they were presented to the royal family:

> The Indian King had on a scarlet jacket, but all the rest were naked except an apron about their middle and a horse's tail hung down behind. Their faces, shoulders, etc., were painted and spotted with red, blue and green. They had bows in their hands and painted feathers in their heads.[15]

One element in the Cherokee personality which merits special mention is their deportment. William Bartram remarked of this quality:

> The Cherokees in their dispositions and manners are grave and steady; dignified and circumspect in their deportment; rather slow and reserved in conversations; yet frank, cheerful, and humane; tenacious of the liberties and natural rights of man; secret, deliberate and determined in their councils; honest, just, and liberal, and ready always to sacrifice every pleasure and gratification, even to their blood, and life itself, to defend their territory and maintain their rights.

In times of peace white men like James Adair found the Cherokees especially generous and hospitable.[16]

Another trait among Cherokees which usually captured the interest of visitors was the status of females. Women occupied a surprisingly high place in the village life. Land was inherited and kinship traced exclusively through their side of the family. They participated in council meetings and elections of chiefs, and they frequently took part in Indian warfare. One of the small streams in the Cherokee country was named "War-woman's Creek"; Bartram was told that it was so called in honor of a Cherokee woman who had gained a great victory through her valor and stratagem. Perhaps the most famous of these feminine leaders was the celebrated Nancy Ward, who rose to a position of considerable prominence near the turn of the century.[17]

The striking equality between the Cherokee sexes is indicated to some extent by marriage arrangements. Early custom usually demanded that elaborate negotiations be carried on by kinfolk of the couple, during which the groom would send the bride a ham of venison as a pledge of ample food supply, while she gave him an ear of corn as a token that the fields would be tended and food prepared. It seems certain that the life of the Cherokee women was not one of drudgery and unrequited toil. Far from it. They were a respected group whose family ties were highly important in the village and social economy. Bartram wrote, with obvious admiration: "The women are tall, slim, and of a graceful figure, and have captivating features and manners, and I think their complexion is rather fairer than the men's."[18]

Perhaps because of the very independence which women possessed, Cherokee marriages were often of short duration. Adultery was frequent enough to provide occasional remarks by European visitors. James Adair, who lived among the Cherokees long enough to become an authority on their society, thought that "the Cheerake are an exception to all civilized or savage nations, in having no laws against adultery. . . ." Attributing this lack to the rule of their "petticoat-government," he added, "their marriages are ill observed, and of a short continuence." Adair described an unusual example of revenge meted out to a Cherokee adulteress:

> Once in my time a number of warriors, belonging to the family of the husband of the adulteress, revenged the injury committed by her, in her own way; for they said, as she loved a great many men, instead of a husband, justice told them to gratify her longing desire—wherefore, by the information of their spies, they followed her into the woods a little way from the town, (as decency required) and then stretched her on the ground, with her hands tied to a stake, and her feet also extended, where upwards of fifty of them lay with her, having a blanket for a covering.

On one occasion a white man who wanted his marriage to a Cherokee woman to endure, took her to a white preacher, where he sought to have her understand and be converted to Christianity and its conception of marriage. Lieutenant Timberlake also noted the short-term marriages, but seemed to find some improvement:

> There is no kind of rites or ceremonies at marriage, courtship and all being . . . concluded in half an hour, without any other celebra-

tion, and it is as little binding as ceremonious; for though many last till death, especially where there are children, it is common for a person to change three or four times a year. Notwithstanding this, the Indian women gave lately a proof of fidelity, not to be equalled by politer ladies, bound by all the sacred ties of marriage.[19]

Household tasks provided the chief duties of women. The care of home and children, the manufacture of clothing, and the preparation of food were their immediate responsibilities; but they also assisted in agricultural duties. For sewing they used needles bought from traders, or "very fine slit Sinews." Timberlake reported that men often helped in sewing clothing. The women, he added, made "pretty belts, and collars of beads and wampum, also belts and garters of worsted."[20] There was some manufacture of home goods, too, such as baskets, mats, and pottery; presumably these chores were performed by women. Red and white clay was available for pottery, which was said to be able to withstand "the greatest heat."[21]

Because of the bounties of nature and their own interest in agriculture the Cherokees enjoyed a fairly varied diet. Fish, wild fowl, deer, bear, buffalo, and hogs were barbecued, roasted, boiled, or fried. Potatoes, pumpkins, beans, peas, squash, and peaches supplemented the more staple corn, which was boiled, roasted, and made into Indian bread, hominy, corn cakes, or mush. At a ceremonial meal attended by Timberlake in 1761, the vegetables were served on "small, flat baskets made of split canes, which were distributed amongst the croud [*sic*]." Buffalo, bear, and deer meat were served, but the visitor found it "greatly overdone." He was highly discomfited at having to eat "without knives and forks, and being obliged to grope from dish to dish in the dark." Timberlake, who was fascinated by the baking which he witnessed at a private home, described the product as

very good Indian bread, baked in a very curious manner. After making a fire on the hearth-stone, about the size of a large dish, they sweep the embers off, laying a loaf smooth on it; this they cover with a sort of deep dish, and renew the fire upon the whole, under which the bread bakes to as great perfection as in any European oven.

Salt for cooking and meat preserving was obtained from salt springs, or "licks," where possible. Otherwise, if salt could not be had from traders, salt ashes from burned stream-weeds or hickory were used.[22]

William Bartram found the hominy mush very tasty. At a meal with an Indian chief in 1776, he was served "a refreshing repast," which concluded with "a pleasant cooling liquor made of homony well boiled, mixed afterwards with milk . . . served up . . . in a large bowl, with a very large spoon or ladle to sup it with." While in the town of Kahiti, Schneider was invited to eat some peaches which had been boiled in a kettle. "My fingers served me instead of forks," he wrote. "They make themselves Earthen Ware . . . but these never washed otherwise than by the licking of the dogs." The Moravian thought the hominy distasteful: "Their most common & for us the worse Tasted Dish, is Homony, which they let grow sour, & handle it very unclean."[23]

Beverage seems to have been far less varied than food. Other than water the Cherokees apparently had little use for drinks with their meals. In 1761 Henry Timberlake noted that water was "their only drink," and that it was handed about in "small goards." One beverage which was fairly common, although not at mealtimes, was alcohol. With the coming of white men rum, whiskey, and brandy found their way into the Indian country in appalling quantities. Laws enacted against the sale of these intoxicants were the most numerous type on colonial statute books; but smuggling was the all-too-frequent and troublesome answer to this legislation. Martin Schneider recorded his disgust at the liquor traffic: "They must give 2 Deer skins for one quart of miserable brandy."[24]

During the eighteenth century, with its accent on militarism, the primary sources of food for the Cherokees were forests and streams. Some dependence was necessarily placed on the products of the somewhat primitive agricultural system. Temperate climate and fertile soil reduced labor to a minimum; as Timberlake expressed it, the soil required "only a little stirring with a hoe, to produce whatever is required of it. . . ." Women and old men could thus be expected to do the farming when warfare required able-bodied men elsewhere. Between wars men did most of the cultivating with some assistance from women.[25]

The calamities of fighting, disease, and famine must have been fairly frequent in the eighteenth century, for each Cherokee village seems to have used a communal granary as a starvation preventative. Foods for the granary were furnished by the individual from his cultivated patch, or from the "Town Plantation." The latter usually consisted of several lots which were farmed jointly. Responsibility for getting this work accomplished was delegated to an overseer, who called the workers together at appointed times and led them to and from the fields. Of this activity Schneider wrote:

In the midst of every Town is . . . a round Tower of Earth about 20 Feet high . . . on which is a little House. . . . Here the first Chief climbs up every Morning at the Time of the Work in the Field, & calls the People with a loud voice together; these must come with their Indian-corn Hoes, & go together in proper order to work. And tho' every family has its own field, yet they begin fellowshiply on one End and continue so one after the other till they have finished all. As every one must come & hoe it seems they prevent thereby that not easily a Family can come to want by carelessness. They dare not go from their work till evening but the Women must bring them their victuals into the field.[26]

An important source of labor supply in the production of food was slavery, both Indian and Negro. The use of Indian slaves for tilling the ground had been noted as early as the 1540's by the De Soto party. The Spanish themselves seem to have led other Europeans in taking Indian prisoners for slavery; a royal proclamation authorized the practice early in Spanish colonial history, with the stipulated excuse that it was the only way to expose Indians to Christianity! Indian slavery existed in French colonies though it did not have legal sanction until the eighteenth century. In English colonies, however, a direct bid was made for control of the traffic in Indian prisoners. South Carolina was especially active in this trade. As early as 1693 a Cherokee delegation protested to the royal governor of South Carolina that the Congaree, Esau (Catawba), and Savannah Indians were capturing Cherokees and selling them to the English. That Cherokee slaves were still in demand in the middle of the eighteenth century is evident from the inducements held out by North Carolina when it sought to raise troops for the Cherokee War in 1760. Those who could capture "an enemy Indian," said the recruiting posters, could hold him in slavery.[27]

Although Negro slaves were held by Cherokees during the eighteenth century, their numbers appear to have been negligible. The Negroes may have been booty of warfare, or runaways captured in the Cherokee country. The red masters often worked side by side with their slaves, and intermarriage was not unknown.

Assistance rendered by the Negro laborers during the difficult period after 1750 must have been greatly appreciated.[28]

Cherokee agricultural methods were noted by Bartram in 1776. Near Cowe on the Little Tennessee River he rode through several corn and bean fields. The corn was about eighteen inches tall and seemed free of weeds; he found that "the Beans planted at the Corn-hills were above ground. . . ." At nearby Whatoga it seemed to him that the fields extended right up to the council house. As he rode into the little town Bartram saw that "on every side, appeared little plantations of young Corn, Beans, &c. divided from each other by narrow strips or borders of grass, which marked the bounds of each one's property, their habitation standing in the midst." An indication of the quantity of Cherokee agricultural production is revealed in the report made by the successful Colonel Christian, following his invasion of the Indian country in October, 1776. In discussing the abandoned provisions which gave "variety to the dietary" of his forces, Christian reckoned that in the Over Hill Towns there were more than forty thousand bushels of corn, and over ten thousand bushels of potatoes.[29]

The Cherokees seem to have grown the tobacco used for ceremonial and medical purposes and to have obtained most of their smoking tobacco and pipes from traders. On formal occasions, such as those terminating war, the smoking of the peace pipe was an important ceremony. Peace pipes were made of red and black hued stone, had stems three feet long, and were decorated with quills, dyed feathers, and deer's hair. Fraternal smoking of a less formal character might have followed the procedure described by Bartram in 1776 on the occasion of his visit to the home of a chief. After supper, he wrote,

> Tobacco and pipes were brought; and the chief filling one of them, whose stem, about four feet long, was sheathed in a beautiful speckled snake skin, and adorned with feathers and strings of wampum, lights it and smoaks a few whiffs, puffing the smoak first towards the sun, then to the four cardinal points, and lastly over my breast, hands it towards me, which I cheerfully received from him and smoaked.[30]

The usual stock found on Cherokee farms during the early part of the eighteenth century consisted of swine and horses. Hogs were apparently treated in the manner described by Adair:

> they are forced to feed them, in small penns, or inclosures, through all the crop-season, and chiefly on long pursly, and other wholsome

weeds, that their rich fields abound with. But at the fall of the leaf, the woods are full of hiccory-nuts, acorns, chestnuts, and the like; which occasions the Indian bacon to be more streaked, firm, and better tasted, than any we meet with in English settlements.

Horses were generally abundant among the Cherokees, although pressure of hunger in the Indian villages caused an occasional depletion of stocks. Adair noted that the Cherokees had "excellent horses," of which there were "a prodigious number" before 1760; but the famine resulting from white invasions in the Cherokee War of that year forced the Cherokees to "eat the greatest part of them." The Indian horses were particularly useful to traders either for riding or as packhorses, while the Indians themselves made all-round use of them.[31]

Owing to a strange prejudice cattle were seldom found in the Cherokee country before 1750, and relatively few were observed in the quarter century following. Cows were regarded as the "white man's buffalo"; often they were among the first beings killed in raids, since their nervous lowing might prevent a successful surprise attack. Furthermore, the Indian had several other reasons for disliking cattle. They required fencing of corn and other crops and demanded considerable personal attention. Also, the salt method of preservation was not as effective with beef as with pork.[32] Toward the close of the century the Cherokees lost much of this prejudice and the presence of cows on their farms became a common sight. Part of the credit for this development must go to the famous female Cherokee leader Nancy Ward, who learned about the dairy values of cattle during a period of captivity among the whites. Throughout the century young turkeys were seen on Cherokee farms, as well as an occasional hive of bees. Tamed dogs were also kept.[33]

Although agriculture took firmer hold upon the tribal economy as the eighteenth century progressed, hunting and fishing continued in popularity both as means of providing food and as recreation. Throughout the century the supply of clothing was largely dependent on the hunter's skill, as were to a lesser degree food stores. Both males and females participated in the hunt, which often lasted two or three months; children and aged remained behind to look after crops. Varying types of weapons were employed. The bow and arrow were the main reliance for killing buffalo, wild turkeys, opossum, deer, squirrel, pheasant, and quail. Blow guns (hollow reeds of cane) were often used on small game.

Winter was the usual hunting season, during which hunters would frequently remain out in the woods.[34]

Fishing was another valuable food source. Fish were speared, caught on hook and line, and trapped in fish weirs or wooden snares. When water conditions permitted, the Cherokees would frighten fish into a shallow area where they could be scooped up. A Cherokee fish trap seen in 1761 was described thus:

> Building two walls obliquely down the river from either shore, just as they are near joining, a passage is left to a deep well or reservoir; the Indians then scaring the fish down the river, close to the mouth of the reservoir with a large bush, or bundle made on purpose, and it is no difficult matter to take them with baskets, when inclosed within so small a compass.

Nets were also used, possibly before Europeans could have introduced them.[35]

The problem of transit had never been a serious one for the Southern Indian. Prior to the nineteenth century his chief need for transportation had been that of moving himself from home to hunting grounds, or to enemy territory for raids. If his direction was northeast, he might paddle up the Holston, hide his canoe on its banks, and walk up the Shenandoah Valley. To the west or northwest the Tennessee River offered a convenient entry into the Ohio or Illinois country. The Cherokees preferred the dug-out type of canoe to the lighter bark model. In 1673 it was noted that the Cherokees at Chota kept "one hundred and fifty cannoes under ye command of theire forte," and further that "ye leaste of them will carry twenty men, and [each one is] made sharpe at both ends like a wherry for swiftness." During the following century the use of canoes somewhat declined. The later Cherokee vessel was described as being made of "a large pine or poplar, from thirty to forty feet long, and about two broad, with flat bottoms and sides, and both ends alike." At first these boats, which were capable of carrying about fifteen men, were hollowed out by fire; subsequently tools were used.[36]

Numerous foot trails supplemented the waterways but few of them traversed the loftier mountains. Some of these paths acquired such fame as to merit "war trail" designations. The Warrior's Trace, running from north to south through the Cherokee country, was such a path, upon which the Iroquois and other enemies swept down on swift raids.[37]

Perhaps the most striking feature of Cherokee government in the eighteenth century was the absence of any effective centralization. The mountainous terrain undoubtedly accounted for this, creating a situation not unlike that of the ancient Greek city-states. Some particularism resulted. The Lower Cherokees, for example, derisively referred to their northern Cherokee kinsmen as "frog-eaters" and "pipe-makers." Localism also found expression in weak tribal discipline. A Cherokee chief told Colonel Chicken in 1725 that "the people would work as they pleased & go to Warr when they pleased, notwithstanding his saying all he could to them. . . ."[38] Attempts were made both by white individuals and white governments to consolidate the many Cherokee towns, chieftains, and clans under one native or group of natives, but these efforts (as will be indicated below) were ineffective. The failures serve to etch more clearly in the pages of Cherokee Indian history the prevalence of a trait common to many Americans: a love of land and liberty. Bartram noted that the Cherokees were not only jealous of their territorial integrity – "ready always to sacrifice every pleasure and gratification, even their blood, and life itself, to defend their territory" – but that they were "quite tenacious of the liberties and natural rights of men." The early Tennessee historian John Haywood declared that "their darling passion is liberty. To it they sacrifice everything. . . ."[39] While this may be an overstatement, the Cherokees' love of liberty was a dominant facet of their political philosophy, a devotion fostered and encouraged by a life in the out-of-doors.

The towns were the most important units of government, and among them seven "Mother Towns" were of particular authority: Tennassie, Kituwah, Ustenary, Tellico, Estoetowie, Keowee, and Noyohee. Chief executive power in each was vested in a person usually termed "king" by Europeans, and elected by the Town Council. The king's capacity was chiefly that of a magistrate presiding over the Council in its daily sessions. Among his other civil functions was supervision of the public granary. For times of crisis, however, there was at hand a Great War Chief, chosen by the leading warriors; his place at Council sessions was beside the king.[40]

Unlike most of their Indian neighbors, the Cherokees had few clans. Only seven in number, they were Aniwahiya (Wolf), Anikawi (Deer), Anidjiskwa (Bird), Aniwodi (Red Paint), Anisahoni (Blue), Anigotigewi (Wild Potatoes), and Anigilohi (Twisters). Of these, the Wolf was considered the most important. In earlier times the seven "Mother Towns" were clan headquarters. The Cherokees established clan kinship through the maternal side of the family only. Intermarriage within clans was expressly forbidden.[41]

The "kings" and the "Great War Chiefs" represented the top levels of a vast two-pronged social organization in the Cherokee Nation. These were the Red (War) and the White (Peace) groups. In theory, the whole tribe recognized the authority of a White civil leader, whose headquarters was located in the principal Cherokee city and who was known variously as "Uku," "Ookah," or "Ugutuyi." Under him were the following officials: a deputy chief; a group of seven counselors who represented each of the seven clans; the council, consisting of the elder men of the tribe (or local region); a "chief speaker"; several messengers; and a number of persons connected with various governmental and religious ceremonies. This same pattern of officials occurred, with local variations, in each of the other important towns in the entire nation. Local leaders were normally subordinate to the Uku and his staff. In times of emergency the local chiefs were supposed to assemble and, with the seven clan leaders, deliberate in a sort of national council. Eligibility to the position of Uku was usually hereditary through the female side, the oldest son of the Uku's sister being next in line. Sometimes a Uku's wife might hold the office until a successor could be chosen or approved.[42]

When war threatened the Red group assumed command for the duration of the emergency. The ranking official of this regime was the "Great Red War Chief," sometimes called the "Captain (Skayagustuegwo)" or "High Priest of War." His staff consisted of an assistant called the "Great War Chief's Second"; a group of seven Counselors of War, upon whose shoulders rested the responsibility of declaring war or ordering any military action; several females called "Pretty Women" or "War Women," who could determine the disposition of captives or the direction of strategy; a Chief Speaker to the warriors, called the "Skatiloski"; a standard-bearer, or "Katata kanchi"; the "Dunikoti," who was a surgeon-in-charge with three assistants; a number of messengers; and three special scouts, the Wolf, the Owl, and the Fox, who wore the skins of those animals as they scouted to the right, left, and rear, respectively, of the military party. Forward scout was the Great War Chief himself, who was called "The Raven" while in that capacity.[43]

Thus there existed in the social structure of the early Cherokee

Indians a dual governmental organization. In case of conflict in authority, the White group seems to have had control over the Reds. The peace faction was more stable, since its officials were subject to appointment through heredity or favor of the Uku. In the war body, however, the officials usually received office at frequent popular elections. Also, the Uku had a reviewing power over the nomination of War Chief.[44] It is possible that after 1750, when trouble with white men brought devastating warfare and greatly curtailed tribal landholdings, this elaborate system was modified considerably to such an extent that it was hardly noticeable to white visitors.[45]

Occasionally the Cherokees responded to the pressure of whites and agreed—at least in council—to plan for nationwide organization. In 1721, at the request of Governor Nicholson of South Carolina, they chose a principal chief or delegate with whom the governor could deal. A decade later Cherokees went even further. In spite of their feeling of independence, their "darling passion" for liberty, they were persuaded by the English in 1730 to accept a single "Emperor" to govern their entire nation. On April 3 of that year, in elaborate ceremonies attended by thirteen Englishmen headed by Sir Alexander Cuming, Chief Moytoy was given the new position. Other Cherokee leaders present vowed their full allegiance to Moytoy (and thus through him to King George II) resigning "their Crown, Eagles Tails, [and] Scalps of their Enemies, as an emblem of their all owning his majesty's sovereignty over them." It was at this meeting that seven Cherokees were chosen to go to London and cement the Anglo-Cherokee bond.[46]

A fantastic plan for a great Cherokee Imperial Nation was projected a few years after Cuming's scheme. Although the undertaking was a dismal failure, its nature was breath-taking in scope. Early in 1736 a former resident of Saxony, Christian Gottlieb Priber, arrived at Great Tellico with a box of books, some writing materials, and a set of ideas as grandiose as any ever projected in a wilderness. Until the occupying European powers could be driven from America, proposed Priber, the Cherokees should organize and perfect an empire. Moytoy, already holding down an "emperorship," was accepted by Priber; in a formal ceremony the Cherokee leader was proclaimed "Emperor of the Kingdom of Paradise," and Priber assumed for himself the title of Prime Minister. The German actually sent an ultimatum to the royal governor of South Carolina, ordering his entire British staff to evacuate! Meanwhile this Utopian dreamer perfected his plans for the new Cherokee state: the "Kingdom" would become a "Republic," and property ownership would be communal; furthermore, social classes and ranks were to be eliminated. The Law of Nature would be the only acceptable law, marriage would be abolished, and the State become the guardian of all children. Headquarters of the new Indian government was to be at Coosawattee, near the Creek boundary in North Georgia. Priber hoped that the Creeks and other Southern Indians could be persuaded to join.[47]

Priber's imaginative scheme had little chance for success. Aside from the lack of any comprehension or appreciation of its purpose by the Cherokees themselves, his project was sabotaged and finally destroyed by the British who regarded him as a dangerous French agent. There was some justice for this suspicion. After all, France was England's most powerful rival in the contention for the New World, and Indian alliances were common weapons in this titanic struggle. Furthermore, Priber himself used the name of "Pierre Albert." After several unsuccessful attempts, English officials finally captured Priber in Creek territory in 1743, and placed him in Frederica Prison in Georgia. There he died a few years later.[48]

Despite these pseudo-national Cherokee governments, and the ancient dual orders of War and Peace groups, the local controls of "kings" or head men continued to exert the major influence on the life of the individual Cherokees. There were few laws such as governed white men; serious problems like murder were handled through clans on the old Mosaic principle of blood for blood. Some forgiveness was possible, but, as Adair observed, the enthusiasm of war dances or the effects of liquor might bring a quick tomahawk to wipe out the pardon and avenge the original crime.[49]

An interesting criminological custom prevalent among the Southern Indians was the practice of designating one or more towns as places of refuge. The Cherokee sanctuary of this sort was usually their "old beloved town" Chota. Criminals, especially murderers, who could get to Chota could bask in its protection unmolested. Although the ancient tradition guaranteed perpetual immunity, and sometimes amnesty, actual practice in the eighteenth century worked against the criminal's security. In the first place, the lust for clan revenge might supersede the respect for such immunity and cause the injured clan to plan an ambush. Furthermore, the demands of the English for Indians who were thought to have committed crimes against the whites were often sufficient to force the Cherokee chiefs to bring an Indian out of sanctuary, or to prevent his entry therein. Adair wrote of these towns: "They seem to have been formerly 'towns of refuge,' for it is not in the memory of their oldest people, that ever human blood was shed in them; although they often force persons from thence, and put them to death elsewhere." Occasionally refuge might be sought at the home or near the person of a white chief. In that case the peace leader then either called an immediate hearing or ordered a regular trial to determine the guilt of the fugitive.[50]

In Cherokee tradition the City of Refuge had assumed extreme importance because it was the headquarters of the priesthood and often the leading city in the White party organization. Originally, according to Cherokee legend, there had been a priest class of extremely high rank in the social order. By the eighteenth century, however, little remained of such a class. According to the tradition, the priests had so abused their privileges that they were set upon and massacred. Therefore the matter of administering to religious needs was left for the individual "shaman" or conjuror. The average Indian conjuror was "something of a cross between a fortune-teller, a judge, an arbitrator, a consoler, and a general diagnostician," and the Cherokee counterpart was no exception. The Cherokee medicine men were "the Persons consulted in every Affair of Importance, and seem to have the Direction of every Thing." A leader named Old Hopp said of these medicine men, "We do nothing without consulting our conjurors, and always abide by what they tell us." A cynical interpretation of the conjuror's method and importance is shown by Adair:

> In Tymahse, a lower Cheerake town, lived one of their reputed great divine men, who never informed the people of his seeking for rain, but at the change, of full of the moon, unless there was some promising sign of the change of the weather, either in the upper regions, or from the feathered kalender; such as the quacking of ducks, the croaking of ravens, and from the moistness of the air felt in their quills; consequently, he seldom failed of success, which highly increased his fame, and profits; for even when it rained at other times, they ascribed it to the intercession of their great beloved men.[51]

The most important characteristic of the Cherokee religion was its simplicity. Cherokee natives had only the vaguest knowledge or conception of a Creator, and there appears to have been no such thing as a personal religious relationship between them and a God. Individuals were on their own so far as religious philosophy was concerned, which generally accepted a great superior being or spirit. Cherokee traditions of origin and existence were closely associated with their myths, a set of fables which sought to explain through animal stories the origins of various phases of existence. The conjuror, shaman, or High War Priest performed all the functions of a holy man, calling upon superstition, prestidigitation, and showmanship.[52]

Although personal religion was of little moment, superstitious belief was of considerable daily importance in connection with the War and Peace groups and their functions, medicinal practices, harvest celebrations, burial customs, diet, and the like. Anciently the Cherokees attached much supernatural significance to the actions of War and Peace chiefs, and few important steps were taken by either without considerable ritual and ceremony.[53]

Superstition affected Cherokee dietary habits. Good health was supposed to result from the practice of throwing fat meat into the fire, prior to eating a meal. For good luck, hunters usually cut a choice piece of meat from the thighs of deer. Adair stated that he never saw a venison ham without such a piece cut out. Some foods were regarded as unclean, especially meat from birds and animals of prey such as foxes, dogs, wolves, snakes, moles, polecats, opossums, buzzards, crows, cranes, fish hawks, eagles, owls, wood-cocks, eels, catfish, and garfish.[54]

Some symbolism appeared in burial customs of the Cherokees. The death of a chief was of course an event of special significance. In reporting the burial of one leader, Adair stated that the deceased was "washed and anointed" and placed in a sitting position upon skins with his property piled around him. After a flowery eulogy, he was interred under thick logs and clay. The custom of burying personal property with the corpse was fairly uniform in the early part of the eighteenth century. Later an inheritance custom developed; this change may have been brought about by the influence of traders, who were probably shocked at seeing such possessions go into the ground. Warriors killed away from home were commemorated by cairns which grew in size as Cherokee passers-by added stones to the heaps as tokens of respect, and possibly to insure good luck in coming encounters.[55]

In medical practice some religious emphasis was attached to

allegedly miraculous powers of certain medicinal drugs or special rites. The ginseng root, for example, was highly regarded, and its preparation prescribed by local conjurors. Women sometimes wore beaded strings of buffalo hair as preservatives against miscarriage or severe labor pains.[56] Typical application of an Indian herb might have been like that made by a white man whose leg was pierced by a "cane stab" while travelling in the Cherokee country in 1766. Obtaining "bark from the root of a lynn tree" for "Indian medicine," he had it "beat on a stone, with a tomahawk, and boil[ed] it in a kettle, and with the ooze I bathed my foot and leg; what remained when I had finished bathing, I boiled it to a jelly, and made poultices thereof."[57]

In 1738-1739 smallpox, possibly introduced from South Carolina, struck the Cherokees with alarming incidence, and against its ravages the efforts of shaman and superstitious practice were of no avail. Having no precedent for treating this disease, most conjurors made the serious mistake of prescribing a cure which was for them a traditional panacea: the cold plunge. As this and other treatments failed, and the pestilence spread from town to town, universal despair beset the Cherokees. Hundreds, possibly thousands, died as a result of this epidemic.[58]

As might be expected from a social order which emphasized ritual and superstition, ceremonies were frequent in the Cherokee country. White visitors of importance were usually met in a formal council gathering attended by the leading warriors. In 1725 Colonel Chicken was greeted by "the head men of five Towns in the Upper Settlements who . . . came and Sing'd before me and faned me with their Eagles Tailes." Sir Alexander Cuming received much the same treatment several years later, for "the Warriors strok'd him with 13 Eagles Tails and their Singers sang from Morning 'till Night. . . ." Of perhaps chief importance among Cherokee ceremonials was the Green Corn Dance, a custom which has persisted in various forms throughout Cherokee history. Timberlake stated that the dance was performed "in a very solemn manner, in a large square before the town-house door; the motion here is very slow, and the song in which they offer thanks to God for the corn he has sent them, far from unpleasing." Other important rites included those for the curing of disease and those preceding war and important games.[59]

The favorite athletic contest of the Cherokees was one which was simply referred to as the "ball-play." This game was a spectacular brawling affair, which required a strong body and a fairly agile mind. Common among the Indians of North America, and probably dating back to pre-Columbian times, the ball-play has a modern counterpart in lacrosse. The Cherokees were apparently quite fond of the game and frequently staked large amounts on its outcome. One persistent Cherokee tradition claims that the spoils of an ancient ball-play victory over the Creeks was a huge tract of land in present-day North Georgia. The game was played with sticks about two feet long with an animal-skin netting on one end. The ball was made of deer hide. The team of twelve or more on a side strove mightily to drive the ball between the opponent's two goal posts. Personal encounters were frequent and violent. Man-handling was somewhat difficult owing to use of slippery oils on the body, but, even so, it was not uncommon for good players to be deliberately knocked unconscious.[60] The use of the ball-play as a stratagem in warfare is indicated in an entry dated May 4, 1714, in the minutes of South Carolina's Board of Indian Trade: "A man named Clea swears he has heard that 'there was a design among the Cherikees to Cut off Chestowee 10 dayes before ye sd town was cut off and that ye Cherikees designed to invite the Euchees to a ball play in order to cut them off.' . . ."[61]

Another favorite game was Chunkge, largely a performance of skill. A common sight in Cherokee villages was the "Chunkge Yard," consisting of an acre or more of cleared ground. Discus-shaped stones were rolled in a wide arc while competing players sought to throw seven-foot poles near the approximate point of the stone's stopping.[62]

As the eighteenth century drew to its close, Cherokee development was entering a new phase. By 1789 the Cherokees were in prime condition for the civilizing policy of the United States government – a policy which was to have a deep effect on their domestic economy and industry, and bring more stability to their political set-up as well. Unsettled in civic affairs, the Cherokees within two decades were to acquire a legal code and a constitution. Lacking a strong religion, they were to offer little resistance to missionary endeavors, which they utilized for educational and cultural gains. These influences were to transform Cherokee culture from one largely savage in character to one patterned on the white man's ways.

THREE

FRONTIER STRIFE

CROWDED AGAINST the eastern and northern borders of Cherokee territory at the close of the Revolutionary War were roughly six hundred miles of semi-circular white frontiers. Land-hungry speculators and settlers, following victorious armies and successful treaty writers, had spilled over into Indian regions, and the resulting map changes presented a triangular enclave in which the Cherokees found themselves backed up against Creek and Chickasaw borders (See Map A). Destruction by South Carolina troops had forced the Lower Cherokees westward into the valleys of the Etowah and Chattahoochee rivers (in present-day North Georgia). Similar pressures farther north pushed the Middle Cherokees into the area between the Coosa and the Hiwassee, while the Over Hill people were compacted in a smaller mountain area between the Hiwassee and the Holston. White settlers along the Holston and the Cumberland contested Cherokee claims to traditional hunting grounds.

Frontier country for late eighteenth century Cherokees and whites alike was no mere boundary line dividing two peoples. Instead, it was a busy region of claims and counter-claims, of raids and counter-raids, of land occupied in some places by white and red men alike. It was a frontier of depth and trouble.

Conflict and confusion made the era between the Revolutionary War and the end of the eighteenth century a troublesome one for the Cherokee Indians. In many small-scale brushes with frontiersmen the Cherokees suffered personal and territorial losses. Their lands seemed to beckon adventurous white men. In defiance of the British prohibition of 1763, surveyors, land speculators, hunters, and settlers ventured into the Cherokee country.

After the Americans wrested a claim to the land from the British in the Revolution, migrations through Cherokee valleys, onto Cherokee bottom lands, and beyond Cherokee frontiers furnished a constant irritant. The pattern was usually the same: white settlers found rich fertile country within Indian bounds and sought recognition from federal authorities. Indians, incensed at the apparent treaty violation, found recourse either in raiding parties or in appeals to the government for justice.

At the close of the American Revolution, the Congress of the Confederation was faced with the problem of making peace with the Cherokees and other Indian tribes who had sided with the British. The Treaty of Hopewell, written in November, 1785, officially ended the war between the Cherokees and the Americans. The negotiations were noteworthy from the Indian's standpoint because the treaty included no demands for land. Instead, the discussions sought to draw the existing boundary along Cherokee territory, crystallizing, at least temporarily, the Indian possessions in stipulated areas.[1]

Before the ink was dry on the Treaty of Hopewell difficulties were again arising. The American government was plagued with the problems of the white settlements already established within the Indian boundaries. By terms of the treaty the claims of squatters living between the French Broad and Holston rivers were to be referred to Congress for disposition. Other settlers who had crossed the lines were expected to leave in six months or forfeit the protection of United States troops and officials. Congress failed to make any provision for the first group, while the second ignored government orders to leave. Finally, on August 26, 1790, President Washington issued a proclamation warning United States citizens of the intention of the government to enforce the Hopewell provisions.[2]

In 1786 the Congress of the Confederation improved the management of Indian affairs by creating two federal Indian departments. The areas of jurisdiction were northern and southern with the Ohio River serving as the dividing line. Superintendents of each department were to supervise and control trade within their territory and were to restrict the issuing of annual trading licenses to United States citizens who could give bond for three thousand dollars. The superintendents themselves were to be bonded for six thousand dollars and were prohibited from engaging in any trading operations. The first appointee for the southern department was James White.[3]

Several factors prevented the smooth operation of this program, especially in the southern area. Jealous of their right to deal with neighboring Indians, the states declined to give way before federal authorities. The difficulty was increased by Georgia's claim to western lands, and confusion over the cession of North Carolina, which involved the claims of the "State of Franklin." The Cherokees found themselves dealing with both federal and state agents; and during the Confederation period the latter, owing to the greater aggressiveness with which they pushed their state and personal interests, usually predominated.[4]

Inadequacy of organization and the incompetency of Superintendent James White further hampered the Confederation's Southern Indian program. White had no deputies to whom he could delegate authority; apparently he was expected to deal singlehandedly with Cherokees, Creeks, Choctaws, Chickasaws, and others. The task was one for a genius and White was not of that stature. Moreover his own interests were divided. He was deeply involved in negotiations with Spanish authorities; apparently he preferred that connection, for he resigned his superintendency early in 1788. From the Cherokee viewpoint White's appointment was incomprehensible and his administration ineffective. He confined most of his attention to the Creeks on the Spanish borders, disregarding other Southern Indians.[5]

Richard Winne of South Carolina was appointed to succeed White on February 29, 1788. Winne was deeply interested in the Southern Indians. Moreover, he had the advantage after a few months of the assistance of Joseph Martin whom Congress had designated as special agent to the Cherokees and Chickasaws. But Winne's term expired in 1789 and he had little opportunity to carry out the program for which the superintendency had been created.[6]

The Hopewell treaty did not bring peace. The Cherokees were dissatisfied with the boundary, while the white settlers inside it wanted to stay. Another difficulty lay in the weak nature of the government under the Articles of Confederation. Attempts to make the states respect Indian rights were largely futile and during the Confederation period there was no official ratification of treaties. All in all, the Cherokee situation was one of confusion and a better treaty was an early project of the new Constitutional government. In July, 1789, Secretary of War Henry Knox urged the "serious consideration of Congress" to the "disgraceful violation of the Treaty of Hopewell."[7]

Cognizant of the critical situation and of the guarantees promised the Cherokees by the treaty, President Washington sent word to the Senate on August 11, 1790, that "notwithstanding the said treaty and proclamation, upwards of five hundred families have settled on the Cherokee lands," excluding the groups on the French Broad and the Holston. He then asked the Senate for authority either to maintain the terms of the treaty or to "arrange a new boundary with the Cherokees, embracing the settlements, and compensating the Cherokees for the cessions they shall make on the occasion." The Senate resolved that the President should not only enforce the existing treaty as well as possible but also that he should make every effort to have the Cherokees cede additional lands not to exceed a cost of one thousand dollars annually. Instructions were promptly issued to the Governor of North Carolina to obtain such a cession. The eventual result was the Treaty of Holston, July 2, 1791.[8]

This comprehensive agreement with the United States government was of great importance to the Cherokee Indians. It stipulated the drawing of a boundary line and prescribed its course. A tract of land one hundred miles broad was ceded, in return for which the Cherokees were to receive "certain valuable goods to be delivered immediately." In addition an annuity of one thousand dollars was granted, which was later increased to fifteen hundred dollars. The treaty delegated to the United States complete control of Cherokee trade and forbade diplomatic agreements between Cherokees and any other "foreign Power, individual State, or with individuals of any State." An immediate exchange of prisoners was agreed upon. "Perpetual peace and friendship" was asserted, and the United States guaranteed to the Indians all their remaining lands. Non-Indians settling on Cherokee lands were declared beyond American protection, but Cherokees committing crimes against persons or property of the United States or its inhabitants were to be given up by their council. White persons perpetrating crimes against "any peaceable or friendly" Indians would be punished by the proper American authorities. Hunting parties were to avoid Cherokee lands in the future and no whites were to travel through the Indian country without permits from state or territorial governors. Furthermore, Cherokees agreed to report any activity among themselves or neighboring Indians which seemed to be inimical to the interests of the United States.[9]

The clause of greatest import to future Cherokee development was Article Fourteen, the contents of which had been suggested by forward-looking commissioners at Hopewell six years earlier. The inclusion of this item represented a new departure in Cherokee relations with the white man:

ART. 14. That the Cherokee nation may be led to a greater degree of civilization, and to become herdsmen and cultivators, instead of remaining in a state of hunters, the United States will, from time to time, furnish gratuitously the said nation with useful implements of husbandry. And further, to assist the said nation in so desirable a pursuit, and at the same time to establish a certain mode of communication, the United States will send such, and so many, persons to reside in said nation, as they may judge proper, and not exceeding four in number, who shall qualify themselves to act as interpreters. These persons shall have lands assigned them by the Cherokees for cultivation, for themselves and their successors in office; but they shall be precluded exercising any kind of traffic.[10]

Senate ratification of this important treaty was prompt. Some credit for this was due to the Senator from North Carolina, Benjamin Hawkins, who had previously demonstrated his interest in Indians both in Congress and as a Hopewell commissioner.[11]

Administration of the Treaty of Holston was the responsibility of the Governor of the "Territory South of the Ohio," a post created by an act of May 26, 1790, which provided that the person holding the office of Governor should also be Superintendent of Indians in the territory. The first incumbent of the new position was William Blount of North Carolina. A frontier opportunist, Blount became an important force in Cherokee life. He had little of the humanitarian approach toward the Indians which characterized later administrations. Once Governor Blount admitted to the Secretary of War his own preference for "decided and positive measures" in dealing with the Cherokees. He favored a policy of demanding instant satisfaction when murders were committed by Cherokees, even though it "should bring on a National War." Such a war, he thought, "could be terminated in the course of a few months, at less expense of Blood, and Treasure, than defensive protection would cost upon so extended and exposed a Frontier." In November, 1792, Blount wrote to Congressman John Steele:

I can assure you that no Man ever laboured with more . . . Zeal for Peace or more earnestly wished to preserve it than I have done but now it is essential that Congress should and I think will declare war.

—The Creeks must be scourged and well too and the Cherokees deserve it.

Blount added that in his opinion the inhabitants of Georgia, Virginia, and the Carolinas would regard the total destruction of the Cherokee Indians as "a Party of Pleasure."[12]

The Territorial Governor made some efforts, however, to maintain peace on the frontier short of an actual declaration of war. In February, 1793, he notified Secretary of War Knox that he was trying to prevent the attempts of white settlers "to invade the Cherokee nation"; that he had issued proclamations against invasion; and had called on the military to patrol. "I found it necessary," he wrote, "to order a Lieutenant of Cavalry and fifteen men to range from Holston to Little River on the frontiers. This destroyed one of their strongest arguments 'that they had no protection.' "[13]

Owing probably to Blount's and North Carolina's interest in the Tennessee country, the new supervisor of federal Indian affairs concentrated his efforts on the Cherokees. Apparently the Cherokees were not happy with this arrangement. They regarded Blount correctly as an avaricious land-seeker, their title for him being "The Dirt Captain." Moreover, they wanted a United States agent to operate from within their territory. In response to a request from the Indians for someone to serve as counsellor and protector, Secretary Knox sent a Princeton graduate, Leonard Shaw, in 1792. Shaw, as Knox informed Blount, was "an amiable young man" who desired "from the purest motives," employment in the Indian Department.[14]

The War Department's instructions to Leonard Shaw reveal strikingly the government's paternal interest in Southern Indians as well as the hard practical need for peace and friendship:

> You will . . . endeavor . . . to infuse into all the Indians the uprightness of the views of the President . . . and his desire to better the situation of the Indians in all respects.
>
> You will endeavor to learn their languages: this is essential to your communications. You will collect materials for a history of the Southern tribes. . . . You will endeavor to ascertain their respective limits; make a vocabulary of their respective languages; teach them agriculture, and such useful arts as you may know or can acquire.

Shaw was not destined to carry out much of this worthy prospectus. A year after his appointment he was removed from office by Governor Blount at the request of Secretary Knox, on grounds of "inebriety and great want of prudence." Shaw had acquired a Cherokee wife and was thought to be influencing the Cherokees against Blount. An interpreter named James Carey reported in March, 1793, that Shaw was instructing the Indians to by-pass Blount and deal directly with the authorities in Washington, preferably Congress. According to Carey, Shaw gave as one reason for avoiding Blount that the governor had "wronged them out of their lands."[15]

Succeeding Leonard Shaw as special deputy to the Cherokees was John McKee, a man who seems to have been more familiar with Indian requirements and more acceptable to Governor Blount. Writing to Secretary Knox in 1794, Blount urged that the War Department let McKee continue to reside in the Cherokee Nation as temporary agent, for:

> besides his having a great share of the confidence of the Nation, he is from his abilities & knowledge of Indians, their habits and dispositions, the most proper man within my acquaintance or knowledge for a Deputy, and it should be necessary to his continuance that he should be an officer, I can assure you that he is not only qualified by his bodily & mental abilities to perform the duties of a Captain but of a Field or General Officer.[16]

Blount and his deputies were faced with serious problems in maintaining peace on the frontier. The normal friction resulting from the rubbing together of diverse elements in the Cherokee area was made even more acute by the presence of unscrupulous whites. White raids and organized horse-stealing, sometimes abetted by Indian accomplices, were frequently blamed on the Cherokees as a nation. Furthermore, there were belligerent Cherokees who consistently preferred retaliation to passive resistance. By Cherokee custom revenge on any white man whether or not he were the perpetrator was considered sufficient repayment.[17]

One group of Cherokees in particular maintained an aggressive policy. These were the Chickamaugas, or the "Cherokees of the Five Lower Towns," who, in protest against the sweeping cessions of lands and submission to the white man's greed, had finally withdrawn from the main body of the tribe and settled on Chickamauga Creek (near present-day Chattanooga). In 1782, however, their towns at this location were hard hit by an expedition under the leadership of the experienced Indian-fighter John Sevier. Subsequently the Chickamaugas moved farther down the Tennessee. The shift was influenced somewhat by a belief that their creek was "infested with witches." The following year their separate existence was noticed by the Moravian missionary Schneider: "This Nation has been much weakened in the last War by the Separation of the Chikamakas or lower Cherokees. . . . They separated because the upper Cherokees would no longer take any part in their Hostilities against the white People & moreover often discovered [disclosed] their designs."[18]

In 1792 Governor Blount described the villages of the Chickamauga-Cherokees, by then familiarly known as the Five Lower Towns. In a report to the Secretary of War, Blount mentioned that Running Water, the most northerly of the five (see map A), consisted of a hundred huts and was a "common crossing place for the Creeks." Three miles below was Nickajack, which contained about forty houses. Long Island village, "which comprehends an island called the Long Island in the Tennessee, and a number of huts on the south side," consisted of about a dozen houses and was located five miles below Nickajack. Farther on was Crow Town, considered "the lowest town in the Cherokee nation," which had about thirty habitations. Fifteen miles south of Running Water was Lookout Mountain Town, located on the creek of the same name. Containing eighty huts, it was situated in a valley about three miles wide next to Lookout Mountain. In all, reported the governor, these five towns contained approximately three hundred warriors, in addition to various groups of visiting hostiles such as Shawnees, Creeks, Northern Indians, and "white Tories."[19]

An important strife-producing factor on the Cherokee frontier was the Spanish colonial administration to the south and west. A Spanish trading post was operating on the Tennessee River as early as 1783, and by the following year Spanish tradesmen were to be found in the Cherokee country. Diplomatic relations, including trading concessions and amity agreements, followed. On May 14, 1792, for example, at Fort Nogales near the mouth of the Yazoo in the Mississippi territory, Spain made a treaty with Choctaws, Chickasaws, Creeks, and Cherokees. Several Spanish forts were built which penetrated even deeper into the Southern Indian country and strengthened relations with the red man.[20] In addition, much influence from the Creek country was exerted on the Cherokees by the powerful quadroon chief, Alexander McGillivray, a recognized Spanish agent, and by William A. Bowles, an English soldier of fortune. Closely linked with McGillivray in promoting the cause of Spain among the Southern Indians was the firm of Panton, Leslie & Company, which established a strong trading network from the Floridas to the Mississippi and as far north as the Cherokee country. Through the Panton connections Spain employed as its Cherokee agent the old trader John McDonald of Chickamauga, who was especially influential among the Five Lower Towns.[21] On March 15, 1797, a Territorial agent named David Craig reported to Governor Blount that "at the house of Richard Justice [a Cherokee chieftain] is a painting of Bowles, and two Cherokee Chiefs, on each side of him, under which is written, 'General Bowles, Commander-in-Chief of the Creek and Cherokee nations.' "[22]

Fortunately for white security, and perhaps for the preservation of Indian lives, considerable factionalism existed within the Cherokee ranks. While many young and belligerent "outcast Cherokees" joined the Chickamaugas, few of the chiefs in the upper settlements followed. The most prominent Cherokee leader at this time was The Little Turkey (or The Turkey), who largely favored peace and settlement of difficulties through negotiation. David Craig reported to the Governor that The Little Turkey had sent the following message to the Five Lower Towns:

> That he (the Little Turkey) was tired of talking to them; that he had heard what they had lately done: that he did not intend to travel the path to them anymore, to hold talks; if they wanted to go to war, go, and he would sit still and look at them; that they must stay on their own side of the mountain, (Chatanuga) and not mix with the other parts of the nation. That he would go and inform Governor Blount where they lived, and that they were for war; that he was done talking to them, and the Governor and they might settle matters as they would.

The Turkey also issued this plain message to several subordinate chiefs among the Cherokees, including Path Killer, The Hanging Maw, and John Watts.[23]

In the Lower Towns Little Turkey's message fell on unreceptive ears. In March, 1792, it was Craig's opinion that

> the present prospects and information warrants a belief, and hardly leaves a doubt, that many of the Creeks and the Cherokees, generally

of the five Lower towns, will join the Shawanese in war, and that they will murder, and steal horses of the frontiers, and from all weak parties, wherever found, if they do not engage in a general national war.[24]

Spanish agents were quick to utilize the continued belligerency of the disgruntled Chickamaugas. On September 2, 1792, The Little Turkey told Governor Blount that most of the frontier unrest was owing to the Five Lower Towns. He continued, "The Spaniards has gave them ammunition and guns, hatchets, knives, guns, &c, and told them it was not to go to war, but to keep it a reserve by them: you may blame no body for all this, only the Spaniards." John Watts, half-breed War Chief of the Chickamaugas, took a party of Indians down to Pensacola in Spanish West Florida where Governor Arturo O'Neill gave them presents, including weapons and ammunition, and apparently promises of aid in recovering lands previously ceded by the Cherokees to the United States. On his return Watts attended a nation-wide Cherokee council meeting at Willstown. He told them of benefits to be derived from Spanish support and friendship. In reporting on Governor O'Neill's conversations, Watts revealed much of the subtlety of the Spanish approach to Indians:

The Governor . . . received him with open arms; asked him if he had seen any Spanish settlers before he arrived at Pensacola; assured him that the Spaniards never wanted a back country; wherever they had landed, they sat down; . . . they are not like the Americans, first take your land, then treat with you, and give you little or nothing for it; this is the way they have always served you, and, from time to time, killed some of your people. . . . That the King, his master, had sent in powder, lead, and arms, for the whole four Southern nations, in plenty; and that then was the time for them to join quickly in war against the United States, while they were engaged in a war with the Northern tribes; . . . that the talks which that part of the nation who had been to visit the President had received, was not from the heart, but only from the teeth; that, besides guns and ammunition, they should be furnished with swords, caps, pistols, bridles, and saddles . . . and that a magazine should be erected for the Cherokees at Willstown.[25]

The Spanish influence helped to encourage a young minority war party in the main body of the Cherokees who began actively to aid the Chickamaugas. The malcontents not only sent small war parties to aid their belligerent brothers, but occasionally exerted influence over the nominal heads of the tribe. In April of 1792, General Andrew Pickens of South Carolina commented with some anxiety on this situation: "While a part, and that the ostensible ruling part of a nation, affect to be at, and I believe really are for peace, and the more active young men frequently killing people and stealing horses, it is extremely difficult to know how to act." A year later it was reported by James Thompson, an interpreter, that The Little Turkey had deliberately claimed lands in areas where he knew privately that the Cherokees had no rights because "the Turkey . . . only meant to please the young warriors, who were always grumbling that the old Chiefs had sold their lands and they had none to hunt on."[26]

Several of the older chiefs of the Chickamaugas who were opposed to war with the United States removed with small bands of adherents to other parts of the nation. Blount reported these "four principal chiefs" as "the Glass, and Captain Charley, of the Running Water, the Breath of Nicajack, and Dick Justice, of Look-out Mountain." Such desertions by men of peaceful intentions, however, were insufficient to curb the Chickamauga warriors. In September, 1792, they officially declared war on the United States — a curiously non-Indian procedure. Assisting the Chickamaugas in war preparations were a group of Creeks and about forty Shawnees. The whole war party was expected to number about four hundred. Although warned that the first blow might hit the Cumberland area, the Secretary of War also alerted the Governors of South Carolina, Virginia, and Georgia.[27]

Peaceful leaders in the main body of the tribe attempted to convince Governor Blount of their utter inability to curb the belligerents. Writing from Turkey-town in September, 1792, the Boot (or Chutcoe) reported, "We are sorry to acquaint you of bad news [the declaration of war], but we can't help it; we done all that lay in our power to hinder them. . . . You know I myself, and others, are at peace, and gives out good talks to our young men." At the same time, The Turkey expressed shame for the actions of the Chickamaugas and their allies and asked that vengeance be meted out to them.[28]

The scheduled war of 1792 failed to materialize as announced. By September 15, Governor Blount was reporting that it had been called off. At first it appeared that the older leaders in the Five Lower Towns had prevailed in their arguments against the proposed conflict. Blount identified this "peace Crowd" as The Glass and Bloody Fellow, with the assistance of John Watts. It later developed that the aggressive element had decided that the times were not propitious for an all-out frontier war. James Carey reported that The Glass, Bloody Fellow, and Watts merely pretended to have peaceful inclinations, hoping to deceive the Americans "until such time as they and their warriors could go down to Pensacola to Governor O'Neal [*sic*] and receive their arms and ammunition, and get their crops from the ground, and hid. . . ." Blount forwarded to the Secretary of War two statements from men who had just come from a trip through Spanish country and Creek lands, and who had witnessed the council gathering at Willstown where the Cumberland raid was planned. Both of these informants, Richard Finnelson, a Cherokee half-breed, and Joseph Deraque, a Canadian, verified the information that the peace-talking chiefs were lying. Finnelson stated in particular that the Cherokee Council at Willstown had "determined to write to Governor Blount, and inform him, that the rumor of war in the lower towns arose from a few drunken young fellows, and that the heads, who were for peace, had stopped them. This . . . would prevent any bad consequences from the information given by Carey . . . and would put the Governor off his guard." Finnelson identified these "heads" as "Watts, Taylor, the Glass, Talohtiske, Fool Charlee (by some called Captain Charley), and the Breath."[29]

But this report was not needed to make Blount and other Americans aware that the expressed desire for peace was merely a ruse. On the last day of September, 1792, an invading war party raided Buchanan's Station (near present-day Nashville). Chief John Watts led the group, which consisted of Chickamaugas, Creeks, Shawnees, and a few Cherokees. The Indians failed to take a central fortified position and were forced to withdraw.[30]

The raids and counter-raids which followed in other parts of the frontier were typical of developments during this era of Cherokee history. Horse-stealing also remained a concomitant problem. Blount reported in May, 1792, that it was a "Subject of complaint (almost continual) to me without my being able to give any redress." Usually, he issued passports to owners enabling them to enter the Indian country and look for their stolen steeds; but little came from these visits. The crux of the difficulty seemed to lie in the fact that both whites and Indians were engaged in the horse-stealing, and were able to get the animals out of the Indian country into seaboard states for sale. The usual depots for this illicit traffic were Swannanoa in North Carolina, Tugalo in Georgia, and the Oconee mountain area in South Carolina.[31]

One incident which clearly revealed the state of confusion existing on the Cherokee frontier occurred in June, 1793, when a party of whites, seeking revenge for the killing of a friend, invaded the "old beloved town" of Chota. The house of Chief Hanging Maw was attacked, the chief wounded, and his wife killed. Yet Hanging Maw had been particularly friendly to Governor Blount, and had worked for peace. Although depredations on both sides continued for several years (over two hundred whites being killed or captured in the period from 1791 to 1794) some leaders continued to seek peace. One of these, remarkably enough, was Hanging Maw, who led the Upper Cherokees in a series of cooperative endeavors during 1794 to punish such warlike elements as parties of Creeks and raiding Cherokees from the Lower Towns.[32]

Other events occurred to keep the cauldrons of war bubbling. Northern Indian tribes, encouraged by British agents, sought Cherokee aid against the United States. Cherokees continued to regard the huge unsettled lands between Virginia and Kentucky, and between Kentucky and the Cumberland as legitimate hunting grounds. General John Sevier maintained his fearsome reputation as an Indian fighter by leading slashing attacks upon Cherokee villages and by taunting and deprecating their warriors. These deeds brought retaliation, although mostly by small parties of Indians. The efforts of Hanging Maw and other friendly chiefs of the Upper Cherokees were little respected by war-weary or land-hungry frontiersmen, who plotted the kind of revenge wreaked upon Hanging Maw and his fellow townsmen of Chota in June of 1793.[33]

Governor Blount made some attempts to stop such actions. On January 26, 1793, he issued a ringing proclamation against certain "disorderly, ill disposed persons" who seemed intent on invading the Upper Cherokees. This edict called upon American citizens to desist from any such intentions and urged that they return to peaceable habits. Further, he commended them to respect the Cherokee territorial limits as established by the Treaty of Holston. Finally, Blount ordered all civil and military officers under his command to prevent any violations of the peace.[34]

Frontier troubles were enhanced by occasional atrocities. An example was the murder and mutilation in 1793 of Captain William Overall and a man named Burnett by a party of Cherokees led by Doublehead. After killing and scalping the white men, confiscating their goods, and drinking their whiskey, the Indians cut up the bodies and proceeded to cook and eat chunks of the human flesh. Presumably this act was designed to indicate red prowess rather than to satisfy mere hunger. But it was a terrible deed, and it fired the frontier to new resistance and new aggressions.[35]

Continuing incidents and threats on the part of the Cherokees, Chickamaugas, Creeks, and Shawnees brought in 1794 a determination to put an end to the frontier troubles. A series of fresh attacks by white militia and volunteer units in that year broke the back of most Cherokee resistance. Especially hard-hitting and effective was the devastating raid led by Major James Ore into the Five Lower Towns, during which Nickajack and Running Water were destroyed, many Indians killed, and numbers of prisoners taken. Surely the white settlers of Ore's home District of Mero, as well as neighboring areas, must have felt satisfaction over this long-desired event. But while they exulted over the victory, Mero and other districts were feeling the pinch of continued—if sporadic—raids; and William Blount was publicly disavowing any responsibility for the Ore attack.[36]

Late in 1794 peace seemed at last in the offing. In November Governor Blount saw three hopeful indications: Ore's attack on Nickajack and Running Water; the defeat of Northern Indians by General Anthony Wayne at Fallen Timbers; and the "decided part taken by the Upper Cherokees against the Creeks." Early in the following year, President Washington notified Congress that apparently "hostilities with the Cherokees have ceased, and there is a pleasing prospect of a permanent peace with that nation." Some depredation continued on both sides; even the famed John Sevier's home was raided late in 1794.[37] But in general hostilities dwindled to small-scale incidents involving small numbers of people. These were more or less characteristic of frontier life throughout the period of Indian occupancy of lands in the Old Southwest.

FOUR

OUT OF THE FOREST AND ON TO THE FARM

CHEROKEE DEVELOPMENT was necessarily limited during the troublous times of the late eighteenth century. Disruption resulting from frequent raiding by whites was augmented by internal dissensions. Despite all these impediments, some progress was made. The tribe was influenced by peaceable chiefs, who sought to "get along" with the Americans. The hunting lands decreased and the southward shift of the Indian population tended to force a dependence on the greater expanse of agricultural lands. Also the strength of mixed-breeds brought about a subtle change of attitude toward white men. Many of these changes within the Indian nation were carefully fostered or approved of by United States government officials.

The government's benevolent program as expressed in the Treaty of Holston depended for its proper execution upon the Indian superintendents and agents. During most of the 1790's, this responsibility in the Cherokee country rested upon the shoulders of Territorial Governor William Blount. Through him and his deputies in the Cherokee Nation the Indians were kept in contact with the United States government. Occasionally, some of them went to talk with the Great White Father themselves; usually, however, these visits accomplished little, especially since they were often unexpected. From the government's point of view, more good could be achieved by its representatives in the field, and the agents were so instructed.[1]

In 1795 comparative peace came to the Cherokee frontiers. Only small parties of raiding Creeks and a few white-Cherokee skirmishes rippled the subsiding waters. In the last months of his administration, Blount took credit for the achievement of peace:

To promote the happiness of the White People it was essential to use my utmost efforts to preserve peace with the Indians, and I can truly add it was ever my most Sincere wish, and how far my efforts have been well directed let those who witness the present Peace . . . , and the first of that description for 10 years, determine.

With the creation of the State of Tennessee in 1796, Blount was retired from the post of Governor of the Territory South of the Ohio and Superintendent of the Southern Indians. In summarizing his service, he wrote the Secretary of War: "I received the appointment . . . with pleasure, . . . I found the execution of its Duties very arduous & painful and . . . I left the frontiers in a perfect State of Peace."[2]

After Blount's departure the Superintendency of Indians seems to have temporarily terminated as far as Southern tribes were concerned. An interim appointee served for the time being, however, in the person of Benjamin Hawkins, a distinguished North Carolinian whose previous experience both in Congress and as commissioner at various Indian treaty gatherings made him a fortunate choice. Hawkins, whose life after 1796 was "devoted entirely to the Indian," was given the title of "Principal Temporary Agent for the Southern Indians." Although he made his headquarters at Colerain in the Creek country, he visited the Cherokees frequently, particularly during the late 1790's.[3]

Benjamin Hawkins was especially interested in carrying out the provisions of Article Fourteen of the Treaty of Holston. He talked to Cherokees of advancements in home industry and agriculture, and urged his deputies to sponsor such improvements. Encouraged by signs of Cherokee interest in the idea of development along the white man's pattern, Hawkins sought progress for as many Indians as possible, both Creek and Cherokee, throughout his administration as Indian Agent.[4]

Hawkins' method was designed not only to aid the Indians materially, but also to dispense justice without regard to color or status. He seems to have had not the slightest interest in using his position for personal gain; indeed he performed his valuable services at some risk to his health, reputation, and personal possessions. On his first tour through the Cherokee country in 1796 he was received with such cordiality as to suggest that the red men sensed his interest and fairness.[5]

On April 15, 1797, Hawkins instructed Silas Dinsmoor, whom he had designated Temporary Agent to the Cherokees, to supply "in the usual course" a group of chiefs who were soon to convene at Tellico, with meat and meal, or corn. Recognizing other customary procedure, Hawkins also stated that "in particular cases" Dinsmoor could issue some whiskey. Less than ten days after the conference began, however, some Cherokees petitioned Hawkins himself for "a little whiskey." Hawkins' reply indicates his own sincere intentions toward the Indians:

> He answered no, not one drop till the business they convened on was completely adjusted. They replyed this was not usual, they heretofore were indulged and expected a continuance. He rejoined he saw but little good in their past transactions, that he did not come to continue abuses, but to remedy the past, and he should, for himself make a point of doing what he judged proper regardless of the past. After some hesitation, the chiefs agreed that this decision was just and they expected some good from it, as heretofore much injury had been done them when in a state of drunkenness.[6]

Hope of promoting general progress among his charges moved Hawkins to plan the establishment of special posts at which white craftsmen could be permitted to reside and work at their various trades, with the stipulation that they take Indians as apprentices. Some artisans had already approached him for such permission and one of them, a hatter, was approved on condition that he find a Cherokee apprentice as soon as possible.[7]

But frontier conditions and Indian tribal customs plagued Hawkins in the performance of his duties. In 1798, after hearing that Tennessee had complained of his apparent inability to round up wanted Indians, the agent somewhat petulantly wrote a friend in the War Department:

> If you in the course of your researches have found out the secret of making Indians fulfill their public engagements where there is no law and it belongs to individuals to take personal satisfaction, and to the family of the individual to avenge the wrong, and you will communicate that secret to me, I hereby bind myself and my successors in office to send you six princesses in full dress.[8]

One of the important functions of the Indian Superintendent was that of controlling trade. Both Blount and Hawkins sought to meet this responsibility. In colonial times it had become evident that not only regulation of individual traders was required, but actual governmental operation of the trading itself. The tendency therefore was for the establishment of trading houses, which came to be called "factories"; the agent in charge was a "factor." This system was adopted by the United States. Regulation of trade in the Indian country by the new American republic began in 1790 when Congress passed an "Act to regulate trade, and intercourse with the Indian tribes." According to this law, licenses were to be issued on a biennial basis to traders who could post a thousand dollar bond. The Superintendents of Indian Affairs were charged with the responsibility of issuing these licenses, and could revoke them whenever the conduct of the traders warranted. The earliest occasion on which Blount seems to have used this authority was August 4, 1794, when Barclay McGhee, Matthew Wallace, and John Lowrey were issued a joint license to trade with the Cherokees.[9]

Another Congressional act in 1795 authorized the President to establish such trading factories in the Indian country as was deemed necessary, and eventually $150,000 was appropriated for the expenses of the project. The purpose was humanitarian in that an eminently fair trading policy was contemplated with strict controls on prices, weights, and measures; and practical in that the program was designed to counteract the influence and prestige of British traders and Spanish agents. The factory which dealt with the Cherokee Indians was built at the Tellico Block House, on the Tellico River near its junction with the Tennessee River; this site was chosen because it already had a small garrison and because the Indians were "accustomed to resort thither for friendly conferences and negotiations."[10]

As a whole the program failed to produce the results which had been anticipated. Too often the price levels were exceeded, and measuring standards tampered with. The federal appropriations which finally trickled down to the Cherokee factory were too small. Futhermore, the competition from British traders generally, and Panton, Leslie & Company in particular, was too strong for the little establishment on the Tellico. The goods sent there were usually inferior to those carried by traders. Credit was prohibited, despite the fact that Cherokees usually had to wait for their money until the end of the hunting season. The factors themselves posed another difficulty, for although they were supposed to restrain themselves from improper financial gains, many of them grew rich. Finally, in spite of the meager appropriation, an abortive attempt was made to supply the Chickasaws from Tellico Factory. On February 5, 1801, a Congressional committee appointed to investigate the expediency of continuing an Indian trade founded on American capital, reported to the House that the returns from the Creek factory at Colerain and the Cherokee-Chickasaw factory at Tellico were insufficient to warrant a new appropriation. The committee recommended, however, that the laws providing for these two experimental factories be extended for another year.[11]

Despite the inadequacy of the factories, it seems evident that the Cherokees made good use of them. A traveller in 1802 saw "a kind of warehouse where the Cherokees carry ginseng [a medicinal herb] and furs, consisting of bear, stag, and otter skins. They give them in exchange for coarse stuffs, knives, hatchets, and other articles that they stand in need of." A report of Secretary of War Henry Dearborn in 1801 indicated that the factory system had some advantages, including "a very salutary effect upon the minds of the Indians." The financial report showed that of the original $150,000 appropriated, $90,115.90 had been withdrawn and invested in the two Southern factories. Of the two, the Colerain factory showed a greater profit, apparently because water transportation of its supplies and products was far cheaper than overland carriage to and from Tellico. Altogether, reported Dearborn, "the business of the two houses has been so managed, as, from the best information to be obtained, not only to save the original stock from diminution, but even to increase it about three or four percent."[12]

Of all developments which affected the Cherokees during these years under United States auspices, none had more social significance for the nation than the program which grew out of the Fourteenth Article of the Treaty of Holston. That stipulation, so unusual in an Indian treaty, had guaranteed United States aid in leading the Cherokee Nation "to a greater degree of civilization," and had promised to send both tools and agents to implement the program. For the Cherokees this provision represented a new attitude of the white man, and one to be regarded with some skepticism. But the program had little chance of complete success in the 1790's. In the first place, although there had been a promise to send agents to carry out the new design, no full-time agent particularly for the Cherokees was named by the War Department until 1801. As has been seen, the Cherokees came generally under the larger administrations of Blount and Hawkins. The latter, of course, was extremely interested in the program, and he and his deputy Silas Dinsmoor made some progress toward its accomplishment.

The Cherokee attitude toward the civilizing program was perhaps best expressed by a chief named Bloody Fellow, who was a delegate to the United States capital in January, 1792. Referring to the Holston agreement, Bloody Fellow told the Secretary of War:

> The treaty mentions ploughs, hoes, cattle and other things for a farm; this is what we want; game is going fast away from us. We must plant corn, and raise cattle, and we desire you to assist us. . . .
>
> We wish you to attend to this point. In former times we bought of the trader goods cheap; we could then clothe our women and children; but now game is scarce and goods dear, we cannot live comfortably. We desire the United States to regulate this matter.

Apparently the United States was willing to "regulate this matter." General Henry Knox, upon whom as Secretary of War rested the responsibility of getting such a program into effect, had already expressed his views on the matter in 1789. Deploring the idea that the Indians might be extinguished, he preferred to hope that "our knowledge of cultivation and the arts might be imparted to the red men." Knox's views were shared by President Washington; and the latter's influence was appreciated by at least one Cherokee leader, Charles Hicks, a half-breed who later became Principal Chief of the Nation. According to Hicks, Washington "encouraged the men to cultivate the soil, by the offer of the plough and the hoe; and the women to domestic industry by holding out the wheel and the loom over the nation."[13]

Owing to the difficulties previously described — frontier fighting on both sides, lands and hunting-ground losses, and lack of sufficient personnel to carry out the government program — Cherokee movement toward the high-sounding goal suggested by Article Fourteen was slow during the 1790's; but progress was made, due in part to the changing economic conditions of the Cherokees themselves. Depletion of hunting lands and pressures of frontiersmen were pushing the Cherokees southward to lands where raising food and livestock was more feasible.[14] Such hunting as continued was probably for supplying peltry to the government factories or to Spanish and British trading posts.

The greatly increased dependence on livestock, particularly beef cattle, was another encouraging development. In October,

1793, John Sevier reported to Governor Blount concerning a sortie he had led into the Indian country following a Knox County massacre. Included in the report was this brief but revealing item: "We took and destroyed near three hundred beeves many of which were of the best and largest kind."[15] Three years later Benjamin Hawkins reported seeing two Cherokee women on horseback taking "ten very fat cattle" to market, and noted other cattle on several farms.[16]

Benjamin Hawkins was particularly interested in the Cherokee agrarian progress and in their reaction to his government's program. During his trip through the Cherokee country in 1796 he conducted frequent interviews designed to further native progress. On the 28th of November, he talked to a half-breed woman who lived alone near Pine Log. She stated that she had once made as much cotton as purchased a petticoat, that she would gladly make more and learn to spin it, if she had the opportunity. The following day a group of neighboring women echoed this approval of the government's program. They told Hawkins "that they rejoiced much at what they had heard and hoped it would prove true, that they had made some cotton, and would make more and follow the instruction of the agent and the advice of the President." Other women who then were able to make sugar and grow cotton and who could manufacture baskets, sifters, and earthen pans and pots told Hawkins they were anxious to receive even more instruction, so that "if they could be directed how to turn their labour to account like the white people, they should be contented."[17]

Two of the many farms Hawkins visited while in the Cherokee country may serve as examples of the Indian progress in agriculture. At the home of an old Cherokee named The Terrapin, the government agent noted that "the old fellow lives well, the land he cultivates is lined with small growth of saplins for some distance, his farm is fenced, his houses comfortable, he has a large stock of cattle, and some hogs. He uses the plow." Near Etowah, Hawkins spent the night of Sunday, December 3, 1796, at the home of Half-breed Will. "The father and mother were out hunting, his daughters received me kindly and furnished plentifully," he wrote, adding:

They gave me good bread, pork and potatoes for supper, and ground peas [peanuts] and dried peaches. I had corn for my horses. The hut in which I lodged was clean and neat. In the morning I breakfasted on corn cakes and pork. They had a number of fowls, hogs and some cattle, the field of 4 acres for corn fenced, and half an acre for potatoes.[18]

A year later Benjamin Hawkins had news of pleasing progress from Silas Dinsmoor, who by this time was residing with the Cherokees under orders to improve them in civilized pursuits.[19] Summarizing a report from Dinsmoor, Hawkins told a friend: "Among the Cherokees everything progresses as well as I had a right to expect it would. My daughters are spinning and weaving. He [Dinsmoor] saw at one place 42½ yards of good homespun and some more ready for the loom." A few days later Hawkins repeated the gist of this information to the Secretary of War, and highly complimented Cherokee progress.[20]

Continued Cherokee advancement in civilized arts was noted in 1802 by the French traveller F. A. Michaux. During his visit to South West Point, a military post fifty miles northwest of Tellico, he learned from several white men that the Cherokees had made considerable improvement "within these few years." He was told that "Some of them have good plantations." Spinning and weaving accomplishments by women constituted further gains, and all in all, Michaux found, "they make a rapid progress."[21]

Of considerable importance to the process of civilizing the Cherokees was the presence of a large number of influential whites and mixed-breeds. Ever since the early days of Indian relations with the white men, there had been a tendency for some of the whites to settle with the natives. When the better class of traders began to reside in the Cherokee Nation about the middle of the eighteenth century, an important new element was infused into the native culture. The descendants of Scotch, Irish, and Scotch-Irish tradesmen rose in power during the 1790's to become strong contenders for leadership in the nation. Tories who entered the Cherokee country during the American Revolution furnished another important source of white blood. Many of these men had enjoyed a relatively high degree of culture in tidewater areas. Some had brought slaves along. Most of the Tories, as well as some of the traders, saw to it that their children received as much education as possible. A third group entering the Cherokee Nation, especially during the last of the eighteenth century, were itinerant artisan-traders, mostly German; those who decided to remain furnished the Cherokees with still another trait — a sturdy dexterity. A less welcome group were the white fugitives from prosecution or prison. Their presence was resented by the Indians and by the neighboring governments alike, and they were a continual source of difficulty.[22]

Most Cherokees seem to have been glad to receive the whites and their institutions into the Indian culture. The law-abiding whites were also welcomed by agent Hawkins and his successor Return J. Meigs, who saw advantages for the Cherokees from this immigration. But there were dissenting voices. Frontiersmen who hated Indians, state governments that resented the federal benevolence, and men like Blount, who saw the Cherokees as troublesome enough to handle without these new disturbing elements, formed a bitter opposition. Discussing Indian depredations in a letter to Secretary Knox in 1792, Governor Blount stated:

> Another reason for these depredations is, that the white people living among the . . . Cherokees, (the greatest of all rascals) and the half-breeds, who are numerous, and mostly traders, encourage the Indians to steal horses from all the citizens of the United States, to the end that they might purchase them. Thus encouraged, the Indians go into the frontier settlements in search of horses, and if they find an unarmed person or family, they fall on them; and if they take horses and are pursued, kill in their own defense.[23]

The late eighteenth century witnessed settlement in the Indian country of some particularly outstanding traders who left a rich heritage among the Cherokees. A typical example of this group and their influence is offered in the story of the Ross-McDonald family, out of which emerged one of the greatest of all Cherokee leaders, John Ross.

Ross's maternal grandfather was John McDonald, a Scotsman who arrived at Charleston, South Carolina, in 1766 at the age of nineteen. Following a brief employment in Savannah with a mercantile establishment, McDonald so impressed his employers that he was sent to Fort Loudon on the Little Tennessee to supervise the company's Indian trade. After a rapid success at this work, aided by his ability to get along with the Indians, he decided to establish his own business. Shortly thereafter he married a half-breed Cherokee woman named Anne Shorey, a descendant of prominent Cherokees. When steady pressure of white settlers on the Indian borders forced a steady withdrawal of the natives, McDonald accompanied one group into northeast Georgia, settling and building a home near Lookout Mountain. Here he re-established his business, the expansion of which brought him into close relationship with Panton, Leslie, & Company, and Spanish agents.[24]

John Ross's father, Daniel Ross, was equally resourceful and daring in his efforts to find business success among the Cherokee Indians. Made an orphan in Baltimore by the Revolutionary War, young Daniel and an experienced trader named Mayberry entered on a river-hauling venture. In Tennessee the partners constructed a flatboat, loaded it with goods, and embarked for Cherokee lands to seek furs. Unfortunately an Indian passenger proved to be a chief unfriendly to the Lookout Mountain Cherokees. When the Mayberry-Ross expedition neared Lookout, the chief was recognized, and the entire party taken prisoner. Controversy as to the proper disposition of their captives led the Cherokees to seek advice from John McDonald. He urged that the party be released, and caused an invitation to be issued to Ross and Mayberry to remain and establish their own trading posts. Daniel Ross did so, and soon became well-liked among the Cherokees. He was "a man of irreproachable character and sturdy honesty," and became noted for his fair dealings with white and red alike. Ross settled in a house at the foot of Lookout Mountain, about three miles west of McDonald's home, with Mollie McDonald as his wife. This union produced nine children, of whom John Ross was the third.[25]

Of especial interest in connection with the effect of the infiltration of whites into the Cherokee national blood and culture, is the fact that Daniel Ross established a private school on his own property in order to educate his children. The local Cherokee Council approved the appointment of John B. Davis to teach at the school, which was probably the first such educational institution in the Cherokee Nation. When young John Ross was ready to enter business, he formed a partnership with his brother Lewis and John Meigs (son of the Indian Agent). They established a trading post near Lookout Mountain at Ross's Landing. As their business grew and prospered, John Ross became particularly well-liked and respected by the Cherokees, whom he preferred to call brothers—although he possessed but one-eighth Indian blood. Known by the Cherokees as "Guwisguwi" (or "Cooweescoowe"), Ross was an attractive young man of supple body and medium height, with blue eyes and brown hair. He had a reserved, quiet manner, and seems to have inherited much of both the Ross and McDonald shrewdness and charm.[26]

Other leading Cherokees of mixed-blood ancestry during the late eighteenth century included the following: the famous Nancy Ward; John Watts, who succeeded Dragging Canoe in leadership of the Chickamaugas, and who was referred to by Governor Blount at one time as "unquestionably the most leading character of his nation";[27] Charles Hicks, an important interpreter during the 1790's who was "much relied on by the chiefs";[28] James Davidson, "a distinguished chief of the Valley and Overhill Towns";[29] James Carey, a Cherokee interpreter "of substance and repute"; and such figures as Doublehead, George Lowrey, James Vann, Richard Justice, Bushyhead (a descendant of Captain John Stuart),[30] and numerous others.

As early as 1789 it was thought by one observer that the Cherokees had progressed to the point of being able to absorb the white man's culture. William Bartram wrote that "if adopting or imitating the manners and customs of the white people is to be termed civilization, perhaps the Cherokees have made the greatest advance." Later historians have echoed this idea, notably Theodore Roosevelt, who asserted that "the Cherokees were a bright, intelligent race, better fitted to 'follow the white man's road' than any other Indians."[31] After a generation of frontier tribulations, the Cherokee Nation of Indians was largely ready to "follow the white man's road" a little farther if it would bring peace, security, food, and shelter. During the thirty years which lay ahead, many of them would find these comforts, leaving tribal life farther behind and learning much of the white man's economy. Of great importance to this growth was the administration of Return Jonathan Meigs, who was to be their agent and counsellor during the first twenty years of their remarkable progress at the beginning of the nineteenth century.

FIVE

RETURN JONATHAN MEIGS AND CHEROKEE PROGRESS, 1801-1823

FATE SMILED on the Cherokees in 1801 with the appointment of Return Jonathan Meigs as Indian Agent. A seasoned frontiersman and Revolutionary War hero, Meigs had a thorough knowledge of the Indians and a deep sympathy for their problems. Sensible, just, firm, and above desire for personal gain, the new agent devoted himself to promoting the well-being of the Cherokees. Diplomatic in spite of his rough background, he ably served his government, successfully dealt with state authorities, and generally gained the confidence of Indians. After the confusion of frontier crises Colonel Meigs was a stabilizing force in a crucial period of Cherokee history.

Return J. Meigs was born at Middletown, Connecticut, on December 17, 1740. At the age of thirty-two he was commissioned a lieutenant in the Sixth Connecticut Regiment, and during the Revolutionary War he rose to the rank of colonel. He participated in Arnold's ill-fated march on Quebec, and later led the "brilliant" Sag Harbor expedition in 1777, for which Congress gratefully awarded him a sword. After retirement in 1781, he became interested in the Ohio Company, which appointed him a surveyor. In April, 1788, Meigs led a group of settlers from New England to the Ohio country. There he suggested a "code of rules" which the community adopted. Meigs eventually settled down at Marietta. In May, 1801, he accepted a dual appointment as Cherokee Indian Agent and Agent of the War Department in Tennessee.[1]

Arriving in the Indian country in the middle of June, Colonel Meigs went to work promptly. His first task was to set up a combined Indian and War Department Agency at South West

Point, about sixty miles northwest of the Tellico factory. At the request of James Vann and other Cherokees, Meigs obtained War Department approval to establish a subsidiary agency at Tellico to which Major William L. Lovely was assigned late in 1801.[2]

During Meigs' twenty-two years as Indian Agent he fulfilled the pledges of the United States by guiding the Indian Nation along the path of the white man's progress. He distributed farming implements and household utensils, along with expert advice on their use. He stood up for Indian rights at treaty conferences, and encouraged Cherokee efforts to establish a republican government of their own. The Agent recovered stolen property, arbitrated disputes, gave medical aid, and ordered out intruders. When the War Department told him to cooperate with religious efforts, Meigs made numerous visits to the mission stations and frequently aided them in construction and other problems. From the moment of his arrival, the sixty-year-old Indian Agent was an active and guiding force on Cherokee development, serving his Indian wards as parent, adviser, doctor, lawyer, and home demonstration agent.

First among the Indian Agent's duties was the maintenance of peace and order. The chief source of difficulty lay in the friction caused by unscrupulous men of both white and red races. The white men who provoked Indians were generally of four categories: land-hungry farmers who settled illegally on Indian territory; traders who took advantage of their legalized presence in the nation; travellers, soldiers, and itinerant artisans who appropriated Cherokee property; and criminal fugitives. Before Meigs entered the Indian country he was instructed by the War Department to report unauthorized settlers to the nearest commanding officer of a United States army detachment. A month later the agent was warned to keep out any trouble-making whites. Secretary of War Henry Dearborn wrote, "request your vigilant attention . . . in order to prevent our peace from being disturbed by the licentiousness of daring & unprincipled men." The problems brought by some of these "daring & unprincipled men" were described thus by a group of Georgia commissioners to the Cherokees: "There are Numbers of white people in the Nation who have wives among the Natives, Carry on a Triffling Commerce with them and are averse to any further, or better understanding [between whites and Indians] than now exists. Several of these characters have fled from punishment."[3]

White men who arbitrarily possessed themselves of Cherokee lands were a constant problem for the Agent. Specific complaints about these intruders were usually reported to Meigs by the individuals concerned. In 1807, for example, John Boggs wrote:

> Friend and Brother I had a Piece of Land allotted for myself upon . . . [Sequatchie River] the head men allotted it for me Since that there is a white man Come and Settled upon it which I do not like his name is James Blair I don't Like him as he has left his own wife and Taken up with an Indian woman I look upon Him as a Base man.
>
> As you are my friend and Brother I hope you will See me Justice Done –

Meigs tried to "See Justice Done" in removing intruders. Usually he investigated each complaint. If whites were found in illegal residence, the military officer nearest the point of intrusion was requested to remove them. The Agent's attention to his duty was revealed in 1808 when Captain A. B. Armistead of the Hiwassee Garrison was instructed to remove a James Chisholm, "residing on the Indian lands as an aggressor." Meigs remarked at the close of the letter, "it is my wish that he may be taken with the least possible distress to his family; which is only involved in difficulty by his bad conduct."[4]

The "bad conduct" of trespassers kept some sections of the nation in anxiety, and added considerably to the problems of Return J. Meigs. His plaintive description of their actions expressed acutely not only the menace to law and order but the threats to successful treaty negotiations:

> The conduct of these intruders is just such as that of others in numerous instances on the frontiers of the Cherokee country –Under some pretext they enter on the Indian lands disturb the peace & quiet of the Indians; then teaze the Government to purchase the land, which raises the price, & embarrasses the Government in effecting purchases – If they are moved they complain of hardship, while at the same time they are the sole cause of all they suffer. . . .[5]

White men were not the only aggressors in the Indian country. Cherokees occasionally robbed and murdered; and Meigs received the brunt of complaints on these scores. Here again he dispensed justice to persons wronged. If investigation proved red men at fault, his agency made restitution in money or goods; in cases of homicide Meigs secured retribution from the National Council.

Shortly after the Agent reported to duty, for example, he settled a case involving a white man named Attwood, who complained to Meigs that he had been held prisoner by a Cherokee named "Tus'ke'ge'ti'hi" who forced him to pay a ransom of three dollars. After a few days' investigation Meigs reimbursed Attwood.[6]

On the occasions when white men ignored the Indian Agent and meted out their own punishment Meigs lost no time in asserting his authority. When two Tennesseans named William Russel and Stephen Copeland forcibly dispossessed several Indians of a hunting camp in retaliation for livestock losses, Colonel Meigs reported the incident to the Governor of Tennessee. In the message he summed up his grievances on such matters:

> What they allege with respect to the Indians killing some of there Stock may be true but as the Law Guarantees satisfaction in such cases, they should have ascertained the facts & made complaints to the Agent – An attempt to obtain private Satisfaction by Violent measures deprive them of recovery damages, & has a tendency to induce retaliation without end, & may finally if not restrained envolve us in a quarrel with the Indians –[7]

One Cherokee successfully evaded both federal and local punishment for his crimes. This was the notorious half-breed town chief James Vann. A peculiar combination of benevolent leader and rip-snorting hoodlum, Vann was a constant trouble-maker. When Moravian churchmen sought to bring a mission to the Cherokees in 1801, Vann was outstanding in his aid to them. After helping to obtain Council approval for the missionaries, he gave generously of his time, advice, and property when the mission station was begun at his home. Yet his carousing was a constant source of anxiety among his church friends, who tried unsuccessfully to reform him. Finally in March, 1804, Meigs sent the Secretary of War a list of Vann's deeds, including a report that the Indian had recently murdered a Georgia militiaman named Leonard Rice. Dearborn's reply indicated a sensible policy for his agent: "If the citizens of Georgia will take due measures for punishing him for his crimes, there can be no objection on the part of the General Government." But Fate caught up with James Vann before "due measures" could be taken. A shooting affray with his brother-in-law brought on a duel; and in 1809 Vann was shot to death.[8]

Most of Meigs' relations with the Cherokee Council were more pleasant than those involving Vann. Anxious to receive the instruments of civilization promised them by the federal government at Holston in 1791, the Cherokees found Return J. Meigs eager to continue the plan of improvement. The Agent carried on the civilizing program in the spirit of his predecessor Benjamin Hawkins, encouraging the Cherokees as individuals and as a nation. At the outset of his work Meigs found the Indians in excellent condition to receive aid. He wrote the Secretary of War for a greater supply of implements, remarking

> It appears to me from the present temper of the Indians, that the raising of Cotton & Sheep & manufacturing the produce of these articles may be easily carried to a very considerable extent & thereby accelerate civilization, even amongst those who have been strongly attached to the hunting life —[9]

The United States government fully intended to "accelerate civilization" among the Cherokee Indians. The policy to be carried out was epitomized in a letter of instructions from the Secretary of War in July, 1801. Referring to a delegation of Cherokee chiefs who had recently visited Washington, Dearborn wrote:

> They have represented to me that the blacksmith who is established at the Muscle Shoals will be much more useful if removed to the great town in the interior of their country: you will therefore be pleased to have him removed thither and furnished with iron to make light iron apparatus for ploughs, &c and direct him to instruct such young Indians as may be willing in the trade.
>
> If a sober, orderly Carpenter can be procured to reside in their country for about Six months to make the wood work for ploughs, &c, & instruct the young men I request you to engage one.
>
> One hundred pairs of Cotton Cards will be sent to you to be distributed in presents to the industrious as occasion may require; a like number will be forwarded to the Tellico Factory to be sold to the Indians.[10]

In the execution of these and similar orders Agent Meigs showed energy and initiative. He immediately made arrangements to move the blacksmith, for example, sending him to the Wills Town area (near present-day Fort Payne, Alabama). A short time later he placed another blacksmith at the request of Indians in a different region. When possible he also supplied the Cherokees with "Wheel Makers," carpenters, and other artisans.[11]

Late in 1801 Colonel Meigs pondered the question, "How shall we give to this people an impulsion which shall draw it towards the aim we have in view i.e. to a degree of Civilization — while the ancient usages are so much esteemed [?]" He arrived at a possible solution which reflected a deep interest in Cherokee improvement, and at the same time forecast Indian governmental developments:

> It cannot be done by an individual: but by forming the whole [nation] into civil divisions, creating officers in each, to attend to the manners, employments, Virtues, & Vices, — to advise, instruct, & encourage virtuous actions — discourage and apprehend vice; in fine, to have an eye on the little community & to report annually at a meeting of the principal Men and Fathers — the moral Virtues may spring up from this mode of cultivation — Vice will hide its head, industry encouraged.

Meigs presented this proposal to the Council, with the further recommendation that the "civil officials" include in their annual reports "the quantity of Cloth manufactured during each year, that when the year came about they would at once have a View of the State of their people, with respect to morals, manufactures, & agriculture. . . ."[12] Although the Cherokees made no immediate effort to adopt Meigs' suggestion, his proposal for civil reorganization found fruit seventeen years later in the creation of the Cherokee Republic.[13]

Requests for assistance poured into the Agency from individuals all over the nation, most of whom desired tools and equipment. Writing for the "Head men of the towns" near Ellijay in November, 1801, for example, an Indian named "Dredful Waters" asked for "ten pair Cotton Cards as they stand in need of them now cotton have come, and four wheels, and two screw augers, and four gimblets and two draw Knives. . . ." On many occasions Cherokees visited the Agency to ask for implements. A letter from Big Half Breed gave warning of such a visit early in 1807:

> Vans villey [valley] febuwerey 7 1807 freind and brother we intend to pay u a viset the third of Next month and have the pleasur of Convering with you Likewise we beg that you will pervid one plow and one whele apese for us. . . .
> Fore of each
>
> Big halfbreid X
> Jobber Sam
> Bird Eye
> George Miller

One prominent Cherokee town chief heard from frequently was The Glass. His requests were mainly those needed by his town, and included writing paper, a blacksmith, and agricultural implements. On one occasion he wrote, "I want you to Lay by for my town fore plows and for widen hos [four weeding hoes] and fore Axes and fore gruben [grubbing] hose and I want you to Lit John Lowery the Same quanty of the Same arttickels for the pore people abot him. . . ."[14]

A scarcity of corn caused by a drought in the Cherokee Nation during the year 1804 was a crisis which Meigs faced in his typical fashion. The first request for food came from Doublehead and other Cherokees in the Muscle Shoals area on the Lower Tennessee River. The Agent immediately sent them three hundred bushels of corn, for which the Indians paid $110. Meigs, however, requested and received permission from the War Department to return the money; he thought it his duty "to give the necessary relief – believing that humanity and interest combine to make it proper especially when Interesting negotiations with them are now soon to be opened." Meigs' policy pleased his government. Henry Dearborn sent him the President's congratulations, urging Meigs to continue helping needy Indians: "You will embrace so favorable an opportunity for impressing the minds of the Cherokees with the fatherly concern and attention of the President to the distresses of his red children."[15]

Occasionally Meigs' "red children" were distressed by disease, and those who turned from native conjurors and traditional herbs found Meigs sympathetic and helpful. When a smallpox epidemic struck the nation in 1806 the Agent, at Council's request, obtained for them the services of a Tennessee doctor named William McNeill. Upon the conclusion of the physician's work, Meigs paid him $150.[16] In 1801 a prominent Cherokee native whose sickness was cured partly through Meigs' assistance thanked him: "Honoured Sir I have Sent to let you know I have Recovered of my Sickness & am perfectly Well I am Greatly Obliged to you Sir for the favours I Ricieved from your hands . . . I Return my thanks for [your] Goodness to me in the time of my Sickness I hope in a Short time to see You all again soon."[17]

One of the more important duties of the Indian Agent was to distribute the yearly annuities paid the Cherokees by the United States. Payments in money and goods were made at annual gatherings, usually at the Indian Agency. Traditional presents to Indians had long included colorful gew-gaws, and some annuity payments were made in these items. The Cherokees, however, were on the threshold of a higher degree of culture, and consequently requested more practical materials. Shortly after Meigs became Indian Agent he notified the Purveyor of Public Supplies in Philadelphia that the Cherokee Chiefs requested goods "that are really usefull for them in their curcumstances." The Indians complained to Meigs that the previous annuity had brought them "Fine muslin, Tamboured [embroidered] muslin, Silk Stockings, Ostrich Feathers, Gold & Silver lace, fine dimity, Earrings, Cambrick, Diaper & Damask Table Cloths, Morocco Shoes, & one Sett of Officers Canteens complete."[18]

The Cherokee Council continued to press for better assortments of annuity goods. In 1803 it presented to Colonel Meigs a list of items to be included in that year's payment, which indicated the Cherokees' interest in the government's civilizing program:

> 50 Brass Kettles of different sizes, 100 Tin Kettles of all the different sizes, 200 pairs of Cotton Cards, 1000 Blankets, 80 Fur Hats, 50 lbs. Thread, 100 ps. [pieces] Callico, 50 ps. Common Cotton Stripes, 100 ps. Strouds [coarse blankets], 100 yards of Scarlet Broad Cloth – Second quality, 50 ps. Broad Ribbon, 6 Gross of Silk Handks, 10 m. Needles, /12 Gross Quality bandings, 30 ps. Linen not fine, 4 lbs. Vermillion, 1 Gross of Scizzars.[19]

The annuity distribution of 1807 is illustrative of supply problems. The annuity of that year consisted of four thousand dollars worth of blankets and five thousand dollars cash. The blankets were shipped from Philadelphia to the Agency (then located on the Hiwassee River) by way of Savannah and Augusta; transport from Augusta was by wagons sent down by Meigs. The cash was sent directly to the Agency by courier. The chiefs requested the money earlier than the usual time for annuities; and Meigs complied with the request by issuing the money on August 25. The following signed (all with an X) a receipt "in behalf of the Cherokee Nation": Black Fox, Sower Mush, Davis, Chulioa, Big Half Breed, Quoleguskee, Tolunluskee, Will Shorey, John Lowery, and Toutchalee.[20]

Normally annuities were distributed in the autumn to huge throngs. When in 1802 he discovered that subsistence for the gathering Cherokees was furnished by the federal government, Meigs tried to cut down the number of attendants. In spite of the suggestion, however, fifty-two chiefs and a considerable number of followers turned up. Subsequent gatherings were also large. In 1803 Meigs ordered "Fifteen thousand rations of Bread, Meat, & Salt" for annuity time.[21]

The annual assembly of such large numbers of Indians was a constant source of trouble for Agent and Council alike. Subsistence problems, speculative ventures, and the disorder and confusion that often prevailed when whiskey was brought along made such occasions difficult. After a republican form of government was organized in 1817,[22] a new plan for the handling of annuities was arranged. The National Council authorized a delegation of chiefs to inform the government at Washington that

> our annuity has been embarrassed by speculation both by whites and red people which has continued from Double Head's time to the present day and that the nation now had Elected thirteen warriors to have the superintendence of it in the settlements with limited Powers subject to the unanimous acceptance or rejection by the members of our council and chiefs of the Cherokee nation. and that the Chiefs have resolved that hereafter the National Committee shall meet at the Agency to receive annuities, &c with the above limited power, as these great national meetings have of late produced quarrels among our people and division among our warriors &c[23]

A prime function of the Cherokee Agent was to serve as a liaison officer between white and red governments and to arrange treaty conferences as they became necessary. It was Meigs' task to maintain a climate of opinion among Cherokee leaders favorable to territorial cessions. During the period of Meigs' agency from 1801 to 1823 numerous attempts were made by federal and state commissioners to secure land grants from the Cherokees. Nine of these attempts were successful, reducing the Cherokee Nation to an area of some ten million acres. Most of the land cessions were in North Georgia, as that state was especially active in efforts to expel the Cherokees. Anxious to see the Indians removed and eager to rid herself of the vexatious Yazoo problem, Georgia ceded her western claims to the United States in 1802.[24] In return for this region, which became part of the Mississippi Territory, Georgia was to receive a payment of $1,250,000 and the Yazoo claims were to be assumed by the United States. Furthermore, the United States guaranteed to "extinguish, at their own expense, for the use of Georgia, as early as the same can be peaceably obtained, upon reasonable terms, the Indian title to the lands lying within the limits of that state."[25] For the next thirty years Georgians demanded with ever-growing impatience that the federal government remove the Cherokees and Creeks in accordance with the "Compact of 1802."

Shortly after Meigs' arrival at South West Point he began to receive requests from his government and the surrounding states to obtain land cessions from the Cherokees. He found the Cherokee Council adamant in its determination not to cede any more lands. His policy, however, was to persuade the chiefs that the payment was more to be desired in some cases than the lands given up. He was told by the Secretary of War that

> the money & goods which they will receive for the lands, more especially that part which will be paid annually will be of more real benefit to the nation under their improved state than the lands can be: that they will be enabled to make still greater progress in the useful arts, & will more & more rely on agriculture & domestic manufactories for their support & of course become a happy people.

That Meigs successfully used this approach early in his Indian dealings was evidenced in 1802 when the Cherokees agreed to sell the Long Island in the Holston River. In reporting the agreement, the Agent wrote Henry Dearborn that the Council "have desired me to request in their behalf, that the Island may be sold for the benefit of their Nation, & say that they think the Island is worth two thousand dollars — & desire that it may be sold for cash. —"[26] Although the treaty for this particular cession was not arranged for several years, it is significant that through Meigs' intercessions the Indians seemed to have initiated the action.

The first land cessions negotiated during Meigs' agency were arranged in 1804 and 1805.[27] On October 24, 1804, the Cherokee Nation gave up a small tract in northeast Georgia known as "Wafford's Settlement," in return for an immediate payment of five thousand dollars in goods or cash, and an addition of one thousand dollars to the yearly annuity. A year later, two large cessions in central Tennessee and southern Kentucky were taken from the Cherokees. The Indians received $15,600 at the time, and three thousand dollars in extra annuities. They also gave road concessions in each of the 1805 treaties.[28] These agreements were negotiated by Meigs and General Daniel Smith of Tennessee. Their success after other commissioners had failed may be attributed partly to Meigs' influence, and partly to the reprehensible use of "secret articles" which gave special concessions to Chief Doublehead as a reward for helping push the treaty through Council.[29]

During the next two years Colonel Meigs was busy with boundary-making problems created by the recent cessions, for he was appointed as United States Commissioner to superintend surveying of the new lines. In the meantime another treaty was arranged. On January 7, 1806, final negotiations were made for selling the Long Island of Holston by a delegation of Cherokees in Washington; this treaty also included a large cession in western Tennessee and Alabama between the Tennessee and Duck rivers.[30]

A decade elapsed before the Cherokees could be induced to part with more land, although South Carolina and Tennessee were importunate in seeking treaties. Finally in 1816, after Colonel Meigs took a delegation of Indians to Washington for personal negotiations, three agreements were reached. On March 22 the last Cherokee portion of South Carolina, a small triangular strip in the state's northwestern corner, was relinquished for five thousand dollars. Another treaty of the same date settled several long-standing problems, notably Cherokee claims for depredations suffered when American troops marched through the Indian country during the Creek War of 1813-14.[31] Other terms of this agreement clarified the Cherokee-Creek boundary between the Coosa and Tennessee rivers, and granted to the United States "the right to lay off, open, and have the free use of all roads through their [Cherokee] country . . . necessary to convenient intercourse between the States of Tennessee, Georgia, and Mississippi Territory; also the free navigation of all rivers within the Cherokee territory." A stipulation which may have won over some of the reluctant Indian signatories provided that individual Cherokees could erect and maintain public-houses along the roads. The third treaty of 1816, ratified by Cherokees on October 4, ceded a large area in present-day northwestern Alabama, bounded by the Coosa and Tennessee rivers, for which the Indians were to be paid five thousand dollars in cash and sixty thousand dollars in ten annuities.[32]

A year later further grants ate away more lands on the Tennessee, Alabama, and Georgia borders. A growing sentiment on the part of some Cherokees favoring westward removal to richer game areas offered a prime opportunity to obtain more lands from the red men. United States Commissioners Andrew Jackson,

Joseph McMinn, and David Meriwether sought an exchange of eastern for western lands. Despite the obvious disapproval of numerous Indian leaders, the commissioners arranged an exchange treaty with some forty-three chiefs, fifteen of whom represented western Cherokees. Signed July 8, 1817, the agreement ceded to Tennessee a triangular area bordering on the Sequatchie River; Alabama received two rectangular strips north of the Tennessee River west of Muscle Shoals; and Georgia was given a large irregular L-shaped region on the east bank of the Chattahoochee extending about one hundred miles north and south. In return for these grants the Cherokees were given an area of equal size on the Arkansas and White rivers bordering on the Osage country.[33]

An unusual feature of the treaty of 1817, and one which offered new hope to those Cherokees anxious for security and agricultural prosperity in their southern homelands, was the "reservations" clause: "Each head of a Cherokee family residing on lands herein or hereafter ceded to the United States who elects to become a citizen of the United States shall receive a reservation of 640 acres, to include his or her improvements, for life, with reversion in fee simple to children, subject to widow's dower."[34] Although this offer was probably intended as a sop for those chiefs opposing western removal, a considerable number of Cherokee land-holders accepted with alacrity.

As an inducement to further the westward removal of Cherokees, the commissioners inserted in the treaty of 1817 several seemingly beneficial clauses to allay the suspicions of undecided lower-class Indians. The stipulations guaranteed payment for improvements abandoned by the emigrants. "Poor warriors" departing for the west would be given "a rifle, ammunition, blanket, and brass kettle or beaver trap each, as full compensation for improvements left by them." Others leaving more expensive property were to be paid full value. Furthermore the federal government promised to pay transportation costs and subsistence for the journey to Arkansas.[35]

Since the 1790's various bands of Cherokees had wandered westward, especially those dissatisfied with the federal civilizing policy. In 1794 a Cherokee Chief named Bowls led a group to the Arkansas country.[36] At the suggestion of Spanish agents, a few families later went to the area around the River St. Francis. By 1805 these Cherokees, with vagabond Indians from other tribes, had become a constant source of danger to passing white boatmen and frontiersmen. But most of the Cherokee Indians were opposed to westward emigration. The topic was broached to them by the United States government shortly after the purchase of the Louisiana Territory in 1803. President Jefferson proposed that eastern tribes of Indians be removed to the newly acquired western lands. Vociferous objections from white inhabitants of the territory temporarily ended that project.[37]

At various times during the next decade the Cherokee Indian Agent discussed removal possibilities with the Council. In 1804 he reported that most Indians disliked the idea, although several leaders were willing to support it "by motives of personal Interest." Four years later prospects seemed brighter, and Meigs received authorization from Washington to attempt a removal treaty. In 1809 the Agent sent a delegation of Cherokees headed by the young mixed-blood John Ross, into the Arkansas River country on an inspection trip. This group's favorable account of the region provoked a temporary enthusiasm for migration, and plans were begun by the Agent and Council. But when it was learned that no federal appropriations were available to finance the movement, only a few went west.[38]

By 1817 there were beyond the Mississippi some two thousand Cherokees who were usually referred to as "Old Settlers West" or "Cherokees West." When the treaty of 1817 was proclaimed, federal and state authorities hoped that a majority of the eastern Cherokees would emigrate. This did not occur. Indian anger over the minority treaty was rampant, and those who signed it were calumniated and persecuted until they and a few others left for the western territories. Meanwhile protests and delegations went to Washington seeking a fairer agreement. Most Cherokees were probably perplexed at the shift in the federal government's attitude. This change and the typical Indian reaction to it were reported thus by a group of missionaries near Chickamauga Creek:

> The Indians say they don't know how to understand their Father the President. A few years ago he sent them a plough & a hoe—said it was not good for his red children to hunt—they must cultivate the earth. Now he tells them there is good hunting at the Arkansas; if they go there he will give them rifles.

These clergymen resolved to keep out of the controversy, although they felt that a "general removal would greatly distress" the Cherokees, and would probably retard "the benevolent design of bringing them out of their state of darkness to the light of divine truth & the privileges of civilization."[39]

Meanwhile some 3,500 Cherokees enrolled for westward removal, filed their claims for improvements abandoned, and prepared for the journey. White officials began protesting to the Cherokee Council that more territory was going to be required in the west than had been given up in the east, and that further cessions were required. The Cherokee leaders were also badgered by protests from their own countrymen for better evaluating arrangements, and more satisfactory guarantees of repayment. Finally on February 27, 1819, another treaty was concluded by which thousands of acres of territory on the eastern, northern, and southern Cherokee boundaries were ceded. The United States reiterated its offer of 640-acre reservations, guaranteed a fair payment for abandoned property, and promised to keep intruders out of the ceded lands until January 1, 1820.[40] Following the vast cessions of the period 1816-1819, the Cherokee Nation refused to make any more land treaties until the 1830's.

The "reservations" clauses in the treaties of 1817 and 1819 proved to be troublesome for Indians and white governments alike. Those Cherokees desiring to retain the 640-acre lots declared their intention to the Indian Agent. Meigs then had to issue an acknowledgement and maintain a record of names and locations. The usual notification from Cherokees was like Walter S. Adair's, dated June 7, 1819:

> In the late treaty between the United States and the Cherokee Indians I see there is a reservation of six hundred and forty acres of land is made to me, provided I Give notice in due time that I intend to become a perminent residinter on the land, these are therefore to inform you, I except of the reservation agreeable to the articles of said treaty.

Nearly 150 reservations were filed in Meigs' office; the list included such prominent mixed-blood progressive Cherokees as John Ross, George Lowrey, John Martin, and Walter S. Adair.[41]

The chief difficulty arising over the reservations, however, was a legal one, and emerged from conflicts between the Cherokees and whites who entered the ceded lands. Many of the Indians were forced by white prejudice to leave their homes and withdraw within the boundaries of the nation. George Lowrey, for example, had to give up his Battle Creek (Tennessee) plantation.

He moved his family to Wills Valley in the Alabama area, where he soon became prominent in local and national affairs.[42] The aftermath of these withdrawals was a long series of litigations between Indian owners and white claimants. As Indian Agent, Meigs was called upon to represent the Cherokees in many of these cases, especially those which were heard in Tennessee courts.[43]

Despite ill-feeling engendered by removal controversies Return J. Meigs was able to maintain a generally friendly Cherokee attitude toward his government; and in this he performed one of his most important services as Indian Agent. The value of his placating influence was effectively demonstrated during the War of 1812, when hostile Indians went on the warpath against the United States. Those nearest to the Cherokees were the Upper Creeks, whose desires to destroy white supremacy on the American continent had been drummed up earlier by Tecumseh and other agents of his short-lived Indian confederacy. When this neighboring branch of the Creeks launched raids against United States posts in 1813, the Cherokees were showered with requests for assistance. Pleas came not only from the hostiles and the United States government, but from Lower Creeks as well, who sought Cherokee help in crushing the revolt. Reactionaries within the Cherokee Council favored abandoning the path toward the white man's culture and joining the attacking Creeks. The friendly overtures of Agent Meigs and the active opposition of Cherokee progressives led by John Lowrey and The Ridge (later Major Ridge) swayed the Indian council. A force of volunteers was organized to fight along with the United States and the friendly Lower Creeks under the leadership of General Andrew Jackson.[44]

Altogether some eight hundred Cherokee participants in the Creek War of 1814 gave valuable assistance through their bravery and knowledge of Indian fighting. Led by capable native officers including Colonel Gideon Morgan, Major John Lowrey, and Captain Richard Brown, the Cherokees gave a particularly good account of themselves at the final important affray of the war, the Battle of Horseshoe Bend. At a crucial point a group of Cherokees under Chief Junaluska silently swam the Tallapoosa River to the enemy's rear and took all hostile canoes. Then, using the same canoes, Cherokees pressed into the battle and fought beside Jackson's victorious forces.[45]

The Creek War had unfortunate accompaniments for the

Cherokee Indians. American troops marched through the nation going to and coming from the Creek country and inflicted serious depredations on Cherokee property. Meig's office received many complaints about these unwarranted losses, which became sources of contention in subsequent treaty discussions. Although the treaty of March 22, 1816, promised justice for the losses, no serious attempt to repay Cherokees was made until the 1830's. On January 15, 1814, a "Claims Journal" containing more than seventy claims for troop damages was presented to Colonel Meigs. The total amount requested was $5,885, mostly for stolen and butchered livestock. One of the largest claims was made by William Chambers, who reported $725 worth of cattle, sheep, and swine taken. A more typical loss was suffered by The Big Cabbin (or Cabbin Smith): "17 bushels corn, 1 bull, 1 cow . . ., 1 sow . . ., total $27." This Cherokee asserted that

> he met several white people going on to his house himself going to Fort Armstrong and informed him they wanted corn, which he directed his negroe man to go back and let the men have the corn which he did and Demanded for pay. and one white man pushed the fellow with his gun and had never recd pay for the corn. the bull was killed above the garrison and the cow was killed there also—which lay in the water and found by George Chambers the Sow was killed on the Blount Waggon road and left the pigs.[46]

In handling these and the other problems of an Indian Agent, Return Jonathan Meigs performed useful service both to his government and to his red wards. Although he must have appreciated his position as a buffer between Indians and Washington, Meigs attempted to help the Cherokees. His interest in their welfare was revealed in numerous instances of individual counsel and assistance, some of which were probably beyond the call of duty. Meigs' concern for Indian development in the white man's pattern blended with a desire to end frontier fighting. In 1819 he wrote Jeremiah Evarts, Secretary of the American Board of Commissioners for Foreign Missions, on the subject of Cherokee missions, promising full support and cooperation. He hoped that attention would be concentrated on educating Cherokee children, since "the sentiments of those of adult years, a few excepted, cannot be altered." After further encouraging statements for the missionary group, Meigs enlarged his remarks to include his own opinions on improving the Cherokees. He urged that the missions actively instruct in "the measures of civilization," to give the Indians information about "useful arts and the knowledge of letters." He pointed out that Indian fighting was a costly and mortal experience, and that although the instructional program might eventually cost "millions of dollars," it would be worth it to save "far vaster sums in human misery, death, and wars."[47]

No deed of Return Jonathan Meigs more clearly suggests his deep affection for the Cherokees than that which brought an end to his life. On a cold night in January, 1823, the eighty-two-year-old Agent slept in a tent so that an aged Cherokee Chief might have Meigs' comfortable quarters. The result of this kind and generous act was a siege of pneumonia which led shortly to his death.[48]

SIX

A REPUBLIC IS BORN

PERHAPS THE MOST striking development in Eastern Cherokee history occurred during the first three decades of the nineteenth century when the traditional tribal-clan system of government was discarded in favor of a republican organization. The individual steps in the process were slow, beginning in 1808 with the adoption of written law and accelerating in the following two decades until a constitutional, three-branched government was in existence by 1830. These changes may have occurred because of an increasing awareness of the need for unity in dealing with the land-hungry white man, or they may have been inspired by American example and suggestion. The rising power of mixed-breeds may also have been a factor. Whatever the causes, a definite shift to republicanism took place.

Belligerency and factionalism among their own people were consistent problems for Cherokee national leaders during the closing years of the eighteenth century. The Chickamaugas were constant trouble-makers, and unfortunately they had many adherents throughout the nation. The white men were also a serious detriment to peace and security in the international jockeying for power in the Old Southwest. The nation had a nominal head chief but his powers were little more than titular. Occasionally a National Council convened for some specific emergency; its jurisdiction, however, was limited to the particular business for which it had assembled. Such a council met at Ustanali (near present-day Calhoun, Georgia) on June 26, 1792, to discuss peace and land cessions with Governor Blount. The make-up of this group was fairly representative of a Cherokee national body during the 1790's. Membership in the council was not definitely fixed nor were its decisions to be considered as representing those of the entire nation. Below are listed the Cherokee chiefs who participated in what was termed the "Grand Cherokee National Council" of 1792, with the titles shown for them in the records of the meeting:

> The Little Turkey, great beloved man of the whole nation; The Badger, the beloved man of the Southern division; The Hanging Maw, beloved man of the Northern division; The Boot, The Black Fox, The Cabin, Path Killer, &c, head-men of the Little Turkey's town [later Turkeytown]; Keatchiskie and Sour Mush, of Hightower; Nontuaka, of Cheestie; Teakakiskie, of Hiwassee; Richard Justice and The Glass, of the Look-out Mountain town; The Thigh, of Celicae; The Big Bear and the Kingfisher, of Estanaula [Ustanali]; Charley, of Alljoy [Ellijay]; Nanotey, of Kautokey; The Terrapin, of Kiukee; The Breath, and his nephew, of Nickajack; and Chickasautche, of Big Savannah, and warriors.[1]

Ustanali was clearly the "capital" village of the Cherokees by this time, replacing Chota in the north, and indicating the population shift southward.[2]

Little Turkey had obviously become the leading chief among the Cherokees at this period, despite his inability to control the more belligerent elements of his tribe. His title in the journal cited above, "great beloved man of the whole nation," seems proof enough of his accepted leadership. Some additional power fell to Little Turkey in 1795 when the Upper Cherokee leader Hanging Maw, previously noted as a chief friendly to Blount and to white peace efforts, passed away. During the same year, The Turkey began affixing his signature as "Principal Chief."[3]

The position of Principal Chief held little security for its incumbent, for leadership in the growing nation continued to fluctuate from one person to another. A local chieftain named Doublehead usurped much of Little Turkey's influence and authority, especially in dealing with white governments. Among the Cherokees he rose to the office of Chief Speaker in National Council sessions and frequently dominated conferences and treaty sessions until his death in 1807. Another important leader at this time was James Vann, a half-breed "of considerable ability and shrewdness," who was regarded by some as "perhaps the most influential chief among the Cherokees." Other chiefs rising to national power during this era were Black Fox, Path Killer, The Glass, Charles Hicks, and George Lowrey. From 1801 to 1811

Black Fox was Principal Chief, save for a two-year period (1808-10) during which he was "broke" from power because of his leading role in an unpopular scheme to effect westward movement of the tribe. Replacing him during his suspension, and succeeding to the title after Black Fox's death, was Path Killer.[4] The latter held the office until 1827—although it seems certain that with the subsequent rise of such prominent leaders as Major Ridge, Charles and William Hicks, and John Ross, the venerable Path Killer became a mere figurehead.

An important step towards the white man's pattern of government was the adoption of a written legal code, beginning in 1808. A law passed by the Cherokee National Council on September 11 of that year recorded in English that "regulating companies" were to be established, listed their complement, and stated that they were to "suppress horse stealing and robbery." This act legalized an existing system of patrols which had been in operation at least since 1797 when, according to a report from Benjamin Hawkins, the Cherokees "appointed some warriors expressly to assist the chiefs in preventing horse stealing. . . ." Later these units came to be called the "Light Horse Guard."[5] The edict of 1808 stipulated that there were to be six men to each company, headed by a captain and a lieutenant. Yearly salaries, to be paid "out of the National Annuity," were fifty dollars for the captain, forty for his second in command, and thirty for each of the four privates. The decree further announced a scale of punishments for convicted criminals beginning with "one hundred stripes on the bare back."[6]

One tribal custom which had long plagued white efforts to maintain peace was the clan-revenge system. By this time-honored scheme, retaliation for murder was meted out into the clan of the murderer without any effort to seek out the actual killer. When the slaying was perpetrated by a white man, the usual procedure was for the injured clan to seek out the nearest white man to receive the "eye-for-an-eye" punishment. Aware that the clan procedure brought trouble with the Americans, and anxious for internal peace, the Cherokee Council took steps early in the nineteenth century to replace it with other means. The law of 1808 provided that in the event an accused person resisted and killed a regulator "the blood of him . . . shall not be required of any of the persons belonging to the regulators from the clan the person so killed belonged to."[7]

Two years later the Council completely discarded clan revenge in its second written law:

> *Be it known,* that this day [April 10, 1810], the various clans or tribes which compose the Cherokee Nation, have unanimously passed an act of oblivion for all lives for which they may have been indebted, one to the other, and have mutually agreed that after this evening the aforesaid act shall become binding upon every clan or tribe; and the aforesaid clans or tribes, have also agreed that if, in future, any life should be lost without malice intended, the innocent aggressor shall not be accounted guilty.
>
> *Be it known, also,* That should it happen that a brother, forgetting his natural affection, should raise his hand in anger and kill his brother, he shall be accounted guilty of murder and suffer accordingly, and if a man has a horse stolen, and overtakes the theif [*sic*], and should his anger be so great as to cause him to kill him, let his blood remain on his own conscience, but no satisfaction shall be demanded for his own life from his relatives or the clan he may belong to.[8]

By this act the burden of punishing murderers devolved on the National Council and its agents of apprehension, the Regulating Companies. The official power of clan control was thus sapped by a written law; and future developments were to see an even greater deviation from tribal principles.

The establishment of a near republic was the next important governmental development. Return J. Meigs had suggested such a step to the Cherokees as early as 1801. In January, 1809, after learning that Upper Town Cherokee Chiefs wanted to have the Indian nation formally split into Upper and Lower groups, President Thomas Jefferson urged conciliation between the two factions and suggested that the entire nation acquire unity through organizing a democratic type of government. He recommended referral of important problems to some assembly which also should enact necessary laws. He further hoped that judges would be elected or appointed to interpret these laws. Wishing them success in such a venture, the President promised that "in this you may always rely on the council and assistance of the government of the United States."[9]

Whether through such American influence, or from the wishes of the strong half-breed element in the Cherokee government, the Cherokees took steps in 1817 to establish a republic. In May of that year the Cherokee Council registered its disapproval of a recent move on the part of "fifty-four towns and villages" to "deliberate and consider on the situation of our Nation . . . without the unanimous consent of the members of Council." With this published excuse, the Council proceeded to create a national bicameral legislature. The upper house, called the "Standing Committee," was to be chosen by the Council from its own members. The Council was continued as a lower house. The Committee was to be made up of thirteen members elected for two-year terms and eligible for re-election. This group, which came to be known as the National Committee, was given the responsibility for "the affairs of the Cherokee Nation," including settlement with the United States Agent for annuity payments. The Council, however, retained reviewing power over actions of the Committee. With reference to relations with the federal government, the chiefs further stipulated that "the friendly communications between our head Chiefs and the Agency shall remain free and open."[10]

Two additional articles of this sweeping decree settled current problems of property rights. Article Three announced that persons leaving the Cherokee territories forfeited any claims to communal property. The next edict, stemming from the time-honored custom of matriarchal inheritance, stated that "the improvements and labors of our people by the mother's side shall be inviolate during the time of their occupancy."[11]

Three years later a further step toward centralization was taken by the National Committee and National Council, with approval of Principal Chief Path Killer. The new measure required the entire Cherokee Nation be divided into eight districts, each of which would contain a subordinate administration for maintenance of peace and justice. Within each district a council house was to be established, "for the purpose of holding councils to administer justice in all causes and complaints that may be brought forward for trial." District judges were to preside over hearings on local matters, while a special circuit judge was to be named for each two districts, to "associate with the district judges in determining all causes agreeable to the national laws." A marshal for each district was charged with the execution of decisions made by his judge, and a company of light-horse was responsible for administering the circuit court orders. District marshals were given the further duty of collecting all debts, of which they were to receive 8 per cent as a fee.[12]

The districts themselves were defined in a separate act. (See map B.) Some idea of the thoroughness of the description may be gained from that for the Third District, to be called "Coosewatee." Its borders were given as follows:

beginning at the widow Fool's ferry, on Oostannallah river, where the Alabama road crosses it, along said wagon road eastwardly, leading towards Etowah town to a large creek above Thomas Pettit's plantation, near to the Sixes, and said creek, northeastward, to its source; thence a straight course to the Red Bank creek, near Cartikee village; thence a straight course to the head source of Potatoe Mine creek; thence a straight course to the most southern head source of Cannasawgee [Connesauga] river, thence a northwestern course to Cannasawgee river, to strike opposite to the mouth of Sugar creek, into the Cannasawgee river, and be bounded by the first and second Districts.

The other districts were Chickamaugee, Chattooga, Amohee, Hickory Log, Etowah (or Hightower), Tahquohee, and Aquohee. The act further stated that the various districts would hold their "Councils or Courts" in five-day sessions on the following schedule: for Chickamaugee, Coosewatee, Hickory Log, and Aquohee districts, beginning on the "First Mondays in May and September." The others were to commence on the second Mondays of those months.[13]

Geographical rather than proportional representation was to be allowed these districts in the national legislature. A joint resolution of the National Committee and National Council stated that every district was to send four delegates to the Council, each of whom was to receive a dollar a day during the sessions. Other salaries were to be as follows: Speaker of the Council, $1.50; Clerk of the Council, $2.50; Committeeman, $2.00; President of the Committee, $3.50; Clerk of the Committee, $2.50; Interpreter of the Committee (to be chosen from the membership), "fifty cents a day in addition to his pay." The Principal Chief (at that time Path Killer) was to receive $150 a year; while, "considering the burden of writing and interpreting which devolves on him," Assistant Principal Chief Charles R. Hicks was given an annual stipend of $200.[14]

In 1822 a visitor to the Indian Nation's American Board missions compiled a list of Cherokee officials. Because of its uniqueness and the detailed view that it gives of organization and personnel under the republican system, the list is given in full below:

Path Killer – King
Charles R. Hicks – Second beloved man
John Ross, President of the national Committee

George Lowrie Richard Taylor Cabin Smith, or Big Cabin John Baldridge Sleeping Rabbit Thomas Forman The Hare John Beemer Kee-la-chu-lee Kur-ro-hee-lih Roman Nose John Downing, jun.	Members of the Committee

Coosawatee District	Major Ridge, Speaker for the Council William Hicks, brother of C. R. H. Terrapin Head Rising Fawn one vacancy		members of council
Etowee	Tonnateehee Walking Stick The Feather Old Turkey	Hickory Log	Slim Fellow Gone to Sleep Tuh-quo Kee-nah-tee-hee
Amohee	Going Snake Choo-no-yuh-kee Wa-nuh-kee Ta-quh-kee	Chicka-maugah	Tah-lee-is-kee Noisy Warrior Three Killer Charles Reese
Chatooga	Tsoo-ee-kullah Big Rattling Gourd Uh-nee-o-lee Samuel Gunter	Aquohee	Uh-nee-ka-yah-no-hee Sik-quh Woman Keeper Kul-lo-skee
		Tawquohee	Tsoo-a-lo-gee Was-to-no-hee A-maw-yee-tah Charley

District Judges

Coosawatee....................	George Sanders	John Martin, Presiding
Amohee	Tee-as-tis-kee	

Hickory Log........	Thomas Sanders	James D........
Etowee	Smallwood	
Tawquohee........	Tee-la-ska-iskee	Richard ....
Aquohee	Tee-sto-e-eskee	(a full blood Cherokee)
Chickamaugah........	Haw-hah-tsee	James B........
Chatoogah	Daniel Griffin	

Coosawatee	– James Foster, Marshal
Amohee	– Archy Foreman
Hickory Log	– Wind
Etowee	– Wah-lah-nee-tah
Tawquohee	– A-lo-tsee-wo-tee
Aquohee	– O-tse-wus-kee
Chickamaugah	– Nathan Hicks
Chatooga	– Davy Vann

Charles R. Hicks, Treasurer of the Nation
Income from United States, $7,200 –
National taxes – small – not collected –
Poll tax – 50 cents a family[15]

In such a fashion did the Cherokees evolve a government far better organized and more unified than that of the previous generation. The decade that followed 1822 witnessed further progress culminating in the writing of a national constitution in 1827 by an elected constitutional convention. Just a year earlier, speaking in a Philadelphia public hall, a prominent Cherokee proudly reviewed his nation's legal progress since the first written law. His account serves as an effective summary of striking developments in his nation's history:

The Cherokee Nation is divided into eight districts, in each of which are established courts of justice, where all disputed cases are decided by a jury, under the direction of a circuit Judge, who has jurisdiction over two districts. Sheriffs and other public officers are appointed to execute the decisions of the courts, collect debts, and arrest thieves and other criminals. Appeals may be taken to the Superior Court, held annually at the seat of Government. The Legislative authority is vested in General Court, which consists of the National Committee and Council. The National Committee consists of thirteen members who are generally men of sound sense and fine talents. The National Council consists of thirty-two members, beside the speaker, who acts as the representatives of the people. Every bill passing these two bodies, becomes the law of the land. Clerks are appointed to do the writings, and record the proceedings of the Council. The executive power is vested in two principal chiefs, who hold their office during good behavior and sanction all the decisions of the legislative council. Many of the laws display some degree of civilization, and establish the respectability of the nation.[16]

A missionary to the Cherokees recalled that by about 1825 they had attained considerable "progress in civil polity." He wrote of their "efficiency in government," and stated that the execution of their laws "meets with not the least hindrance from anything like a spirit of insubordination among the people."[17] In general, the Cherokee progress in acquiring some of the outward characteristics of the neighboring white man's government was steady. It is likely that the inertia of tradition was not easy to overcome. Custom of centuries probably kept alive many tribal tendencies; and local town chiefs undoubtedly retained much of their power. Frequent references by missionaries to Path Killer as "The King" indicate a probable tendency on the part of some Indians to regard the Principal Chief as a tribal rather than a republican leader.[18]

Another lingering custom was the deference to women. Two evidences of this may be cited. Article Four of the government act of 1817 guaranteed property gained through "the mother's side." The second example harkens back to early tribal procedures. In June, 1818, a delegation of Cherokee women delivered a stirring message to their nation's Council, urging that "the bounds of the lands we now possess" be maintained as before. They were particularly opposed to westward removal, stating that the very idea of it was "dreadful."[19]

An interesting picture of Cherokee Council sessions during the early years of the republic was given by the missionary Ard Hoyt on the occasion of his visit to the seat of Cherokee government in October, 1818:

> On entering I observed the King [Path Killer] seated on a rug, at one end of the room, having his back supported by a roll of blankets. He is a venerable looking man, 73 years old; his hair nearly white. At his right hand, on one end of the same rug or mat, sat brother Hicks. The chiefs were seated in chairs, in a semicircle, each facing the king. Behind the chiefs a number of the common people were standing listening to a conversation, in which the king and chiefs were engaged.[20]

Presumably Path Killer represented conservatism in a day of rising

George Lowrey
From a Catlin portrait, courtesy of the Gilcrease Institute, Tulsa, Okla.

JOHN ROSS
From McKenney & Hall, *The Indian Tribes of North America*
Courtesy Bureau of American Ethnology

MAJOR RIDGE
From McKenney & Hall, *The Indian Tribes of North America*
Courtesy Bureau of American Ethnology

Colonel Return J. Meigs
From an engraving in the Library of Congress

Reverend Humphrey Posey
From Fleming's *Life of the Elder Humphrey Posey,* courtesy of Emory University Library

Reverend Abraham G. Steiner
Courtesy of the Moravian Archives, Winston-Salem, N. C.

SEQUOYAH
Courtesy of Library of Congress

ᏣᏆᎩ ᏧᎴᎯᏌᏅᎯ.

PROTECTION.

CHEROKEE PHŒNIX.

VOL. I. NEW ECHOTA, WEDNESDAY JUNE 25, 1828. NO. 18.

EDITED BY ELIAS BOUDINOTT.
PRINTED WEEKLY BY
ISAAC H. HARRIS,
FOR THE CHEROKEE NATION.

At $2 50 if paid in advance, $3 in six months, or $3 50 if paid at the end of the year.

To subscribers who can read only the Cherokee language the price will be $2,00 in advance, or $2,50 to be paid within the year.

Every subscription will be considered as continued unless subscribers give notice to the contrary before the commencement of a new year.

Any person procuring six subscribers, and becoming responsible for the payment, shall receive a seventh gratis.

Advertisements will be inserted at seventy-five cents per square for the first insertion, and thirty-seven and a half cents for each continuance; longer ones in proportion.

☞All letters addressed to the Editor, post paid, will receive due attention.

[illegible Cherokee-script notice]

AGENTS FOR THE CHEROKEE PHŒNIX.

The following persons are authorized to receive subscriptions and payments for the Cherokee Phœnix.

to all other officers within their respective Districts.

New Echota, Oct. 14, 1826.

JNO. ROSS, Pres't N. Com.
MAJOR RIDGE, Speaker.
Approved—CHARLES HICKS.
A. McCOY, Clerk of the N. Com.
E. BOUDINOTT, Clk. N. Coun.

Resolved by the National Committee and Council, That a child under the age of twelve years, whose tender age renders it improbable that he or she should be impressed with a proper sense of moral obligation or of sufficient capacity, deliberately to have committed an offence, shall not be considered, or found guilty of any crime or m[illegible]meanor; nor a lunatic or a person insane without lucid intervals, shall be found guilty of any crime with which he or she may be charged; Provided the act so charged as criminal shall have been committed in the condition of such lunacy or insanity: Be it further resolved that an idiot shall not be found guilty or punished for any crime or misdemeanor with which he or she may be charged; Be it also further resolved that any person counseling, advising, or encouraging a child under the age of twelve years, or a lunatic, or an idiot to commit an offence, shall be prosecuted for such offence when committed as principal, and if found guilty shall suffer the same punishment as would have been inflicted on said child, lunatic or idiot, if he or she had possessed discretion, and had been guilty.

New [illegible] *Oct.* 14[illegible]

[illegible Cherokee-script text]

[illegible], 14 [illegible], 1826.

[illegible Cherokee-script signatures]

CORRESPONDENCE

Between Commissioners on the part of the United States, and the Council of the Cherokee Nation, in the year 1823.

[CONTINUED.]

The following is a reply from the Commissioners to the Council.

NEWTOWN, *October* 21, 1823.

Friends and Brothers: Your communication of yesterday was handed us by your messenger. We feel constrained by duty and instruction to reply, and to reserve to ourselves the [illegible] as ofte[illegible] we may [illegible]

kees and receives them into favor and protection. The language of the Cherokees is submissive, and accepts the offer. So complete was the authority acquired by these memorable operations, that the territory of all those tribes was made the subject of "*allottment.*" All the lands which they now hold, has been "allotted" to them. Their original title is forever gone. First, by discovery. Secondly, by conquest. And, thirdly, by treaty. But the surrenders which have been made from time to time by the Cherokees, go still further, and authorize the United States to "manage the trade of the Cherokees as they may think proper."

Brothers: We have reference to these matters of history and compact, not to shew your humility, but to shew your *dependance*. On the contrary, it does not degrade you to give you the evidence of your dependance: it is a matter of distinction, to be connected *with*, and dependant *upon*, the Government of the United States.—There are twenty-four states and three territories, which are found to acknowledge this connection and dependance. The advantage is mutual. The United States give laws, give stability, and protection, to the states, and the states give obedience, support, and taxes, to the Government. By this union, the Government becomes powerful—by a division, it would be feeble. As relating to the different tribes of Indians who have settlements within the states, the [illegible] is p[illegible] red

moving, and retire within your lines. If they are disposed to become members of the states, they can be secured in a residence, and let into all privileges of ordinary citizens.

Brothers: We have thus laid before you some new topics for discussion. These involve considerations of vast importance to yourselves and to posterity. Listen to them, and answer with calmness and deliberation.

You are not engaged in light disputes or trifling considerations. Nations are parties to this correspondence. If we knew our Government and ourselves, we design you no harm. Our object is the good of the whole American family.

We shall now proceed to notice some of the remarks in your communication of yesterday, and close for the present.

The picture which you have drawn of the separation of friends and relatives at the emigration to Arkansas, is honorable to the sympathies of your hearts. But the heart often bleeds at what the judgement approves. Among ourselves, these separations occur almost daily. You advert with some emphasis to the "circumstances and means which caused the separation."

Brothers: We understand that it was *wholly voluntary*, and that your citizens projected the scheme themselves, as long ago as 1808. At that time the President was aware that the season was unpropitious for so serious an operation. His lord beyond [illegible] contemplated.

THE CHEROKEE PHOENIX
Courtesy of New Echota Foundation. Calhoun, Ga.

liberalism. It seems likely that more and more of the progressive younger men, usually mixed-breeds, came to dominate Committee and Council sessions. The rise of Charles Hicks, John Ross, and George Lowrey offers good examples of this development.

An important step in Cherokee republican progress came in 1822 when the Committee and Council authorized the creation of a "National Superior Court," to meet concurrently with the legislature each autumn. Membership on this bench was to consist of the four district judges; a jury was to be impanelled, however, to bring in the court's verdict. Both civil and criminal cases could be appealed to this body.[21]

The first sessions of the "Supreme Court of the Cherokee Nation," as it came to be called, met at Newtown on October 9, 1823. According to its record-book, personnel present were "their Honors John Martin, James Daniels, Richard Walker, Circuit Judges. James Brown being absent. Jurors chosen for the present term, George Saunders, Foreman [of the jury], Thomas Saunders, Daniel Griffin, Hair Trimmer, Small Wood." The initial case settled a suit for damages between James Griffin and Nancy West, deciding that "the defendant [Nancy West] shall hold the contended farm."[22]

During its first term, October 9-25, 1823, the Cherokee high court heard twenty-one cases. The matters settled involved the following: plea of debt (thirteen), plea for damages (three), plea of defraud (two), ejectment, grand larceny, plea for settlement, and hog-stealing. In the thirteen years of the court's existence a total of 246 cases came up for settlement. Debt cases were by far the most numerous ones heard; seventy-six such suits were listed in the court records. More than fifty other varieties of appeals were made, involving such diverse causes as bigamy, recovery of a ferry, harboring slaves, gambling, and illegal hiring of United States citizens.[23]

A sampling of verdicts in cases heard in the Cherokee Supreme Court indicates the method and approach of the dispensers of Indian justice. In 1823 the court ruled that "on a plea of debt, it is the opinion of the Court that Bushey Head pay unto Samuel Carr sixty-five dollars." In an instance of "harboring neagroe," heard the following year, Richard and John Rattiff were ordered to pay the slave's owner, Lewis Ross, $92.50. Chief Path Killer was sued in 1826 for part ownership in a Coosa River ferry. The court decided "that James Hughes the plaintiff is equally interested in the ferry as the defendant." A week later, the conviction of Elijah Hicks for purchasing liquor from an American citizen was upheld. He was found guilty and fined "$100 principal — $6 cost of appeal." The judgment was executed against Hicks by the Marshal of the Nation, George Hicks.[24]

The adoption of a constitution in 1827 was the climax in the establishment of a republic. On October 13, 1826, a joint resolution of Committee and Council announced a call for a constitutional convention, and designated lists from which each district was to choose three delegates. The election was to be held at stipulated places in the districts where free males who were "full grown" were to meet "on the Saturday previous to the commencement of the Courts for May term, next," and cast ballots by voice vote. Superintendents of voting for each district were also named.[25]

The election was held on schedule. Below are listed the persons elected in the various Cherokee districts for the all-important task of writing a satisfactory constitution; the predominance of names of white origin indicate the strength and importance of the mixed-breed element: CHICKAMAUGA DISTRICT, John Ross and John Baldridge; CHATTOOGA DISTRICT, George Lowrey, Edward Gunter, and John Brown; COOSAWATEE DISTRICT, John Martin, Joseph Vann, and Kelechulee; AMOHEE DISTRICT, The Hair (or Hair Conrad), Lewis Ross, and Thomas Foreman; HICKORY LOG DISTRICT, James Daniel and John Duncan; HIGHTOWER (ETOWAH) DISTRICT, Joseph Vann, John Beamer, and Thomas Pettit; AQUOHEE DISTRICT, Situwakee, Richard Walker, and John Timson; TAQUOHEE DISTRICT, Ooclenota and William Boling. John Ross was named Presiding Officer of the Convention, and Alexander McCoy was appointed by that body as Clerk.[26]

The document produced by these Indians is notable for its liberal provisions. It epitomized nearly a generation of progressive legislation, led to a greater unity in government, and produced a broader system of justice for the Cherokee people. The Cherokee Constitution of 1827, obviously patterned on that of the United States, sought to define and preserve individual liberties and rights, at the same time cementing the desire of these Indians to remain unmolested in their Southern territories. It was in a sense a token of nationalistic defiance — and it probably contributed greatly to an increased resolution on the part of surrounding state governments to remove the Indians.

Strongly reminiscent of its American counterpart, the Preamble reveals the seriousness of purpose which produced the Cherokee Constitution:

> WE, THE REPRESENTATIVES of the people of the CHEROKEE NATION in Convention assembled, in order to establish justice, ensure tranquility, promote our common welfare, and secure to ourselves and our posterity the blessing of liberty; acknowledging with humility and gratitude the goodness of the sovereign Ruler of the Universe, in offering us an opportunity so favorable to the design, and imploring his aid and direction in its accomplishment, do ordain and establish this Constitution for the Government of the Cherokee Nation.

The first of the six articles stipulated the boundaries of the Cherokee Nation (see map B), and asserted the Cherokee government's "Sovereignty and Jurisdiction" over this territory. It also guaranteed to the Indian citizens their improvements and continued rights of occupancy, with the reservation that anyone leaving the Cherokee country would forfeit such rights.[27]

Executive, legislative, and judicial divisions of the Cherokee government were guaranteed in the second article of the constitution. The powers, duties, and make-up of the legislative branch were fully stated in Article Three. The National Committee and National Council were clearly separated for the first time; members of each were to be chosen annually by "the qualified electors of their respective Districts," who would send two delegates to the Committee and three to the other house. Yearly sessions of the legislature, to be referred to as the General Council, were to begin on the second Monday in October at New Echota. Candidates must have reached the age of twenty-five and be free Cherokee male citizens, including the "descendants of Cherokee men by all free women, except the African race, whose parents may have been living together as man and wife." No child of any Negro parentage would be eligible. Rules of voting, names of superintendents, and locations of precincts were also announced. Voting privileges were given to "all free male citizens" who were at least eighteen years old, except those of African descent. Section Fifteen of this article contained a rather sweeping "necessary and proper" clause, thereby granting by implication broad powers of legislation to the General Council. The constitution also stipulated certain types of laws which could not be passed, such as any which impaired contractual obligations.

The Council was given sole right to institute appropriations bills and impeachment proceedings.[28]

The executive department was the subject of Article Four. "Supreme executive power of the nation" was vested in a Principal Chief, to be chosen by the General Council. This four-year position was limited to "natural born citizens" who were at least thirty-five years old. The Assistant Principal Chief was second in rank, and had the same qualifications and tenure. Removal of either or both of these executives could be accomplished by law of the General Council. An interesting duty of the Principal Chief was that he "visit the different Districts at least once in two years to inform himself of the general condition of the Country." He was given a veto which could be overridden by a two-thirds vote of the legislature. The constitution specifically required that the chief executive "attend to the seat of government" during sessions of the General Council. A third executive officer was the "Treasurer of the Cherokee Nation," who was to be chosen by joint vote of the two houses for a two-year term.[29]

The judicial powers of the new Cherokee government were specified in Article Five. A new Supreme Court was created, and "such Circuit and Inferior Courts as the General Council may from time to time ordain and establish." Justices of the Peace were also to be appointed by the General Council as the needs arose. The Supreme Court, consisting of three members elected by joint vote of the General Council for four-year terms, was to meet concurrently with the legislative sessions each October. The closing sections of the judiciary article expressed a desire for justice akin to that previously sought by Anglo-Saxons:

> Sec. 14. In all criminal prosecutions, the accused shall have the right of being heard, of demanding the nature and cause of the accusation against him, of meeting the witnesses face to face, of having compulsory process for obtaining witnesses in his favor, and in prosecutions by indictment or information, a speedy public trial by an impartial jury of the vicinage, nor shall he be compelled to give evidence against himself.

> Sec. 15. The people shall be secure in their persons, houses, papers, and possessions from unreasonable seizures and searches, and no warrant to search any place or to seize any person or things shall be issued without describing them as nearly as may be, nor without good cause, supported by oath or affirmation. All prisoners shall be bailable

by sufficient securities, unless for capital offences, where the proof is evident or presumption great.[30]

The final portion of the constitution was an omnibus article of fifteen sections. Religious liberty was guaranteed except where practices involved were "inconsistent with the peace or safety of this nation"; any person denying "the being of a God or a future state of rewards and punishment" was precluded from office; and ministers were banned from the legislature or the top executive post. Policing in the nation was to be handled by a national marshal, elected for a four-year term, and a sheriff in each district, to serve two years. Double jeopardy was prohibited, the right of trial by jury was safeguarded, and education was encouraged.[31]

A novel effect was provided by the rather detailed amending procedure, which seemed to throw the responsibility upon the district voters, but which actually began and ended in the legislature. According to the plan given in Article Six, a two-thirds majority in both houses was sufficient to pass a proposed amendment. Then the Principal Chief was to direct district officials to announce the proposed change "as extensively as possible within their respective Districts" at least nine months prior to the next general election. Following that election, the new legislature was to take up the measure at its next session. Passage was then to be declared final if at that time two-thirds of each house again approved.[32]

Cherokee support for these progressive governmental developments was not unanimous. A momentarily strong opposition arose from full-blood conservatives led, ironically enough, by a councilman named White Path. This old reactionary conducted a number of meetings near his native Turniptown, advocating a three-point program: repudiation of the constitution; abandonment of the white man's religion, economic life, and social structure; and re-adoption of tribal existence. Popular enthusiasm for the new government and the strength of progressive half-breeds, however, proved too powerful for White Path. He was deposed from office late in 1828; two years later, after making a public acceptance of the constitutional government, White Path was reinstated as a member of the Council.[33]

The most obvious outside reaction to the publication of the new constitution was that registered by state and Congressional leaders in the United States. To some of them the document seemed a flamboyant declaration of independence from American interests and connections. Land-hungry white neighbors were equally disturbed over the greater Indian unity which the new instrument promised. But the attitude which most immediately concerned the Cherokees was that of the government in Washington. Shortly after the constitution was promulgated, the Cherokee Agent met with the Principal Chiefs to discuss the new government. At this conference, the Indians expressed apprehension that the President of the United States might echo the disapproval heard in neighboring states to the effect that "an Indian tribe in the heart of the Union has assumed an attitude of independence, by forming a constitution and ought to be opposed." The Cherokees' fears proved groundless. They learned that President John Quincy Adams had no intention of prohibiting the Cherokees from organizing a constitutional government. Instead, the President announced that the United States welcomed and recognized the change, so long as the relations then existing between the American government and that of the Indians were not impaired.[34]

In 1828 the *Cherokee Phoenix,* official organ of the Cherokee Republic, undertook to answer some of the American criticism. Denying any attempt to undermine Cherokee connections with the United States government, the editor stated that

> This constitution was adopted for the good of the Cherokee people. . . . It did not originate in any desire of such rights which do not belong to us, much less are we so blinded as to suppose, that we can within ourselves change our relation with the General Government. Rights, however, we have, secured to us by treaties, and will the people of this enlightened land, emphatically called the land of freedom, deprive us of these few rights?[35]

Perhaps the first full practical realization of the existence of a new constitutional government came in the summer of 1828, when the first election to the legislature was held. There was some excitement over the campaign, certainly among the more progressive elements who sought either to create a government along the pattern of white democracy and progress or to bring about a greater unity of purpose among the Cherokee ranks. An impressive number of persons entered the various district races for Committee and Council, and comments in the *Cherokee Phoenix* indicate that they campaigned with considerable vigor. A number of individual candidacies were noted by the newspaper in the early stages of the election, such as: "we are authorized to announce RICHARD FIELDS of Creek Path, a Candidate for the Committee, for Chatooga District." On May 28, 1828, the paper began publishing district lists of the many candidates for the two houses. Apparently not all candidates submitted notice to the *Cherokee Phoenix,* for even after six insertions, only six of the districts were represented on the list. Based on this showing, Hickory Log and Chattooga districts indicated the greatest civic spirit, having eighteen and fourteen candidates, respectively, for the General Council.[36]

One of the Cherokee correspondents sent in a stirring message to "The People of the Cherokee Nation," which was published early in the election campaign. "UTALETAH's" communication was a challenge to Cherokee voters, and reflects a deep appreciation of the significance of the election to the Indian development:

FELLOW CITIZENS:

In about three months hence, you will be called upon by the constitution of your country, to exercise a privilege of great importance to yourselves, and to your country. . . .

The welfare of our country should be the order of the day with all who have the interest of their native land at heart. Our nation, as a political body, has reached an important crisis, and bids fair for rapid progress in the path of civilization, the arts and the sciences; while at the same time we can say with no ordinary degree of exultation, that agriculture is gradually gaining an ascendancy amongst us equalled by no other Indian Tribe. . . . It is but just to ourselves and to our country, to endeavor to maintain the eminence we have attained to. . . . As we have put our hands to the plough, and as the art of Legislation is little understood by a majority of this nation, great care should be taken, how we manage our political engine. . . .

The Committee should be composed of men of education, and good knowledge in the affairs of our nation; while the Council should be composed of full blooded Cherokees, known for love of their country, the land of their forefathers, and also celebrated for their good natural sense, justice and firmness. . . .

As a citizen, I must beg your indulgence for these lines, actuated as it is, only by the zeal I feel for my country's welfare.[37]

Although Editor Elias Boudinot printed a number of communications on the subjects of voting and civic responsibility, he came out sharply in July, 1828, against the practice of electioneering.

Not only did he mention the lack of space in the paper, but he made the objection that few persons were interested in the comments.[38] It seems more likely that Boudinot and other Cherokee leaders realized that intense electioneering might promote factionalism, a condition which could be utilized to great advantage by enemies of the Cherokees.

The years 1827 to 1829 were the high points in Eastern Cherokee governmental development and progress. After the Constitutional Convention and general election, the new government had a brief but enthusiastic beginning. In the autumn of 1828 Cherokees began to translate the terms of the constitution into practicable working order. But in 1829 gold was discovered in eastern regions of the Indian country. As prospectors poured in, the long agitation for removal reached a climax, and state governments took extreme steps to destroy Cherokee sovereignty and to effect a westward expatriation. From this point most Cherokee legislation and most political discussion hinged on the question of rights, treaty guarantees, and white encroachments. Little time was left for continuing the remarkable governmental developments of the 1820's.

SEVEN

THE WHITE MAN'S RELIGION IN THE CHEROKEE COUNTRY

A MAJOR FACTOR in Cherokee development during the early nineteenth century was the importation of Christianity and mission-school education. Though primarily interested in the white man's knowledge and literacy, Cherokee Indians also absorbed some elements of his religion.

The American churches most responsible for this great impetus in Cherokee progress were the Society of United Brethren (Moravians), Presbyterian, Baptist, and Methodist. A further source of missionary supply was a semi-independent organization called the American Board of Commissioners for Foreign Missions, which at various times had Presbyterian, Congregationalist, and Dutch Reformed Church connections. Occasionally itinerant or unattached preachers ventured into the Indian country; most of these found little success.

The most difficult problem in attempting to Christianize Cherokees was their apparently lackadaisical approach to religion. The native Cherokee religious creed was brief and vague. It acknowledged the existence of "a Supreme Being, the Creator of all, the God of the red, the white, and the black man." Belief in an afterlife was accepted, in which rewards and punishments would be meted out by the Great Spirit. Numerous evil spirits were also recognized, chiefly one who "resided in the setting sun."[1] In 1823, a prominent Christian Cherokee described his religious belief prior to conversion: "To reverence the great and supreme Being, love my friends deeply & to take vengeance on my enemies. . . . In the Indian devotion there is nothing like pure religion. Tho' they have faint ideas of Deity, yet they are far from loving him with all the heart."[2]

Missionaries could not understand the absence of a personal religion among the Cherokees. To the frontiersman, the Indian's lack of a formal, familiar type of worship seemed to indicate atheism. Many questioned the red man's potential for salvation. A common view was that "an Indian has no more soul than a buffalo; to kill either is the same thing, and when you have killed an Indian, you have done a good act, and have killed a wild beast."[3] Such an interpretation sounds suspiciously like the more familiar saying concerning "the only good Indian," and might well have been due to the usual frontier attitude rather than to careful observation of religion among aborigines. To the missionaries, however, the Indian's soul was something which lay in utter darkness and needed saving.

Prior to the nineteenth century, Protestant missionary activity among the Cherokees as among other American Indians was largely the result of "individual initiative and consecration."[4] The first successfully organized missionary activity among the Cherokees was begun by the Moravian Society of United Brethren.[5] In 1740 a Moravian mission to the Cherokees was projected by Johann Hagan from Georgia; but an untimely epidemic of smallpox in the Indian country prevented the fulfillment of his desires. Hagan's project was not forgotten, however. Moravians from Bethlehem, Pennsylvania, went near the Eastern Cherokee country twelve years later, establishing the community of Bethebara (later Wachovia) on the Upper Yadkin River in North Carolina. From this point they began to make contact with the Cherokee Indians.[6]

The Christianizing of the Cherokees had been a prime purpose in the North Carolina settlement. The Moravian Bishop Spangenberg, after an exploratory trip through the country, observed: "We believe it is the Lord's purpose to confer a blessing on the Cherokee Indians, by means of the Brethren." Soon church agents were attending Cherokee Council sessions, seeking permission to establish their missions. In 1759 a brief unsuccessful conference with several Cherokee chiefs was held at Bethebara.[7]

The first Cherokee conversions by the United Brethren occurred in 1773 when two captives in the Delaware Indian country were baptized by Moravian missionaries. Although this happened outside the Cherokee area, the brethren at Wachovia and Salem (a new Moravian town on the Yadkin) found encouragement in this early success. Taking new heart for their purpose, they sent Martin Schneider to the Over Hill Cherokees to determine the prospects for a Moravian mission. But the times were not propitious, and Schneider was forced to leave for his own safety.[8]

With the arrival of peace on the frontier, the Moravians determined to sound out the Cherokees again on the subject of missions. In 1799 Abraham Steiner went to talk with Cherokee councils; finding them dispersed, he utilized the opportunity to consult with American officials in the Indian country, who promised cooperation in the religious project. In 1800 Steiner had greater success when he and Friedrich von Schweinitz, assisted by the progressive-minded James Vann and Charles Hicks, in a series of conferences won the long-sought official assent to establish a mission. In reporting the action Little Turkey told his council:

> Their desire appears to be good, to instruct us and our children and improve our and their minds and Nation. These gentlemen, I hope will make the experiment; we will be the judge from their conduct and their attention to us and our children, this will enable us to judge properly. Should they not comply as now stated, the Agent will be the judge for the Red people.[9]

Noticeably lacking from this sanction is the topic of Christian evangelization. The Cherokees were definitely more interested in the education which churches had to offer; and this fact was to be a continuing source of disagreement between Indians and missionaries.

Losing no time after Cherokee acceptance of their proposed mission, and capitalizing on the official approval of the Secretary of War, the Moravians sent Steiner to begin the work. A few months later, Gottlieb Byhan and Jacob Wohlfahrt were dispatched as assistants. The brethren and their wives were warmly received by the Vann family; at first James Vann's home was used as a temporary mission. Later, from a Cherokee named Brown, they obtained a nearby plantation which they named Spring Place. Religious instruction began as quickly as possible; as early as July, 1801, Steiner preached to Indians in the Chickamauga area. During the following year the journal of these Christian workers records that they conducted services at Vann's home ("Diamond Hill") for "Negroes, Half-Indians, and others who understood English."[10]

The next few years were severe ones for the little Moravian band at Spring Place. Despite the support of Vann and other Indian leaders the general native attitude continued to be one of suspicion and hostility. Frequently the mission suffered losses of provisions and other supplies. The problem of the strange language, and the small number of Cherokees who understood English, made effective preaching extremely difficult. Furthermore, the Cherokee Council continued to press for schooling at Spring Place. Finally, in 1802 the mission was threatened with banishment if measures were not taken to board and educate young Indians. In short, the Cherokees wanted their children taught "the three r's" rather than the Trinity; and under duress the Moravians complied with the order. They managed, however, to rationalize the decision with these remarks in their journal: "It would be wise to take three or four children, eight to twelve years of age, selected by the Chiefs, partly to content the Indians, and partly to afford our Brethren an opportunity to learn the new language."[11]

By 1805 the Moravian mission was experiencing happier times. After some difficulty the school had been established. On October 8, 1804, the first Cherokee boy was brought to Spring Place by none other than "Gentleman Tom," a Cherokee who had been most vociferous against Moravian missions at Council sessions. From this promising opening, the school prospered, gaining eight students during the succeeding year. Keeping their original purpose in view, the missionaries early integrated their young scholars into the church services. On Christmas Eve, 1804, the children "were able to sing some English verses of Christmas hymns which they had learned during the Advent season. The meaning of the Lovefeast was explained to them and the lighted Christmas taper was given to each. They were very attentive and happy."[12]

The Moravian mission in the Cherokee country expanded in the years that followed, especially after the arrival of the Reverend John Gambold and his wife in 1805. Possessing remarkable talents for educating heathen children, these Christian workers gave new life to the little mission school.[13] But how they must have sorrowed over the slow progress of Christian conversion of Cherokee adults. Nine years passed after the founding of Spring Place Mission before the first conversion of an adult occurred there! This convert was Margaret Anne Scott, widow of James Vann, and soon to be married again to Joseph Crutchfield, Vann's overseer. The next Cherokee to be converted to Moravian Christianity was Charles Hicks, who was baptized in 1813 and given the middle name of Renatus, or Re-born. It was not until November 14, 1819, that the Spring Place Church was completed and consecration ceremonies performed.[14]

In addition to Charles Hicks, other Cherokees who received training at Spring Place included the talented Indian lads Galagina (or Buck Oowatie), John Ridge, and John Vann. Later, while a student at Brainerd Mission, Buck was given the name of a prominent New Jersey friend of missions, Elias Boudinot. It was this young man who later became the first editor of the Cherokees' own newspaper, the remarkable *Cherokee Phoenix*.

The year 1819 was a signal one for the Moravian work in the Cherokee country. A "powerful revival of religion" swept through the Indian nation, and the Spring Place missionaries felt its fervor with gratitude. Their small flock increased from two to fourteen; and numerous others, many of whom had been extremely hostile, visited and inquired about Christianity. The first of these was Wawli Vann, aged mother of the late James Vann, who came to the mission in early January for baptismal instruction. After three months of training she was pronounced ready for the ceremony, which occurred March 14. Attired in a white dress which she had previously designated as her burial costume, Mother Vann was baptized "Mary Christiana." Shortly afterwards, this newest Moravian sent a message to her unenlightened relatives:

> I let you know that God has changed my heart. I have been received by Baptism among the Christians. I am so happy as I have never been all my life. Formerly, for many years and up to within a short time, I thought as you do and lived as you live. God has had mercy on me. May you all make the same experience. Take my words to heart! . . . I am much concerned for you.

One of the first to take her "words to heart" was her white husband, Clement Vann; and he was followed during 1819 by William and Sarah Hicks, Susanna Catherine Ridge (wife of Major Ridge), and nine other Cherokees.[15]

After the death of his wife in 1821, John Gambold was transferred to Oothcaloga (about fifteen miles south of Spring Place), where he established a second Moravian mission. Gambold remained in charge of the Cherokee work until his death in 1827. Spring Place continued, and both missions dispensed religious and secular education until 1838. In 1830 Spring Place could boast of a church membership of thirty-two adults and thirty-one school children; while Oothcaloga had sixteen adults, twenty baptized children, and fifteen female students.[16]

Some indication of the Indians' regard for Gambold may be gained from this eulogy, published in the *Cherokee Phoenix* in 1828:

> His faithfulness, humility, and zeal for the missionary cause, in behalf of which he sacrificed everything, his child-like confidence in the heavenly Father, which was never shaken, even in the most difficult and pressing circumstances, his philanthropic, collected, and highly circumspect behavior in word and deed, which was so peculiarly adapted to the character of the nation, among which he preached the Gospel . . . all these qualities will insure to the dear departed, a grateful and glorious tribute in the ranks of [all previous] . . . missionaries.[17]

Close on the heels of the first Moravians in the Cherokee country had come a Presbyterian missionary from Virginia named John Martin, who reached the Over Hill Cherokees in 1758. For several years he preached to the Indians under the combined auspices of the Hanover (Virginia) Presbytery and the Society for the Propagation of the Gospel, a Scottish organization. But Martin had little success. His friend Lieutenant Henry Timberlake noted that one day after Martin had preached until everyone was tired, the Indians told him "they knew very well, that if they were good, they should go up; if bad, down; that he could tell no more; that he had long plagued them with what they no ways understood, and that they desired him to depart the country." Martin's successor was William Richardson, who seems to have had equally poor results preaching to Cherokees.[18]

Presbyterian missionary activity among the Cherokee Indians continued to be sporadic until the early nineteenth century. The New York Missionary Society, organized largely by Presbyterians in 1796, sent Joseph Bullen to investigate mission possibilities among Southern Indians. In 1799 Bullen reported from Knoxville, Tennessee, that "the Cherokees who reside in the vicinity of Tennessee are desirous of having missionaries among them."[19]

While in the Tennessee country Bullen may have encountered the Reverend Gideon Blackburn, a fellow churchman who was destined to bring to fruition the "first wholly successful work by Presbyterians among Indians in the south." Since 1794 when Blackburn first began preaching in East Tennessee, he had thought about improving the "savage and wretched state" of the

Indians of that region. In 1799 he suggested that a mission be sponsored by the Presbytery of Union (Tennessee), but he was unable to take action on his plan until 1803, when as a commissioner to the Presbyterian General Assembly Blackburn persuaded the Assembly to grant two hundred dollars to educate Cherokee children. Supervisory responsibility for the Indian schooling was given to the newly organized (1802) Presbyterian Board of Missions.[20]

Gideon Blackburn began at once to consummate his plans for civilizing the Cherokees. He approached his task with a practical philosophy, believing that previous attempts had been "abortive" owing to "exalted" instructions given the Cherokees. To his mind, the problem was one of appealing to "ignorance, obstinacy and strong prejudices." If "rightfully managed," he thought, the Cherokees could become American citizens and valuable members of the Union. His plan was to concentrate on the children, since he had little hope of adult conversions. After obtaining approval of the United States government, Blackburn was successful in October, 1803, in persuading a council of "2000 assembled Indians," to accept his mission school.[21] Native sanction must have come quickly, since there was such strong interest among the Cherokees in securing education for their children.

By the spring of 1804, Blackburn's first school was in operation at a location on the Hiwassee, chosen principally because it was "in a part of the nation most unlikely to be civilized." Two Moravians who visited the school several months later wrote approvingly: "Between twenty and thirty Cherokee children are now receiving instruction and are also provided with food and clothes." The conduct of schoolmaster Jonathan Black received their commendation, as well as the good behavior of the heathen children in the school. A typical day's activities, according to the visitors, included rising, praying, and washing; scriptures, praise, and public prayer; lessons until breakfast; one hour of recreations; three hours of lessons, then lunch; two hours of recreations; spelling lessons before supper; and hymn singing, prayer, and bed.[22]

In 1806 Blackburn established a second school at Richard Fields' place near the mouth of Sale Creek on the Tennessee River. Robert Denham was the first teacher at the new school, which enrolled thirty pupils on opening day. Blackburn supplemented the meager church appropriations for his two schools by soliciting donations on speaking tours. These and other exertions proved too much for him. In 1810 poor health forced him to close his Cherokee schools and retire.[23] A few years later other workers in the Indian country summarized Blackburn's notable achievement in these words:

Within about five years, between four and five hundred young persons of both sexes were so instructed as to be able to read with a good degree of facility in the English Bible; were proportionably advanced in spelling, writing, and arithmetic; and at the same time were taught the privileges of the Christian religion. Many Bibles and religious tracts were distributed, and several individuals, some young and some of mature age, became hopeful and exemplary Christians.[24]

For seven years after the close of Blackburn's missionary career the Moravian establishment at Spring Place was the only church mission in the Cherokee Nation. For a brief time in 1815 Robert Donnell and Thomas Calhoun were itinerant missionaries in Eastern Tennessee for the Cumberland Presbyterian Church, during which they held "two protracted meetings for the Indians." In 1816 Calhoun again went into the Indian country; one of his preaching stops was the home of an Indian named Renfro.[25] Little is known of the success of these efforts.

During the years that followed, Presbyterian interest in Cherokee mission work merged with the desires and operations of an interdenominational organization which became known as the American Board of Commissioners for Foreign Missions. Largely Congregationalist-Presbyterian at the outset, and later including Dutch Reformed Church elements, the American Board was established on September 8, 1810, with a definite determination to send missionaries to American aborigines as soon as practicable. In 1816 the Board decided to work among Southern Indians, who were believed to be well suited to receive Christian instruction. This group hoped

To establish schools in the different parts of the tribe under the missionary direction and superintendence, for the instruction of the rising generation in common school learning, in the useful arts of life, and in Christianity, so as gradually, with the divine blessing to make the whole tribe English in the language, civilized in their habits, and Christian in their religion.[26]

Early in the autumn of 1816 the Board sent Cyrus Kingsbury to survey the Cherokee country and to report on the prospects of establishing a mission there. He discussed the project with federal officials in Washington and received the "prompt approval" of President Madison, along with encouraging promises of monetary and other support from the Secretary of War. Arriving at the Cherokee Agency on September 23, 1816, Kingsbury made quick arrangements for presenting his proposals to an Indian council then in conference with United States commissioners. With the encouragement of the leading American delegate present, General Andrew Jackson, the mission program was accepted by the chiefs. They designated one of their number to help Kingsbury find a suitable location. A twenty-five-acre plantation on Chickamauga Creek, two miles from the Georgia line, was selected as the site of the first American Board mission station to the Cherokees, and was named for the creek on which it stood. A year later the name was changed to "Brainerd," in honor of a distinguished missionary to Northern Indians.[27]

Chickamauga Mission began operations on January 13, 1817. The practical Kingsbury made immediate preparations "to cultivate the land" and to open his mission school. Three months later Loring S. Williams and Moody Hall arrived with their wives to assist him. The Chickamauga Journal records the inspiration with which they began: "We are now a little band of Missionaries, who profess to have renounced the world for the sake of Christ. O! that we may be faithful to our covenant vows." Kingsbury's emphasis on teaching received prompt response from Cherokees. By September Chickamauga was a thriving mission school of twenty-six scholars aged four to eighteen, who were being taught "the rudiments of the English language, the principles of the Christian religion, and the industry and arts of civilized life." Six of the Indian students already possessed a good knowledge of English, and they were useful both in school and mission. In his first yearly report, Kingsbury wrote proudly of Chickamauga's accomplishments: "Could the friends of this mission look into our school, and see these tawny sons and daughters of the forest listening to our instructions, sitting at our table, and bowing around our family altar, we do not believe they would grudge the money they have given to commence this establishment." The Cherokees were pleased with the school, Kingsbury added, and more scholars were expected in the near future.[28]

Within a few days of their arrival in the Indian land the men and women from New England formally organized "The Church of Christ at Chickamauga," and wrote a covenant consisting of ten articles of religious belief. Other mission workers arriving later joined this devout little body, and it became the nucleus of what it was hoped would become a thriving white-red-black Christian organization. In July, 1818, membership had been increased by "five Cherokees, three Africans & one white man." But after four years, only nine other Indians had joined the church. The disappointment which the men at Brainerd must have felt at this continued slow progress is mirrored in this comment recorded in the Brainerd Journal in 1819:

> While there is reason to hope, that some are edified every day, there is reason to fear that others are hardening more and more. They attend with decency; hear as if they assented to all as true, and yet remain, like so many thoughtless hearers in old congregations, unawakened and unconcerned. But, through the power of divine grace, some appear to hear in a different manner. We hope for several, who have not yet publicly confessed Christ, that they do indeed receive the truth in love.[29]

Despite disheartening religious progress in the field, the Prudential Committee of the American Board continued to have confidence in the work and ultimate success of Brainerd. By 1819, appropriations for "outfits, travelling expenses, schools, labor, provisions, and various necessary supplies of the Cherokee mission" totalled $6,956.93. True to its promises, the United States government was also aiding the American Board. The annual federal appropriation to Brainerd reached one thousand dollars by 1821. Further support came from various individuals and organizations who donated money, clothing, religious literature, and other paraphernalia.[30] The reports of travellers and inspecting agents were a continuing source of faith in Brainerd's potential.

A very important visitor came to Brainerd in 1819 and caught the mission family by surprise. President James Monroe, accompanied by General and Mrs. Edmund P. Gaines, dropped in to inspect the school whose founding he had approved two years earlier. Monroe not only found much to praise, but recommended the construction of "a good two story house, with brick or stone chimneys, glass windows &c . . . at the public expence" for use as a girls' school. The Brainerd men were quick to take advantage of this offer. As soon as the necessary papers were obtained from the Indian Agent, the new girls' building was planned, and construction begun.[31]

After getting the Brainerd Mission under way in 1817-1818, Cyrus Kingsbury left for the Choctaw country to pioneer another mission. He was succeeded as superintendent by Ard Hoyt, who along with Daniel S. Butrick and William Chamberlin had arrived from Boston shortly before. From its beginning Brainerd served as training ground for an intermittent stream of incoming missionaries, and as a parent institution and supply point for the ten additional mission stations established and maintained by this corps of Christian workers. These branch missions, and the dates of founding, were: Taloney (later Carmel), 1819; Creek Path, 1820; Hightower, 1823; Willstown, 1823; Haweis, 1823; Candy's Creek, 1824; New Echota, 1827; Amohee, 1831; Red Clay, 1835; and Running Waters, 1835.[32] (See map B.)

The missionary headquarters in Boston kept in close touch with the Cherokee work. Detailed reports coming in from each of the various mission families told of daily life, missionary method, and routine. A typical letter from Daniel S. Butrick to Corresponding Secretary Jeremiah Evarts in 1822 described school life at the mission:

> The first year brother Chamberlin had charge of the school, the boys & girls were both under his tuition. He had a full school, & the whole charge of the boys out of school. He attended to them early & late, & had generally evening schools after dark. With the boys, he took care of the cows, calves, hogs, & sheep, cut & hawled [*sic*] all the wood, shelled the corn, attended to the millings & many other things which cannot now be mentioned. The second year he did the same much of the time with the addition of planting a field of corn.[33]

The Boston office also maintained contact with the missions through special agents. The report of one of these itinerant inspectors, made five years after the founding of Brainerd, gives an especially full view of American Board operations in the Cherokee country. This agent (identity not known) first visited Taloney Mission, where he interviewed Moody Hall and Henry Parker on May 1, 1822. He was generally pleased with Hall's school, which numbered thirty regular members, although he found the "great want of attention" disturbing. "The proficiency in writing was as good as among children generally," he reported, adding "in some instances it was remarkably good." While he was present, the first class "read in Murray's introduction, both prose & poetry, & spelt in the long and difficult table of monosyllables . . . with uncommon accuracy." In the evening he attended Hall's regular weekly preaching, at which "10 adults, including blacks & Cherokees, were present, beside the mission family & 5 or 6 children."[34]

The investigator next went to Brainerd, his main destination in the Cherokee country. Here the chief object of his inspection was revealed: an examination of alleged mismanagement, especially on the part of Superintendent Ard Hoyt. Hoyt's unpopularity with other members of the mission family was soon apparent to the investigator. One of the persons interviewed was a Cherokee half-breed named Charles Reese, who had been the second native convert at Brainerd. Reese objected to the manner in which the mission was operated and asserted that many more Cherokees would attend if Hoyt should be removed. He cited the complaint of a native District Judge named Brown, that "his child had repeatedly come home from school lousy; that he had told the [mission] family of it privately, but found no amendment."[35]

Yet there were cross-currents at the mission, personality and character clashes, which may have explained Hoyt's inability to keep the station operating smoothly. Abijah Conger, for example, illegally sold articles to Indians in spite of repeated remonstrances from Cherokees and Father Hoyt. Other friction was caused by Chamberlin's difficulties with classroom discipline, his wife's poor health and consequent inability to perform hard tasks, and the apparent favoritism shown to Hoyt's sons, Milo and Cornelius. Realizing the pettiness of these affairs, the visitor from New England held several very serious talks with the mission family. He apparently inspired them to a new spirit of cooperation, understanding, and dedication to their real tasks. Privately, he reported to Boston: "There is much good here: they all need to have their zeal increased; and they need better direction."[36]

Not everything at Brainerd merited the agent's disapproval. He was pleased with the condition of the buildings, especially the saw and grist mills. The progress of the native converts interested him also. He made a descriptive list of them in the order of their joining the church at Brainerd:

Jane Coodey—She remains uniform & stable considering circumstances. Her husband is a Methodist.

Charles Reese—has had some seasons of disaffection, his religious character good.

Sally McDonald—having moved to Springplace . . . joined the church of the Brethren there.

Susanna Hare—Very stable.
Catherine Brown—is constantly improving—sustains an excellent character.
Lydia (Lowery) Hoyt—leads an exemplary life . . . a very remarkable person. . . .
Anna McDonald—an aged woman—very stable & warm in her attachment.
John Arch—a faithful, good interpreter.
David Brown—an extraordinary youth, now at the Cornwall school.
Anna McPherson—exemplary.
Samuel J. Mills—a very sincere man.

On May 12, 1822, the visitor attended a Sabbath meal at Brainerd, which he found a delightful experience: "There were, beside the mission family, and the children of the school, 35 adult Cherokees, several of their children, & 10 or 12 blacks. The meal was corn bread, & baked meat & beans, prepared on Saturday."[37]

There is much evidence to confirm the impression left by this anonymous agent of the Board's outstanding religious and educational accomplishment in the Cherokee country. One of the most striking testimonials to missionary progress was the roll of natives converted to Christianity. Although the number of converts was relatively small, the prominence of some of them was impressive and the remarkable example which they set in Christian ways was gratifying to the missionaries. Among the better known converts were Elias Boudinot, John Ridge, John Arch, Lydia Lowery (later married to Milo Hoyt), Stephen Foreman, John Huss, and David and Catherine Brown.

Catherine Brown was a young Cherokee girl of mixed blood who knew a smattering of English and nothing of Christianity when she arrived at Brainerd on July 9, 1817. Six months later she was baptized in a "solemn and impressive" ceremony; so favorably did the mission family regard Catherine's progress that her baptism was considered by them as "the first [real] fruits of our labor in this heathen land." A few weeks later Catherine was taken by her parents to Arkansas. Something of this girl's advancement both in literacy and Christianity is reflected in a subsequent letter to Brainerd:

> Dear friends, I weep; my heart is full. . . . Ought I not to praise the Lord for what I have received, and trust Him for everything? . . . Oh that the Lord would search me, and lead me in the way of eternal life. . . .

I am here amongst a wicked set of people, and never hear prayers, nor any godly conversation. . . . When I think and see the poor thoughtless Cherokees going on in sin, I cannot help blessing God, that he has led me in the right path to serve him.

To the great joy of the missionaries, Catherine returned from Arkansas to become again a valued member of the Brainerd group. She joined the church on March 29, 1818; two years later she was sent to Creek Path (near present-day Guntersville, Alabama) to "take the charge of a female school in her Fathers neighborhood." Catherine Brown died there in 1823, of a sudden "pulmonary disturbance." She had conducted a successful mission school among her own people, who termed her "the Priestess."[38]

Atsi, a full-blood, was another Cherokee who developed remarkably under mission instruction at Brainerd. When he first appeared in June, 1818, to enter the school at the age of twenty-four, his appearance was so unprepossessing as to cause some anxiety on the part of the missionaries that he might use the school as "an easy way to obtain his bread," and thereby set a bad example. Their decision to admit him on trial was rewarded handsomely. Rechristened John Arch, he proved himself an excellent scholar and became particularly valuable as an interpreter. At the time of his death in 1825 he had nearly completed a translation of the Gospel of St. John.[39]

Several outstanding Cherokee Christian youths were seen at first hand by New Englanders during the years 1817 to 1826 when the American Board opened the Foreign Mission School in Cornwall, Connecticut. Promising young men from American Board missions all over the world were sent to this school. It was hoped that these scholars would receive sufficient training to help carry on the mission work in their own lands. Ten young Cherokees represented Brainerd at various times: Leonard Hicks, Elias Boudinot, Thomas Basil, John Vann, Tar-chee-chy (David Steiner), James Fields, John Ridge, John Sanders, David Brown, and David Carter.[40]

The most outstanding of these Cherokee college boys were Elias Boudinot, John Ridge, and David Brown. Elias made a brilliant scholastic record at Cornwall, showing especial promise in history, geography, surveying, Latin, trigonometry, and philosophy. Later he entered Andover Theological Seminary for two years of advanced training. Upon his return to the Cherokee country he was assigned the newly opened mission at Hightower. Subsequently he entered the Cherokee political scene, serving as Clerk of the National Committee and later as the first editor of the *Cherokee Phoenix*.[41] Less diligent scholastically than Elias, John Ridge also entered politics when he returned to his nation.[42] But John and Elias were responsible for the school's precipitate closing in 1827. They had fallen in love with two Cornwall girls. When John married Sarah Northrup, and Elias married Harriet Ruggles Gold a year later, a storm of protest arose. Elias and Harriet were burned in effigy by Connecticut townspeople, while the public and the press howled in indignation over the two inter-racial marriages. The offenders were accused of "sporting with the interests of this charitable institution," while those who had permitted the weddings to take place were charged with "insulting the Christian community." On January 27, 1827, the school closed its doors.[43]

One Cherokee whose career exemplified the spirit of Cornwall to the satisfaction of all was David Brown. Brother of the famous Catherine, David made a superb record at Brainerd; the missionaries there regarded him as "a very promising and interesting young man" who seemed to be "more ready & able in prayer than any other Cherokee man in the nation." Seeking to become a minister, David had little difficulty in securing entry to the Foreign Mission School, where his devotion to studies and Christianity attracted favorable attention during his years there from 1820 to 1823. After a year at Andover, David returned to the land of his people and worked unceasingly to evangelize and educate them. He prepared a spelling book for the use of mission children. Under appointment of the Cherokee Council, David and his father-in-law George Lowrey undertook official compilation of Cherokee laws and a translation of the New Testament.[44]

Many of the Cherokees won to Christianity owed their conversion to the efforts of Samuel Austin Worcester, who probably was the most able of the American Board's home missionaries. Worcester's qualifications included an aptitude for language, as evidenced by his mastery in college of Latin, Greek, and Hebrew, and proficiency in such practical skills as blacksmithing, printing, beef curing, mechanics, and carpentry. Furthermore, he was inspired with a missionary zeal to Christianize the Indian.[45]

When Worcester arrived at Brainerd in 1825, the Indians were immediately attracted to him. They named him "The Messenger," and circulated reports of his inspiring messages throughout the nation. Worcester's new name was more apt than they could have realized. His arrival coincided with the first flush of nation-wide acceptance and study of the new invention of Sequoyah, the eighty-six-character syllabary which was to bring a vastly increased enlightenment to the Cherokees.[46] Sensing the value of this invention to the missionary work, Worcester plunged into feverish activity, translating Scriptures and hymns, teaching Indian scholars how to help, and urging the Board to send more books and writing materials. When the Cherokee Council resolved to establish a printing press, "The Messenger" took a leading part in its founding.[47]

In the meantime, two other Protestant groups had sent missionaries into the Cherokee country: the Baptists and the Methodists. Early Baptist efforts came from individuals or local church groups. During the late eighteenth century Baptist preachers Thomas Johnson, Dozier Thornton, and Littleton Meeks of Georgia spent several years among the Cherokees. Little is known of their work, but it is unlikely that many conversions resulted.[48] In 1805 an independent Baptist preacher named Evan Jones passed through the Cherokee Nation. He spent Easter Week at Spring Place. Later at the Cherokee Agency, he baptized a number of persons, some of whom may have been half-breed Cherokees. About ten years later the Sarepta Baptist Association of Georgia established some Cherokee mission schools, but records concerning this and other early Baptist ventures are vague and scant.[49]

A much stronger Baptist missionary program among the Cherokees was begun after the formation of the Baptist Missionary Convention, which held its first triennial meeting at Philadelphia in May, 1817. During the sessions, requests of the Cherokees for schools and missions were discussed, and a resolution favoring such action was passed. In December, 1817, an able Baptist hill-country preacher named Humphrey Posey was appointed to take charge of the Cherokee work. In the year that followed, Posey began four different schools in the nation: at Cowee, Tillanoocy, Eastatory, and at the house of a Cherokee mixed-breed named Edward Tucker. He also preached at various places in the Indian country to audiences comprising both white and red listeners. Furthermore, he found time to tour Georgia and upper South Carolina, preaching and soliciting funds for the mission. His work was highly praised by the *Christian Herald* in 1819: "The labours of the Rev. Humphrey Posey among the Cherokees, have been zealous, and marked with holy prudence. His schools have been well attended."[50]

Baptist missionary work among the Cherokees suffered a temporary set-back in 1819 when Humphrey Posey suddenly left the nation on a westward tour, possibly anticipating an early Cherokee removal. In 1820, however, he resumed his work in the east. Although his four schools had been forced to suspend operations, the new activity proved even more beneficial. With the help of Thomas Dawson, Posey established "Valley Towns," an active mission station in the eastern part of the nation, on Hiwassee Creek about twenty miles from the Tennessee River "in the valley called Peach Tree."[51] During the first two years after Valley Towns Mission began, the Baptist Board of Foreign Missions supplied Posey with a large staff of assistants. Thomas Roberts became superintendent, Isaac Cleaver was blacksmith, John Farrier directed farming, and Evan Jones, Elizabeth Jones, Mary Lewis, and Ann Cleaver were among the teachers.[52]

In May, 1822, Humphrey Posey discussed his mission's progress with a member of the American Board. He revealed the great strides taken in his operations during the comparatively few years of its existence, and stated that his staff of twenty-six persons was educating sixty children at Valley Towns. He reported the living arrangements at his station as follows:

> The pupils eat & lodge by themselves, forming one family, & eating at one table; the family being under the care of the teacher, with the aid of two or three young women. The other families live by themselves, entirely independent of each other, and draw their substantial provisions from the common stock. Beside this they have an allowance from the Treasury of $70 for each man, $50 for each woman, & $20 for each child. . . .[53]

Meanwhile another Baptist missionary station had been founded at Tinsawattee, sixty miles southeast of Valley Towns. Here again the Sarepta Missionary Society showed its continuing interest in Indian missions, for it sustained Tinsawattee for several years before that station became a branch of Valley Towns. The Reverend and Mrs. Duncan O'Bryan (or O'Briant, O'Brien) conducted this new mission school, which consisted of a day school with separate dwelling house for the staff. By 1825 Tinsawattee school had been re-located at Hickory Log, eight miles down the Hightower River. Jesse Mercer and Littleton Meeks, two prominent Georgia Baptists, gave encouragement to the mission by preaching to the Indians there and by soliciting help in Georgia. Meeks reported that he "frequently heard them singing, praying, and exhorting, in their own tongue." On one occasion he baptized "one aged woman, a native Cherokee," and noted that "several more have a hope in Christ, and are expected to join shortly." Mercer learned that about twenty baptisms had occurred at Tinsawattee, and urged that the school be continued.[54]

In the meantime, Valley Towns had been growing. Several buildings of various types had been constructed, land cleared and fenced, a gristmill and a sawmill built, and a considerable amount of livestock and farming utensils procured. Five of the school children had been outfitted by special appropriation of fifty dollars from the General Convention. Their names suggest that the Baptists followed the traditional mission practice of renaming native scholars: Anna Stokes, Obadiah B. Brown, Posey Clagett, Edmund Edmonds, and Edelin Bradford. The daily schedule of the school was described by Superintendent Roberts in 1823:

> In the morning, at sunrise, the horn is blown for worship, when all the children, with as many of the mission family as can conveniently, assemble at the school house. A portion of the word of God is read, and a hymn is sung, in which the Greatest part of the Indian children join. One of the brethren addresses the throne [*sic*], and the meeting is dismissed.
>
> Every child that can read commits to memory 6 verses every morning, which are recited at the opening of the school; and all that is thus committed through the week, is said over again at Sunday school, and various questions asked from the chapter. . . .
>
> The conduct of the scholars is mild and respectful. . . . Many of them write well, and have made considerable advance in figures.
>
> The evening worship is conducted in the following manner. A chapter is read from the Old Testament, and explained to the understanding of the children. . . .[55]

As had been the case at Spring Place and Brainerd, spiritual conversions at Valley Towns occurred slowly. It was not until 1823 that a native joined the church. The Cherokee was John Timson; his wife became a member of the church shortly after, and the two served the mission well as interpreters. "Several chiefs" were interested in the new religion, as were a number of other Indians; and the Baptist missionaries felt greatly encouraged.[56] Roberts described a baptism ceremony occurring in 1827:

> On a pleasant Sabbath morning hundreds of the Indians were wending their way to the beautiful Hiawassa river to see the first fruits of the nation baptized in the likeness of Jesus' death and resurrection. We saw no visible dove descending as when Christ arose from the baptismal stream, but we saw and heard and felt the presence of the Holy Spirit. We saw the big tears chasing one another down the furrowed cheeks of old Indian warriors who never, since their manhood wept before. We heard the prayers of young converts, who, emboldened by the Spirit of God, cried aloud for a blessing to descend upon their benighted nation.[57]

In addition to John Timson, other Cherokees who became valued Baptist workers included Jesse Bushyhead, Kaneeka (renamed John Wickliffe), Oganaya, and James Wafford. Bushyhead and Wickliffe became particularly able ministers. In 1830 the Baptist Board of Foreign Missions resolved to employ Wickliffe "to travel and preach among his countrymen for six months, at a compensation not exceeding $10 per month." Jesse Bushyhead, a descendant of the famed English agent John Stuart, was baptized by a minister from Candy's Creek Mission (ABC) in 1830, and operated a voluntary, one-man mission station in his native Amohee district. From this point he became acquainted with the Baptists at Valley Towns, and was soon drawn into that organization. He and Wickliffe were ordained ministers in 1833.[58]

Personnel at Valley Towns was sharply reduced after the departure of Humphrey Posey in 1824. By the next June only five persons remained: Evan Jones, Superintendent and Preacher; James Wafford, Interpreter; Mrs. Jones, Elizabeth Jones, and Mary Lewis, assistants and teachers. Despite staff curtailment Valley Towns continued to progress under the leadership of Evan Jones. Shortly after his arrival at the mission, Jones began experimenting with the Cherokee language, trying to work out a method of putting it on paper so that the Scriptures and hymns could be translated for the Indians. The success of Sequoyah's syllabary later overshadowed Jones' experiments, and they were abandoned.[59]

By the 1830's Jones and his little band at Valley Towns were busy with schools and circuit preaching. Duncan O'Bryan packed up his Hickory Log Mission and moved west in 1831 with a group of local emigrating Cherokees. But Tinsawattee remained an active church served by the circuit-riders. As late as 1837 Jones and Bushyhead were touring and preaching at Coosawattee, Long Swamp, Tinsawattee, Big Savannah, Amagalolelega, Deganeetla, and at various native homes. Jones stated that within twenty days he and his Cherokee assistant conducted twenty-six preachings, one communion, six conference meetings, and baptized twenty-one persons as follows: "Coosawattee, 4 males, 2 females; Still's, 1 male, 4 females, Cherokees, 1 black woman; Long Swamp, 1 male, 1 female; Deganeetla, 3 males, 4 females."[60]

The last of the large-scale missionary endeavors among early nineteenth century Cherokees was that of the Methodist Church, begun in the Alabama area of the nation in 1822. For several years, Methodist leaders had considered Indian mission work. Bishop William McKendree of the Tennessee Conference, the first native American bishop of the Methodist Church, ardently hoped to Christianize the Indians adjacent to his area, and early in the 1820's began to arouse his preachers to the program. He particularly favored a systematic contributory financial plan for missionary expenses. The Bishop corresponded with Thomas L. McKenney and others, seeking information and suggestions.[61]

The Bishop's dream came true in the Cherokee country almost by accident, through the ambitious circuit ministry of a young Methodist licensed preacher named Richard Neely. Assigned to the Jackson Circuit of Eastern Alabama in 1822 by the Tennessee Conference, Neely came into contact with the Cherokees on the south side of the Tennessee River. He was particularly attracted to an English-speaking half-breed named Richard Riley, who seemed impressed with Neely's messages. On Riley's insistence, Neely enlarged his circuit so as to include the Indian's home at Fort Deposit (a few miles northwest of present-day Guntersville, Alabama). From the spring of 1822 through the remaining conference year, Neely preached at Riley's house once each month. In the summer he reported that he had "organized a society of 33 members, all natives, and appointed Brother Riley class leader."[62]

Bishop McKendree and the Tennessee Conference observed Neely's reports with considerable interest. In October, 1822, they brought his Indian work under their supervision by appointing Andrew J. Crawford as the first assigned Methodist preacher to the Cherokees, with instructions to work in the Riley area. As his mission grew, Crawford reported satisfactory progress. Indeed, if his reports were accurate, his experience was unique, for shortly after beginning the new assignment, he stated that he had "far more success in preaching to the natives than in teaching the children."[63]

The growth of Methodist missions to the Cherokees was steady. In 1824 the work was expanded into the Upper and Lower Missions, directed by Nicholas D. Scales and Richard Neely. At the invitation of a Cherokee named William Coody, Scales' Upper Mission was established at Coody's house and farm near Ross' Post Office; the Indian also aided the mission by voluntarily contributing one hundred dollars annually. A year later this branch mission had 81 Indian and 20 Negro members; while the Lower Mission boasted 108 Cherokees and 43 Negroes. In 1825 the Middle Mission was created, and Isaac W. Sullivan named to its ministry.[64]

The Conference leaders had meanwhile become disturbed that in their zeal to convert Indians, the missionaries might fail to educate and civilize their charges. Bishop McKendree issued a warning in 1824 that preachers in the Indian country were "neglecting intellectual and material instruction." Instead, he recommended that "guidance in agriculture and house-wifery should be taught." Consequently the assignments issued in 1825 specifically ordered Scales and Sullivan first to teach and then to preach. Neely, on the other hand, was given *carte blanche*. He therefore devised a preaching circuit, the description of which gives an excellent picture of the Cherokee area he covered:

> He operated from the two Societies at Riley's and Coody's: a line from Chickasaw Island in the Tennessee River to the junction of the Etowah and the Oostanaula, from here to the point of Lookout Mountain, up the Tennessee River from there to Chickasaw Island. He had no regular stops, but preached anywhere a congregation gathered.[65]

In December, 1825, the Conference answered a request from Cherokees near New Town (New Echota) by sending Francis Asbury Owen to begin a mission school. A few months later, Richard Neely visited the new station, which was finally established at nearby "Ooyokiloke" (Oothcaloga), and found it thriving with twenty scholars and a dozen more expected shortly. Neely's report praised Owen's work, and at the same time revealed the Cherokees' interest in the new Methodist mission:

> This school is composed of sprightly, enterprising youths, who advance with a facility that does honour to themselves and to their teacher;—

and here it may be remarked that this school cost the society nothing.

Nor has brother Owen been less successful as a minister. . . . Since he came to this station he has raised a society of twenty-one members; and there is a great opening in the adjoining settlements for the preaching of the gospel.

It was reported the following year by George W. Morris, who succeeded Owen, that he had not "heard a profane word, nor seen a drunken man, nor witnessed a quarrel, nor heard the sound of an axe on the sabbath day . . . in the neighborhood of the mission."[66]

Methodist work, like that of other missionary groups, was stimulated by intelligent and interested natives. John Ross, for example, was converted at a meeting in the Chickamauga area, and became an active Methodist. Particularly effective support came from native exhorters, such as John Fletcher (The Boot), Edward Gunter, Joseph Blackbird, and Turtle Fields. The last was a veteran of the Creek War who became so enthusiastic over Methodism that in December, 1826, he was appointed regular itinerant preacher in the Methodist Church, the first Cherokee to be thus assigned. He built up a considerable following among his people, and served as an effective example for them.[67] At a special conference ceremony in Tennessee celebrating the sixth anniversary of Methodist missions to the Cherokees, John Fletcher spoke in his native language on the subject of the Indian missions. Edward Gunter then translated Fletcher's message, and added a speech of his own. Turtle Fields completed the program with an oration also in English.[68]

In 1827 William McMahon was appointed Superintendent of the Cherokee Missions. During an inspection tour of his new charge, McMahon was "very much encouraged" to find "a great civil and religious improvement" among the Indians. He conferred with the five ministers then assigned to Cherokee work, two of whom were on circuit, and three engaged primarily in teaching. At "the lower mission in Creek Path" he observed the work of newly assigned George W. Morris, who with his wife was maintaining three societies in a "prosperous state; most of the members . . . are running with patience the heavenly race." He visited W. P. Nichols at Coosawattee, a flourishing mission school with twenty-six scholars and more expected. Nichols reported the station's first society was about to begin. One of the circuit ministers was James J. Trott, who worked in the Wills Valley area. McMahon joined with Trott in a quarterly meeting at Connesauga, where "thirteen adults and seven children were baptized, and eleven joined society." Francis A. Owen was by then back in the New Town Mission, and there McMahon found that the station contained "a large society of pious members," and expected even better progress soon. The fifth white minister in the Cherokee mission area, Nicholas D. Scales, was preaching on an unassigned basis, as was Turtle Fields.[69]

Methodist missionary work among Cherokee Indians enjoyed a steady growth during the late 1820's and early 1830's. The Methodist method was direct, being aimed at personal evangelizing. Much was accomplished at camp meetings, where lively and dramatic exhortations appealed to Indians as much as they had to whites. In the summer of 1830 a series of three- and four-day camp meetings resulted from a revival which swept through the Methodist areas of influence. By the end of the year, 1,028 Cherokee Indians were claimed as members by the Methodists.[70]

Dr. Elizur Butler, an American Board missionary, attended one of these Methodist camp meetings in September, 1830. While obviously displeased by some of the things he observed, Butler made a report of the service which is extremely valuable for the detailed view that it gives of Methodist revival techniques. "Camps or log cabins were built on the margin of about an acre of ground," he wrote. "In the center . . . was a large shed erected — perhaps seventy feet by thirty, set inside was a 'stand' or a floor elevated perhaps two feet, on top of which was a desk or pulpit — In front of this enclosed by railing was a place termed the alter." Describing the service proper, Butler continued:

I was tolerably well pleased with the fore-part of the meeting — Near the close of the discourse the speaker imagined a council held in hell — which extended to some of the state legislatures — and also included the President of the U.S.: all for the purpose of robing [*sic*] the Cherokees of their country and breaking them up as a Nation. He also imagined a council held by Christians, by holy angels, and finally by the Father, Son, and Holy Ghost, for the purpose of saving the Cherokees; and he predicted the Salvation of the Nation — This much affected the minds of some, even produced groaning and tears. — When the sermon closed, a young man addressed them, in Cherokee, with much feeling — When he closed a scene commenced which struck me very unpleasantly — Six clergymen took their places in the alter; and a number of Cherokee preachers, interpreters, and singers — After some persuasion by Cherokee preachers and interpreters, a number came up to the alter to be exhorted, prayed for, and converted. The congregation rushed forward each seeking the nearest place to the alter. Presently some one called on all to pray . . .

voices and perhaps a hundred all broke forth in prayer at once, many of them were vociferous — I stood on a bench by the alter and all the congregation bowed around — As my mind was not solemnized with a religious feeling I took a general survey — Soon the season of prayer was closed — It is not too much to say, there were *many* voices engaged in praying and exhortation, both in Cherokee and English, at the same time, also singing, shouting, spatting of hands, and screaming. In the alter some were prostrate on the ground, some lying on benches, some apparently fainting, some crying &c &c. I thought I had a specimen of the confusion of tongues at Babel, also of the scene of trial between Elijah and the worshippers of Baal — Indeed I came home with my faiths for the Cherokees very much diminished — It seems as if such a religion could never benefit them — a religion calculated to draw the vilest characters into the church. Today a man may be considered a horsethief, an adulturer, a drunkerd, and tomorrow be considered by the methodists a good christian. I left them at half past two disgusted.[71]

Thus by the late 1820's Moravian, Congregationalist-Presbyterian-Dutch Reformed (American Board), Baptist, and Methodist missions were operating in the Cherokee country, teaching and preaching in an effort to advance religion and enlightenment.[72] Their operations were greatly aided by the invention of the Cherokee syllabary. With it the missionaries could translate the Scriptures and hymns into a language which their flock could understand more freely, and they could enlist the assistance of a larger number of native helpers. A still greater aid came with the establishment of the Cherokee press at New Echota and the creation of a national newspaper in 1828, the *Cherokee Phoenix*. The paper and the press contributed much to the Christianizing effort through the dissemination of religious education and news items, especially during the early years of the *Phoenix's* existence. Scriptural translations in Cherokee were offered, as well as hymns and short messages from Christian Indians of all denominations. By printing the English versions of things as rendered into Cherokee, Elias Boudinot offered a practical guidance to missionaries and religious leaders. In 1828, for example, the editor printed Samuel Worcester's contribution of such a translation of the Lord's Prayer:

Our Father, who dwellest above, honored be thy name. Let thy Empire spring to light. Let thy will be done on earth as it is done above. Our food day by day bestow upon us. Pity us in regard to our having sinned against thee, as we pity those who sin against us. And lead us not into any place of straying, but, on the other hand, restrain us from sin. For thine is the empire, and the strength and the honor forever. So let it be.[73]

A further valuable service to the missionary work was rendered by the *Cherokee Phoenix* through its frequent notices of meetings, religious services, and related affairs. Typical of such announcements was one printed in July, 1828: "The annual examination of the Mission School at Brainerd will take place on the last Monday in this month. – All persons interested in the welfare of the rising generation are respectfully invited to attend."[74]

For the most part, relations between the missionaries of the various denominations were good. Frequently they cooperated with each other, and their respective journals generally record good opinions of one another. Brainerd men, for example, regarded Humphrey Posey as a "man of enterprise, and of good feelings . . . very liberal in his regards for other missions." The Gambolds and other Moravians seem to have been very cordial toward their fellow Christian workers. A month after Cyrus Kingsbury began his work at Chickamauga, he received "a letter and some presents" from the Gambolds. The letter brought assurances of "their affections for us, & their deep interest in our establishment."[75]

Some criticism and petty jealousy occasionally existed among the various Cherokee missionaries. For example, when requests came to Brainerd for schools in the Hightower and Chattahoochee areas in 1822, Daniel S. Butrick suggested that "as the Baptist Brethren preached in that part of the nation . . . they ought also to have schools there." The most serious criticisms from Brainerd were aimed, however, at the Methodists; some of the American Board workers, like Elizur Butler, expressed a dislike for Methodist methods. William Chamberlin was particularly disturbed over the idea that Cherokees on whom he and his colleagues had worked for some time might suddenly join a Methodist society after a single meeting. He felt that such emotional reactions would ruin such Indians for further Christianizing effort: "If you say anything to them about a new heart, they will appear surprised and . . . answer, 'Why I joined the Methodist.'" Butrick struck a more tolerant attitude about the rival Methodists when he wrote from Hightower in 1829:

Several who had been suspended from this church united with the Methodist Society; and are now, to say the least, apparently moral, and attentive to religious instruction. Here I feel compelled to state that our Methodist brethren have hitherto conducted [themselves] with great propriety, and I think have manifested a Christian spirit in this place. They know us to be *Presbyterians,* and we suppose them to be Methodists, yet I do hope we love each other.[76]

A specific proposal to avoid exhibiting "sectarious differences" in the presence of Indians was made by Moravian representative Abraham Steiner to the Brainerd men in 1819. It is likely that the recommendation was widely followed. Numerous cooperative religious services occurred, three of which are cited as examples: On a Sunday in May, 1822, Humphrey Posey joined Cyrus Kingsbury in an all-day preaching at Brainerd. Stephen Foreman, a native Cherokee Presbyterian minister, assisted Evan Jones at a Baptist meeting held at Coosawattee in 1837. The *Cherokee Phoenix* reported an inter-denominational gathering at Haweis Mission (ABC) in 1828. About two hundred people attended the meeting, at which "an interesting discourse was delivered by Mr. Chamberlain, a Missionary at Willstown." Ten were baptized, and forty took the Holy Communion. The personnel consisted of Indian converts from the American Board, Methodist, and Moravian missions. The editor observed, "It was a pleasing sight to behold professing Christians of differing denominations uniting in celebrating the love of their common Redeemer."[77]

Yet Editor Boudinot had criticism to make, and perhaps in doing so he reflected the anxieties of all sincere Christians in the Cherokee Nation:

As respects those who are admitted to Church membership in this nation, it becomes us to speak in a very cautious manner, for it is not to be expected that all those who unite themselves with the Church of God will continue steadfast to the end. It is therefore no wonder, particularly in this country . . . that some of those who make a public confession, should go back to the world.[78]

Indeed, the concern of Editor Boudinot over the backsliders seems justified. In spite of the hard work of the brave, self-sacrificing, and sincere men and women who served as missionaries from various denominations to the Cherokee Indians, the practicing Christians of the Cherokee Nation in this era seem to have been a definite minority. The Methodist claim of 1,028

Indian members during the peak revival year of 1829 represents less than seven per cent of a Cherokee population of over 16,000.[79] The memberships of other churches were considerably less. A report published in 1831 indicated that the American Board claimed 192 communicants in the Cherokee country. Baptist church members numbered about 120; and the two Moravian missions had a total of seventy-four.[80]

During the 1830's the missionary situation was unhappily entangled with political affairs, as the efforts of federal and state governments to remove the Cherokee Indians disrupted the mission work. Yet the several decades of religious efforts in the Indian nation had produced notable results. Numerous Cherokees had been exposed to the white man's religion and hundreds of them had accepted its teachings. A few became enthusiastic Christians and gave valuable assistance both to missionaries and to inquiring Indians. As Cherokees came to realize that the energetic white preachers were chiefly interested in Indian welfare and that the missionaries sought no concessions or land grants but only the improvement of the red men, response became more fervent. The presence of numbers of Christians in the Cherokee government and the deference to religion found in their constitution and laws suggest an important influence on Indian affairs traceable to missionary endeavor.

Education for numerous young and old Cherokees, regarded by missionaries generally as a by-product of their main efforts, was of first importance to the majority of Indians seeking progress in the white man's pattern. From the days of Gideon Blackburn mission workers found it profitable to educate prospective converts. Some, like Blackburn and the American Board teachers, entered the Indian country with a deliberate and somewhat successful determination to raise Indian living standards through education and training. Methodists, Baptists, and Moravians also operated schools with beneficial results.

In an era when the Cherokee Indian was receiving and learning to use the white man's basic utensils of existence, missionaries brought further knowledge in those implements along with culture, refinement, and religious improvement.

EIGHT

EARLY NINETEENTH CENTURY CHEROKEE SOCIETY

THE EARLY nineteenth century was a new era for the Cherokee Indians. In an age when their government was undergoing a remarkable degree of national democratization, Cherokees faced sweeping changes in their social structure. Sedentary life, especially after objecting reactionaries found refuge in western areas, brought a concomitant alteration in everyday economics. Missionary enterprise which moved into high gear in the 1820's brought knowledge not only of Christianity but of something more important to the Indians – education in English, arithmetic, and domestic arts. Return J. Meigs sponsored much improvement. An accelerating force in Cherokee social development was the written Cherokee language, the amazing accomplishment of the half-breed Sequoyah. The compound resulting from these diverse elements was a peculiar red-white social structure.

At the turn of the century, approximately 20,000 Cherokees inhabited 43,000 square miles of Southern Appalachian country. Twenty years later, as a result of treaty adjustments and voluntary westward emigration, the Cherokees numbered about 14,000 and occupied some 28,000 square miles. In 1835, near the close of the regime of the Cherokee Republic in the East, an official census revealed the following population data:[1]

	Indians	Slaves	Intermarried Whites
Georgia	8,946	776	68
North Carolina	3,644	37	22
Tennessee	2,528	480	79
Alabama	1,424	299	32
TOTALS	16,542	1,592	201

These sixteen thousand Cherokees lived in some forty towns and villages and on isolated farms and settlements. While there were occasional clusters of houses and cabins at such important localities as New Echota and Oostanaulah, most Cherokee towns of this era were glaringly different from those in white communities. The sharpest point of contrast was that of size. Although the villages were shown as individual spots on various maps, many were actually areas of some distance in length, containing scattered homes and farms. One of the most lasting institutions of Cherokee local government was the office of Town Chief, whose authority extended well into the period of the republic. Judging by the appearance in Cherokee geography of such names as Going Snake's Town, Thomas Foreman's Town, and Vann's Old Town, the Town Chief must indeed have controlled not merely a cluster of houses, but an area more nearly like a township or a city-state. The missionaries in the Cherokee country saw some of this community grouping. In 1818 a preacher from Brainerd reported difficulty in getting groups together to hear his sermons, and ascribed this trouble to the fact that "there is no place near us where a large audience can be collected. As the people do not live in villages, but scattered over the country from 2 to 10 miles apart, to collect in a place 20 or 30 who can understand our language, is as much as can be expected."[2]

Perhaps these missionaries were more accurate in calling the locations "places," rather than the white man's conventional "towns." A "List of Places in the Cherokee Nation," prepared by the Brainerd brethren about 1822, names twenty-one of these communities, and offers illustrations of the types of organization. Hightower (or Etowah) was stated to have "a large population . . . upwards of 200 families," and to be "perhaps 50 or 60 miles in length." Turkey Town, where lived "the king, his first council, & many other old chiefs," was about "30 or 40 miles long." Still further evidence of this widespread community arrangement may be had from the description of Chattooga: "Bounded by Turkey Town, Lookout, Raccoon Town, Turnip Town, and the Creek line." On the other hand, some places like Hickory Log, Saliga, and Pine Log, were stated to be "compact," usually along a creek or river.[3]

The incomplete Cherokee gazetteer compiled by the Brainerd men listed the towns of Wills Valley, Squirrel Town, Crow Town, Sauta, Hightower, Turkey Town, Chattooga, Turnip Town, Hickory Log, Saliga, Pine Log, "Y pu ki lo gi" (Oothcaloga), Shoemake Town, Thomas Foreman's Town, Sleeping Rabbit's Town, Going Snake's Town, Tesy's Town, Broom Town, Raccoon Town, and Dirt Town.[4] Missing from this list were such important places as Newtown (later New Echota), Oostanaulah, Spring Place, Creek Path, Coosawatee Old Town, Taloney (later Carmel), and Chickamauga — the last-named a surprising omission in view of Brainerd's location. (See map B.)

Clearly the principal government town in the Cherokee Nation by the 1820's was Newtown, located near the spot where the Connesauga and Coosawatee rivers come together to form the Oostanaulah (in present-day Gordon County, Georgia). On November 12, 1825, the National Committee and Council of the Cherokee Nation of Indians issued a resolution which marked a high point in their unusual governmental progress. This important document announced that within the next twelve months an Indian city was to be built which would become the new seat of government for the Cherokee republic.

Meeting at Newtown, the Cherokee legislators produced the following resolution:[5]

> Resolved, . . . that one hundred town lots, of one acre square, be laid off on the Oostenallah river, commencing below the mouth of the Creek, nearly opposite to the mouth of Caunausauga river. The public square to embrace two acres of ground, which town shall be known and called Echota; there shall be a main street of sixty feet and the other streets shall be fiifty [*sic*] feet wide.
>
> Be it further resolved, That the lots, when laid off, be sold to the highest bidder. The purchasers right shall merely be occupancy, and transferrable only to lawful citizens of the Cherokee Nation, and the proceeds arising from the sales of the lots shall be appropriated for the benefit of the public buildings in said town; and
>
> Be it further resolved, that three commissioners be appointed to superintend the laying off the aforesaid lots, marking and numbering the same, and to act as chain carrier, and a surveyor to be employed to run off the lots and streets according to the plan prescribed. The lots to be commenced running off on the second Monday in February next, and all the ground lying within the following bounds, not embraced by the lots, shall remain vacant as commons for the convenience of the town; viz: beginning at the mouth of Caunausauga, and up said creek to the mouth of the dry branch to the point of the ridges, and

thence in a circle round along said ridges, by the place occupied by Crying Wolf, thence to the river.

JNO. ROSS, Pres't.N.Com.
MAJOR RIDGE, Speaker
Approved—PATH KILLER (x) his mark
CH. R. HICKS

A. McCOY, Clerk of Com.
E. BOUDINOTT, Clerk N. Council

Thus was New Echota born. The little village soon to be constructed was to serve as legislative, executive, and judicial headquarters of the Cherokee republic until 1830.

Lay-out and construction of New Echota proceeded according to plan. John Martin, George Sanders, and Walter S. Adair, who were named as commissioners by John Ross, superintended the work. One of the early problems was that posed by Cherokees whose lands lay within the proposed bounds of the capital. Finally the Council decided that the nation was not liable for compensation to these owners. Exceptions to this ruling were made to several favored individuals. Alexander McCoy and Elijah Hicks, whose homes lay within New Echota's limits, were to be given the privilege of bidding first for their lots. Two Indians, named Crying Wolf and War Club, lost their locations, but were reimbursed by the Cherokee government. Later McCoy and Crying Wolf were given special permission to plant crops in the New Echota area.[6]

With the intention of creating a national press and newspaper, the Cherokee Council authorized in 1826 the construction of a printing office

20 x 24 feet, one story high, shingle roof, with one fireplace, one door, . . . one floor and a window in each side of the house two lights deep and ten feet long, to be chinked and lined on the inside with narrow plank, with the necessary watering benches and type desks requisite for a printing office.[7]

While the type and press were being obtained in Boston through the assistance of missionary authorities, the printing office was being constructed at New Echota. One of the first printers was John Foster Wheeler, who has left an account of the building:

The house built for the printing office was of hewed logs, 30 feet long and 20 feet wide. The builders had cut out a log on each side 15 or 16 feet long, and about 2½ feet above the floor, in which they had made a sash to fit. This we had raised because the light was below the cases. Stands had to be made, a bank, and cases for the Cherokee type. The latter was something entirely new, as no pattern for a case or cases to accommodate an alphabet containing 86 characters could be found. . . .[8]

From this building the first issue of the *Cherokee Phoenix* appeared on February 28, 1828.[9]

Nearby the Cherokee government constructed another government building. This was for the national supreme court. With a view to creating an efficient and durable structure, the legislature authorized that the court building should be a "framed" house of the following dimensions:

twenty-four feet in length by twenty feet in width, two stories high, lower story ten feet, upper story nine feet high, shingled roof of yellow poplar shingles, one stair case, one door on each side of house, batten shutters, two fifteen light windows on each side of the house, above and below, also two windows in the end of the lower story where the judge's bench shall be erected; the weather boarding shall be rough, but jointed, the floors shall be rough also, but the lower floor shall be square jointed and the upper tongued and grooved; the platform for the judge's bench shall be three feet high, eight feet in length, three feet in width, and banistered, steps at each end, with a seat the whole length of the platform; there shall also be half a dozen other seats of dressed pine plank, ten or twelve feet in length; the foundation of the house shall be of good rock or brick, and raised two feet above the ground. The persons contracted for the building of the above mentioned house shall be required to furnish nails, glass, putty, hinges, locks and other small necessary articles.[10]

The legislative hall of the Cherokee government housed the National Committee and the National Council, an elective bicameral body. The building in which this branch of the government transacted its business was an equally important part of the new capital at New Echota. Unfortunately, few records are available for a description of this structure. However, scattered comments in the records and letters of travellers and the random literary remains of a few Cherokees indicate that the building was largely similar to the others—that is, of frame or hewn-log construction, probably about twenty-five by thirty feet. One differing element in its construction seems to have been its roof, which, following an ancient tradition among Cherokee council houses, may have been conical in shape.[11]

A few houses and taverns were built around the government buildings during the early years of New Echota's existence. Some Indians moved to the capital or to nearby Newtown, while others occupied the capital only during legislative and court sessions during the autumn. Some white men came in also, hoping to capitalize on new business or seeking to help the Indians. One of these was the missionary Samuel Worcester, who operated a mission school and served as postmaster at the capital. Another, and one who may have influenced the appearance of New Echota, was J. S. White. He advertised as follows in the Indians' newspaper:

> HOUSE BUILDER AND CABINET MAKER. J. S. White, from the City of New York, respectfully informs the citizens of the Cherokee Nation, that he intends carrying on the business of house building and cabinet-making in a manner superior to any that has been done and in the most fashionable manner equal to that of New York and Baltimore, and superior to any work of the kind in this part of the country. He will work as cheap as any workman and in a better manner than can be done. He has got mahogany and materials of the best quality.

Other businesses in the New Echota area were operated by Cherokees. These included Alexander McCoy's ferry and Elijah Hicks' store.[12]

Contemporary descriptions of New Echota show the capital city to be a small town of some six buildings centered together, with others scattered nearby. In times of legislative and court activities, the population often exceeded three hundred. During the remainder of the year the area resembled a small crossroads village, with a mission station and post office, while nearby Newtown was larger and more populous.[13]

The wife of the editor of the *Cherokee Phoenix* was Mrs. Harriet Ruggles Gold Boudinot, a native of Cornwall, Connecticut. In 1828 her parents, Mr. and Mrs. Benjamin Gold, visited the Boudinots. Benjamin Gold's appealing descriptions of New Echota reflect the charm and dignity of the simple little village, and at the same time reveal something of a New Englander's surprise and pleasure at witnessing the surroundings in which his daughter lived. To his brother-in-law he wrote: "New Echota is on a hansom spot of ground a little elevated—with a Council House & Court House in the center & two or three Merchants Stores about half a dozen framed Dwelling Houses in sight which would be called respectable in Litchfield [Connecticut]. . . ."[14]

Writing to his immediate family, Benjamin Gold gave more details about the Indian capital:

> This neighborhood is truly an interesting and pleasant place. The ground is level and smooth as a floor; the center of the Nation, a new place, laid out in city form: a hundred lots of an acre each. A spring, called the public spring about twice as large as our sawmill brook, near the center, with other springs on the plat; six new framed houses in sight, besides a Council House, Court House, printing office and four stores, all in sight of Mr. Boudinot's house; but the stores are continued only during the session of the Council and then removed to other parts of the Nation—except one steadily continued. . . .[15]

Some forty years later an old Indian named White Horse reminisced about the appearance of New Echota in the 1830's. He described the sights a tourist might find:

> That long house to our right with beautiful surroundings is the tavern of A. McCoy—clerk of the council, just over the hollow further on is the large beautiful residence of Elijah Hicks,—member of the Senate from Cooseewatah. We pass the stone house of Lewis Ross and Lavender, and also of James Daniel and Co., and the council house to our right, and supreme court building to our left. Further on we pass the office of the Cherokee Phoenix, and on the same street a large two story frame, with garden, orchard, and convenient out-house attached. This is the home of E. Boudinot, the editor. To our left is the handsome cottage residence of Jno. F. Wheeler the printer. Beyond that is the Mission establishment of the Rev. S. A. Worcester. Not far off are two more taverns—one kept by J. Horn, the other by George Hicks. . . .[16]

The most detailed account of New Echota's specific location is the evidence of one of Georgia's surveyors. These agents entered the Indian country in the early 1830's for the purpose of laying it off into land-lots to be handed out to white men in a lottery.[17] The surveyor who passed by New Echota in 1832 was one Stephen Drane, working the fourteenth district of the third section. A study of his records shows that New Echota consisted primarily of a cluster of six buildings located approximately one-half mile southwest of the river forks.[18] Drane also noted the general limits of the capital as being in a wide circular area, just as the Council resolution of 1825 had stipulated.[19]

Meanwhile Cherokees in the early nineteenth century continued the earlier practice of making their houses out of logs.[20] For the average Cherokee, the timber was split and fitted together by notching, forming a one- or two-room house ranging from fifteen to twenty-five feet square. Most cabins had a "puncheon floor" which was made of split logs formed into rough boards with unfinished edges. Open fireplaces were used for heat, light, and cooking; the smoke usually travelled upward through a wooden chimney made of sticks and short logs chinked with clay or mud. Some houses had lofts and porches. Most of them had no windows.[21] Cyrus Kingsbury noted in his journal shortly after his arrival to begin the American Board missions: "The houses . . . in this country . . . have generally wooden chimneys, are without glass, & the doors are obliged to be kept open in the day time to admit light, so that one can hardly eat breakfast without a fit of the ague." Roofs usually were of split-oak shingles called "shakes."[22]

The rising prosperity which followed adoption of the white man's ways resulted in improved dwellings and increased comforts. The Cherokee Census of 1835 revealed the presence of more than 11,000 houses of various types amongst the 2,700 families. The more affluent Cherokees, who usually were mixed-breeds, sometimes built homes that rivalled the dwellings of upper class whites. Such men as John Ross, Major Ridge, John Martin, Richard Taylor, and George Lowrey lived in considerable comfort, owning large frame dwellings surrounded by several outhouses including quarters for their slaves. Probably the most outstanding residence in the entire nation was the two-story brick mansion owned by Joseph Vann, at Spring Place (near present-day Chatsworth, Georgia). Known as "Rich Joe," this son of the enterprising mixed-breed James Vann apparently handled his inheritance wisely. When land-hungry Georgians forced him to move away in 1834, Vann sold his house and improvements for $28,179.75. The imposing dwelling which he left behind in Georgia is still standing, and although time has taken its toll in actual beauty, the red-brick white-columned house, with connecting kitchen, dominates the rolling countryside around it and commands respect with its grim air of lost elegance. The broad veranda and spacious interior impart an air of comfort and convenience, while the still-standing cantilevered staircase and indications of elaborate panelling reflect taste and discernment. Joseph Vann moved to Tennessee, and by 1835 his possessions there included some 35 various buildings, 110 slaves, a mill, a ferry, and 300 acres in cultivation on which he had raised 3,200 bushels of corn.[23]

When the American Board established a branch mission at Taloney, Brothers Hall and Parker took over an existing Cherokee farm which was purchased (improvements only) from a half-breed family named Sanders. The several houses and surroundings as described by a visitor in May, 1822, revealed a relatively high standard of living on the part of the former owners:

After breakfast, visited an old field across the creek purchased by Mr. Hall last autumn for 12 dollars. It contains 4 acres of excellent land, fenced on three sides—it being enclosed with other land, cultivated by one of the Sanderses. Visited, also, the cellar, store-house, kitchen, meat-house, garden, corn-cribs. . . . There are certainly many conveniences attached to this station.

The house is built of hewn timber, & covered with the split oak stuff of the country, which is called *boards*. The principal dwelling house of the station is built in the same manner, & has two rooms. Mr. Parker occupies a little cabin designed for the children.[24]

An opposite view of Cherokee life was related by the English traveller George Featherstonhaugh, who passed through the Tennessee River country in 1837. His report of a short visit to an Indian home reveals a squalid life which undoubtedly existed on the lower levels of Cherokee society. Featherstonhaugh stopped "at a rude log house in a small clearing hemmed in by the woods." Nearby were a few peach trees bearing some green fruit. Inside, the Englishman found the house floorless. He saw a Cherokee man lying on the ground, "near a hideous-looking woman, seated upon her haunches, and an Indian girl, depediculating her mamma's head."[25] Possibly the visitor detected an air of depression, which, considering the imminent removal facing the Cherokee population, was justified.

When actions of state and federal governments in the late 1830's forced the expatriation of the Cherokee Indians westward, many Indians suffered losses of property and improvements. Most of them put in claims for these losses, listing both real and personal property—and in so doing left an important record of the physical evidence of their progress in utilizing the white man's comforts and conveniences.[26] A random sampling of sixty-five claims from the Etowah District, representative of thousands of such documents executed by the Eastern Cherokees at removal time, reveals various types of losses. Thirty-six of the sixty-five put in claims for improved lands, farms, and fields; thirty-five listed buildings of various sorts; thirty-five specified livestock and poultry; thirty-one named orchards and scattered trees; twenty-four enumerated farm equipment and household tools; twenty-three noted household furnishings and personal property; fourteen mentioned food and produce on hand; and ten entered such miscellaneous losses as cash, ferry ownership, and rentals. The predominance of this type of claims suggests the extent to which the Cherokees had adapted themselves to the sedentary ways of the white man. The claims for household furnishings and personal property items indicate a similar trend. Kitchen ware appearing in the lists included dishes, cutlery, pots, pans, coffee pots, coffee mills, bowls, ovens, pails, kettles, irons, churns, and washtubs. Chairs, tables, featherbeds, bedsteads, and cupboards comprised most of the furniture lost; while the clothing left behind included cloaks, hats, hunting shirts, shoes, stays, trousers, and dresses of silk and cotton.[27]

The clothing worn by early nineteenth century Cherokees varied as widely as the social scale. Upperclass Indians, particularly the mixed-breeds, adopted the garb of their white counterparts in the neighboring states. Leaders like John Ross and Major Ridge confounded the traditional picture of "wild Indians" by appearing in Washington and at home in the dress of cultured gentlemen of the Old South.[28] A more standard Cherokee costume, prevailing among the majority of the Indians, consisted of the traditional hip-length "Cherokee hunting shirt," made of buckskin, calico, or home-woven material, and usually fringed at the bottom. Men often wore earrings, which hung from slitted ears. Leggings were generally being replaced during the latter part of this era by trousers of buckskin or cloth, colored a rich tan by the application of dye made from walnut hulls. A curious headdress adaptation was a sort of turban, made usually of calico wrapped about the head. Some Cherokees wore hats. Those who did not adopt the white man's shoes wore moccasins.[29]

The appearance of two contrasting types of Cherokee leaders was clearly described by Elias Cornelius, who, as a representative of the American Board, attended a "council of Chiefs" at Charles Hicks' home in 1817. Of his host Cornelius wrote glowingly:

> He is a half-breed Cherokee, about fifty years of age. He has very pleasant features, and an intelligent countenance. He speaks the English language with the utmost facility, and with great propriety. . . . As a man of integrity, temperance, and intelligence, he has long sustained a most reputable character.

But the other chiefs he portrayed thus:

> They were less civilized in their exterior. Their ears were *slitted,* after the Indian manner, and pieces of silver attached to them. Their dress was the hunting shirt, vest, turban, deer-skin *leggins,* with silk or other garters, and *moccasons.* Some of them had hats. . . . The chiefs were all well provided with horses and saddles, and blankets. Their appearance was that of the utmost contentment.[30]

An ancient Cherokee trait which persisted into the early nineteenth century was the comparatively slight regard for one of the white man's cherished principles – the sanctity of marriage to one wife. As in the preceding eras, most Cherokees apparently accepted polygamy, especially those who did not accept Christianity from the missionaries. James Vann's polygamous marriages must have disturbed the Moravian brethren at Spring Place, who undoubtedly sought to reason with him on the matter. Twenty years later, Puritans of the American Board were disturbed by the same problem. One of Cyrus Kingsbury's early assistants in the Cherokee country was a half-breed named Charles Reece, who became one of Brainerd's first converts. But Reece was another polygamist. Kingsbury noted that the Indian "has had three sisters for his wives at the same time, one of whom is dead; & he has left the other two on account of the insolence of their mother – has left a good plantation, & a valuable stock of cattle, for them & his children, & taken another woman with whom he has begun anew in the world."[31]

The general problem of the Cherokee attitude toward marriage was discussed in the Brainerd journal on September 23, 1818, in connection with difficulties in the mission school caused by separation of families. Often one parent would take from the school a child who had been placed there by the other. A specific case of marital confusion was described, in which it was related how a father of three who had had two wives now had another; while the first two were themselves living with other men. The journal commented: "How much better for this man & his children if he had adhered to the original institution of marriage; few, however, of the natives pay attention to it."[32]

Elias Boudinot declared proudly to a Philadelphia audience in 1826 that in his country "polygamy is abolished. Female chastity and honor are protected by law." He had reference to a series of laws passed by the Cherokee legislature against multiple marriages, and rape. Previously Cherokee law had banned white men in the Indian country from having more than one Cherokee wife, and had urged "all others, also, to have but one wife." In November, 1825, the Council amended these laws by announcing that "it shall not be lawful hereafter, for any person or persons, whatsoever, to have more than one wife." On the same day, the Cherokee legislature decreed that persons convicted of rape should suffer severe penalties: first offense, fifty lashes and the left ear "cropped close to the head"; second offense, one hundred lashes and the right ear cropped; third offense, death. False accusations, however, would result in twenty-five lashes for the perjuring female.[33]

In spite of Cherokee laws, missionary efforts, and desires for civilization along the white man's pattern, some polygamy continued to exist in the Indian nation. In 1835 Daniel S. Butrick asked the American Board to rule on "the propriety of requiring candidates for church membership to put away all their wives but one." David Greene, writing from the missionary offices in Boston, reported that the Board declined to make such a decision, and recommended that either the missionaries in the field decide such matters, or that possibly the question could be "brought before the General Assembly." But Greene himself thought the latter action unwise, owing to the unpleasant publicity which might result. Instead, hinted the Secretary, if such decisions made locally were kept from the general public, the situation might be accepted; for, he remarked, "I will . . . say that I have proposed the question to five or six persons most of them ministers and all but one or two thought that there was nothing in the New Testament to authorize you to require of a man in the circumstances proposed to put away his wives."[34]

Under the influence of the missionary effort, many Cherokees intending marriage had a Christian service performed – and it is likely that this procedure increased marital stability. The *Cherokee Phoenix* published many wedding announcements, such as this one of October 15, 1828: "MARRIED – On Thursday last, by the Rev. Mr. Byhan [Moravian], Mr. DAVID VANN, ESQ, of High Tower District, to Miss MARTHA, youngest daughter of Capt. David M'Nair of Amohee District." Occasionally a description of a wedding was printed. One appeared in May, 1828, when a correspondent named "Waterhunter" sent a flowery account of a marriage ceremony, which at the same time reveals something of the Cherokee native's reaction to the progress of his nation. The writer walked six miles to attend the service, and on his journey described the delights of his native countryside:

> The birds mingled their charming melody with the breezes that gently agitated the leaves of the forest; and my soul glowed in harmony and rapture, as I surveyed the Oostanalee winding its silent course towards the South. . . . The spring had . . . spread her rich carpet of green, white, red, and yellow in the . . . earth. These blessings, are extended for the use and benefit of the Cherokee Indians, who for ages past have lived in ignorance and degradation, but now, no longer savages, are rising from ignorance to the standard of moral, intellectual, religious and political importance.[35]

During the service, Waterhunter interpreted the Reverend Greenberry Garrett's "instructive discourse" for the benefit of Indian friends attending. Then there came "prayer and singing . . . wholly conducted in Cherokee." After a wedding dinner, the marriage ceremony was performed by Garrett, with Waterhunter translating. The correspondent concluded his account with descriptions of the newly wedded couple:

> The Bride is a quarter white, possesses a fine figure, somewhat tall, beautiful complexion, with dark hair and eyes; her features bear the evidence of amiability and good nature; and on the whole she is an interesting woman. She is a member of the Methodist Church. The Bridegroom, a cousin of mine, is a full blooded Indian, of Aboriginal deep copper complexion, low in stature, fine figure, but does not possess a handsome face, though depicted upon it are the marks of honesty, fidelity, and good nature. He was dressed in a clean northern domestic suit, and his bride was in white cambric.[36]

On the other side of the confused picture of Cherokee "progress" was the tendency to cling to older customs. One curious practice, reminiscent of ancient deference to women, allowed a widow to drop the name of her dead husband, reverting to her maiden name. Although non-Christian marriages were apparently less enduring, yet there was considerable ceremony connected with the tribal union. Such a service occurring in the early nineteenth century was described as follows:

> The whole town were convened, all attired in their gayest apparel. The groom, accompanied by the young associates of his own sex, was feasted at a lodge a little distance from the council-house. The bride,

with her maiden associates, was similarly feasted in a lodge equidistant from the Council-house and on the opposite side. First the old men took the highest seats on one side . . . , next the old women took similar seats on the other side. Then all the married men took seats on the side occupied by the old men, and all the married women sat with the old women. At a given signal, the companions of the groom conducted him to the . . . open space between the men and women. . . . The companions of the bride conduct her to the other end . . . , and they now stand with their faces towards each other, but a distance from 30 to 60 feet apart. . . . The groom now receives from his mother a leg of venison and a blanket; the bride receives from her mother an ear of corn & a blanket. The groom and bride now commence stepping towards each other, and when they meet . . . the groom presents his venison & the bride her corn, and the blankets are united. This ceremony . . . is a promise . . . that he will provide meat for his family, and . . . that she will furnish bread, and . . . that they will occupy the same bed.[37]

As in other families the world over, there were happy marriages and unhappy ones, whether Christian or tribal in nature. Charles Reece's experiences with his mother-in-law, cited above, indicate something of the traditional plight of a dissatisfied husband. Some Cherokee wives probably felt about their husbands as did Nancy Badger, in whose name the following complaint was lodged with the Indian Agency late in 1805:

Dear Sir This Coms to inform you that Mr Bager & his wife has parted & She is a Frade that he will take some means to Destrase [Distress] her he will Com perhaps to you with a tale but She says belive nothing he says for the truth is not in him & their is nothing that is to bad for him to say or do & she Can prove it by white & Rade [Red].[38]

Happier circumstances in a Cherokee family were reported by Harriet Gold Boudinot, the Connecticut girl who had married Elias. The young couple lived with the Oowatie family for a few months after arriving in the Cherokee country. In her letters home Harriet had much praise for her husband's people:

My Cherokee father often reminds me of my own Father by his cheerfulness and I think is remarkable for his amiable kind and affectionate disposition . . . and both he and My Dear Cherokee Mother frequently say that I am like an own child to them. Mother is a very feeble woman — but never idle if she is able to be off her bed. She cuts and makes all the clothes for the family except the coats for the men. She is remarked by all who know her for her amiable kind and friendly disposition.[39]

The diet of nineteenth century Cherokees followed the general pattern of the nation's development. Most families enjoyed corn served as a sort of mush, or less frequently, baked into bread. Sweet potatoes, garden vegetables, and occasionally meat provided by the hunters were the usual supplements. With the rise of the Indian's social scale and income, due generally to success in following the lines of economy suggested by the white man, there came a rise also in the quality and variety of his food. During her stay with the progressive Oowatie family, for example, Harriet Boudinot enjoyed "coffee, Sugar, Tea, milk, Corn and wheat bread, Beef, Pork, Venison, and an abundance of fowls," as well as butter, cheese, apple sauce, and pickles. Staple foods for the majority of Cherokees were corn and sweet potatoes. The latter were usually stored for the winter in holes with dry grass or other material packed around them, so that as much as possible the yams could be enjoyed on a year-round basis. But the main source of sustenance throughout the nation was corn. Three methods of preparation were used, producing meal, hominy, or "skin-corn." If hominy or meal was desired, the corn was pounded in a mortar, which was often fashioned from a hollowed-out tree trunk. A tasty and frequent dish was ca-nu-chi (or Car-Nut-Chee) consisting of corn meal mush mixed with crushed hickory nuts. Fresh and dried fruit furnished additional items for the diet, as did honey and fish.[40]

The excessive consumption of liquor was a serious problem in the Cherokee country. Since early days, traders had found it profitable to haul in liquor, legal or otherwise. Sometimes unscrupulous treaty commissioners weakened Indian opposition with "fire-water." Its dangers were of great concern to Cherokee leaders. In 1804, for example, Little Turtle told the United States Indian Agent that liquor sales in the nation must be stopped if the Cherokees were to make further progress. After the Cherokee republic was organized, in an effort to eliminate the "great variety of vices emanating from dissipation . . . so prevalent at public places" the Council enacted a statute which struck at part of the evil. This act forbade any persons from bringing liquor "within three miles of the General Council House," or to Cherokee courthouses in the districts. A subsequent amendment specifically banned liquor from public gatherings under penalty of having it poured on the ground. It seems significant that the Council did not attempt to institute prohibition throughout the Cherokee Nation. Perhaps the Indian leaders felt that prohibition would be extremely difficult to enforce; besides, the nation was receiving some taxes from whiskey sales, and the owners of public houses and general stores sold it freely.[41]

Violation of the whiskey laws is attested by correspondence published in the *Cherokee Phoenix* in June, 1828. The editor hoped that "the examples of these writers would be followed by the aged, the influential, and the patriotic of this Nation until . . . this great evil can be arrested." The letter, signed by nine Cherokees, was addressed to "the newly appointed chiefs, William Hicks and John Ross," and complained that the laws concerning whisky "are not obeyed here: for whenever our young men are assembled together, whiskey is not wanting." After drinking began, the complaint continued, there would be stealing in the community, and dancing. "When they have been dancing all night, in the morning they commence fighting . . . [and] nearly kill each other sometimes."[42]

An unusually ingenious drinking custom seems to have been followed by the Cherokee Indians. An eye-witness of Indian "drinking frolicks" in the 1830's states that "there was always one sober Indian. If two or ten were together, one was sober and took care of all the knives and pocketbooks and had a sad face all the time; but the next time he was the first man to get drunk." This observer also asserted that he never saw a drunken Cherokee woman.[43]

In the *Cherokee Phoenix* Elias Boudinot constantly inveighed against excessive drinking, publishing extracted temperance articles or using the closer personal touch of an editorial. In the issue of May 28, 1828, for example, he commented on a recent murder committed by a drunken Indian:

> The pernicious effects of intemperance, which prevails to an alarming extent in this Country and elsewhere, stand in their order, divested of all palliating circumstances, when instances similar to this case are considered. . . . Can the people of this country look at the prevalence of such an evil with indifference? Will the Patriots of the Cherokee Nation see one victim after another falling before that pernicious vice and not exert themselves to avert its progress?[44]

Associated with the intemperance vice was the great national Cherokee game, the Ball Play, which continued to exist as a popular recreation in this era. Missionary and government agents alike noted the frequent occasions on which it was played. The mission worker saw the Ball Play as a time of riotous drinking and heavy gambling, and sought to deter attendance. The government agent on the other hand took a more tolerant view because of the definite advantage resulting from large numbers of Cherokees gathering occasionally in one place. Particularly outstanding games took place in 1825 and 1834. The first, played at New Echota on a Sunday in August, profoundly shocked the American Board missionaries, one of whom termed the affair "a scene of national iniquity." A full attendance of the Cherokee leaders did nothing to assuage the missionary horror over this apparent wholesale back-sliding. The 1834 match pitted teams from Hickory Log and Coosawattee together in a game on which the rival chiefs wagered one thousand dollars.[45]

Another popular sport among the Eastern Cherokees in the early nineteenth century was "Stalk-Shooting," a game which kept alive the Indian's skill at archery. Less formalized than the Ball Play, Stalk Shooting's rules varied from place to place; generally, it was a contest requiring a player to shoot an arrow at a group of cornstalks in an upright bunch approximately 150 yards away. Points were awarded each archer depending on the number of stalks pierced by his arrow.[46] Very likely this game was especially loved by reactionaries who sought to perpetuate tribal abilities in marksmanship.

Less active enjoyments were found by sedentary Cherokees who were pursuing the white man's culture. Those with sufficient financial resources and literacy in English owned books and subscribed to periodicals. When Adam Hodgson, an Englishman, visited "the house of a very intelligent farmer" in the Cherokee country in 1820, he seemed pleased to behold on his host's bookshelves "Robertson's America, the Spectator, and several periodical publications; a Bible, hymn-book, and other religious works." During the six years of the *Cherokee Phoenix,* reading matter in both Cherokee and English was available to all members of the nation. Boudinot constantly offered his readers stories and articles on interesting matter from all parts of the globe. Indoor entertainments enjoyed by upper-class Cherokees included billiards, gambling at dice or cards, and travelling shows and exhibits.[47]

Among ancient Cherokee customs and rites which carried over into the nineteenth century, the Green Corn Dance was most important. By the 1830's it was sometimes rather aptly called the "Stomp Dance," but it was still associated with the opening of the green corn season. Fires were kept burning throughout the year for special ceremonial exercises in connection with the festival. Frequently a Ball Play also commemorated the occasion.[48] Other "dancing frolicks" were popular, especially with those Cherokees who had remained further behind on the "white man's road." A traveller through the area of the Five Lower Towns in the summer of 1813 witnessed such an affair in which "Indians, White people, half-breeds and Creoles" participated.[49]

A definite tribalism continued in medicinal practices, although practical Cherokees utilized the white man's cures. When fevers struck native families, the usual treatment was by the time-honored medicine-man method of "sweating," during which kettles of hot water were put into the patient's bed. A "cupping-horn," familiar enough in ancient times for blood-sucking, occasionally turned up. The principal diseases which plagued Cherokees were consumption and smallpox. An epidemic of consumption struck the Cherokees in 1823 in such alarming proportions that Elias Boudinot in a fit of depression told friends in New England that perhaps the "Cherokee Nation is destined to fall by this Instrument of Death."[50]

Smallpox brought equally devastating results. During an attack in 1806, Cherokee chiefs called upon a white doctor named William McNeill to help them.[51] The epidemic of 1824 elicited from Moody Hall, a missionary stationed at Carmel, a graphic account which revealed much of the conflict between opposing treatments:

> The Small Pox is raging to an alarming degree within 1½ miles of the Valley Town mission. We have heard that it is spreading very fast, & is now within 20 miles of Calhoun [Tennessee]. Owing to the ignorance & inattention of the Indians it is probable that it will spread generally thro' the country & that 1000 will die with it. In our little Town where it first appeared in the nation, 27 have died; all that had it except one. . . . [Should we obtain from Tennessee] the matter for the cow pox I shall use all my influence to have all the Cherokees inoculated. The Old Conjuror has appointed a great Phys[ic] dance, (as in the case of the measles) promising that all who join him, shall not be afflicted with the disease.

The Christians all say that they think more of a short sincere prayer, than of their seven days fasting & drinking physic.[52]

A logical result of cross-breeding red and white customs was the emergence of strange practices. One of these was witnessed by William Chamberlin during a preaching tour in 1823. The occasion was the funeral of a young man of a mixed-breed non-Christian family. As Chamberlin arrived, the grieving females began "the most doleful lament" he had ever heard, consisting primarily of the words, "Ath quo tse [Oh my son]." After a few minutes the boy's father abruptly said, "It is enough!" Then he "carryed water to each individual, they washed their faces and at once were perfectly calm." Subsequently, as each new visitor arrived, the lamentations were renewed. The body was taken in a coffin to a nearby grave and the coffin reopened. "The brother took one of the hands from under the winding sheet and all the people present, went and shook the hand of the dead body, thus presented to them, bidding him fare well telling him they hoped to meet him above." When the coffin had been placed in the grave, each person in turn threw a handful of dirt into the pit. Upon returning to the house, the women again lay on the floor and began their plaintive moans.[53]

Peculiar indeed was the condition of Cherokee society in this era. Inherited, borrowed, and invented social practices produced oddities in dress, marriage, diet, recreation, superstition, and medicine. Many Indians unable to appropriate the white man's language used his houses, utensils, and clothing. Affluent Cherokees bore close resemblance to white planters save in color — and even there, striking similarities existed. Truly the Cherokee Nation during the early nineteenth century had become a curiously pseudo-white agrarian culture.

NINE

LIVELIHOOD AND LEGISLATION

An encouraging economic prospect for the Cherokee Indians was noted in 1801 by Indian Agent Return J. Meigs shortly after his arrival in the Cherokee country. It was a fitting report, for it summarized succinctly the advances made by the Cherokee Nation during the preceding era, and offered a promise of things to come.

> They begin to taste the Comforts of an agricultural life, therefore place a value on their land. They make a great deal on Cloth & raise a great many Cattle. They have one Mill – they ask for two more. . . . The mills are of the kind called Tub Mills. . . . Many of the Indian women are good spinsters and weavers, & can instruct their neighbors.[1]

During the early nineteenth century the Cherokee Indians made considerable domestic, agrarian, and business progress. An indication of this development may be had from an official census begun by the Indian government in 1824 and published in the *Cherokee Phoenix* in 1828. This survey revealed that a total population of approximately 15,000 Indians owned about 1,000 slaves; 22,400 cattle; 7,600 horses; 40,000 swine; 3,000 sheep; 1,850 spinning wheels; 2,450 plows; 547 "wheels"; 475 goats; 700 looms; 120 wagons; 12 saw mills; 20 grist mills; 55 blacksmith shops; 6 cotton gins; 10 ferries; 9 stores; a turnpike; 6 public roads; and a threshing machine. Elias Boudinot, editor of the Cherokee newspaper, estimated the aggregate value of this property at $2,200,000.[2]

While it seems certain that most of these elements of material prosperity were in the hands of half-breeds or upperclass full-bloods, it appears overdrawn to say that the majority of the fifteen thousand Cherokees lived in hovels, and that the poor were getting poorer and the rich richer. The Charleston *Observer* made such a statement in 1828, and received an emphatic denial from Samuel A. Worcester. He declared that the charge was "entirely without foundation." Instead, he wrote the editor of the *Cherokee Phoenix,* "the condition of the majority of the people, not including those who may be termed wealthy, is, in point of prosperity, constantly improving and never more rapidly than at the present time. . . ." Worcester's claim was buttressed by an unidentified Indian. This writer indignantly refuted the statements of United States Representative Mitchell of Tennessee, who had told Congress about the "abject condition" of the "great mass of . . . the poorer class" of Cherokees. Boudinot's correspondent, who styled himself "one of the mass," wrote:

> I, being one of the "poorer class" feel hurt in reading this sentence. It is certainly humiliating to think after making exertions to raise myself above the level of the most degraded of the human races, and presuming to have succeeded, at least in a small degree, it should still be declared that I have made no progress. This is poor encouragement for Indians. . . . A part of the population of . . . the United States, are more wretched and degraded than the "poorer class" of the Cherokees.[3]

Perhaps if disparagers of Cherokee prosperity had traveled through the fertile regions of the Indian country they might have altered their opinions concerning native degradation. Certainly the many farms and scattered plantations indicated a standard of living far removed from days of war parties and scalp-dances. During the early years of the nineteenth century, more and more Cherokees accepted the invitation of the United States government and, taking advice and tools from the Indian Agent, turned to agriculture as a basic means of support. By 1835, when Federal removal agents conducted a census of Cherokee Indians, it was found that of 2,668 families registered, representing a total of 16,542 individuals, 2,495 (about 93 per cent) had at least one farm. Altogether, 3,120 farms were recorded. A number of Indians had more than one farm: 224 had two, 77 had three, 33 had four, 17 had five, 8 had six, 1 had seven, 1 had nine, and 1 had thirteen.[4]

Detailed descriptions of some of these farms are recorded in the Cherokee Claims Papers, in which individual Cherokees listed their property losses at the time of removal in 1838 or earlier. The claim of Sawnee Vann, a half-breed who lived at the junction of the Oostanaulah and Etowah rivers, is representative of the economic status of many of his type. Sawnee made the following claim:[5]

For being dispossessed of improvement and property lost, in consequence of being forced to remove by the U. S. Troops. in the forks of Estanallee, & Hightower rivers in the State of Georgia. Emigrated under Genl. Smith, in the spring of 1838, to wit;

1836 –	Rent	15 acres of land, dispossessed $3.00 per Acre for one year – $45 – 2 years	$ 90.00
1838.	15	Acres of growing Corn – $10.00 per acre . . .	150.00
	2	Acres of growing Potatoes	50.00
	15	head of Cattle – $8.00 Each	120.00
	50	head of Stock Hogs – $3.00 Each	150.00
	20	head of Sheep – $5.00 Each	100.00
	100	Bushels of Corn – $1.00 Each	100.00
	3	Shovel Ploughs – $6.00 & 3 Gearing $18.00 . .	24.00
	8	Chairs $8.00 & 8 Bee Hives $15.00	23.00
	2	Bed stead $10.00 & 1 Feather Bed $25.00 . . .	35.00
	100	Chickens $12.50 & 9 Pots $25.00	37.50
	3	Dishes $3.00 – 8 Plates $1.00 – 2 Keelers $2.00	6.00
	8	Weeding Hoes $8.00 & 4 Tin Pans $2.00 . .	10.00
	20	lb Clean Wool $10.00 & 100 lb Cotton . . .	10.00
	1	Table $5.00 & 1 Weaving Loom $5.00 . . .	10.00
	3	Large troughs full of soap	10.00
	1	Spinning Wheel $3.00 & 2 pr Cotton Cards $2.00	5.00
	4	Cane Fanners $2.00 & 3 Padlocks $3.00 . . .	5.00
	500	lb. Bacon 12½¢ $62.50 & 3 Augers $2.00 . . .	64.50
	1	Foot Adze $1.50 & 1 Drawing Knife $1.50 . .	3.00
	1	Hand Saw $3.00 & 1 Cradling Sythe $3.00 . .	6.00
	3	Rifle Guns $30.00 & 2 $25.00	80.00
	3	Horses taken & sold by U.S. Officers & $45.00 on sd horses – worth $100.00 each	255.00
	1	Saddle & Bridle & c. $30.00 & 3 axes $6.00 . .	36.00
			$1,250.00

The Census of 1835 credits Sawnee Vann as being the head of a family of six males and two females. He owned two slaves and a farm on which he had six buildings and thirty acres in cultivation.[6] In comparison with other Cherokees, Sawnee Vann ranks among the less affluent upperclass, and his property holdings, listed in detail above, may be taken as fairly representative of that group of his countrymen.

Livestock production in the Cherokee country enjoyed a steady growth. The chief animals raised were swine and cattle. The Cherokee Census of 1824 tabulated nearly forty thousand swine, of which the greatest concentrations were in Chickamauga and Amohee districts. On the other hand, Chattooga and Coosawatee districts recorded the largest amounts of cattle, their totals being respectively 7,018 and 2,944, out of a Cherokee aggregate of 22,400. The primary use of cattle was for beef. Even in Chickamauga, the district ranking fourth in cattle production in 1824, missionaries observed that cattle were not used for labor purposes:

> Few people in this part of the country, either red or white, know anything about working oxen. A few pair, well broken, introduced into different parts of the nation, may do much toward teaching the people that "Much increase is by the strength of the ox." Cattle are so easily raised in this country that the natives might easily furnish themselves with oxen, did they but know their use, & how to train them for work.[7]

Although missionary example might have taught some Cherokees the advantage of utilizing "the strength of the ox," beef production continued to dominate Cherokee cattle interests. In 1831 the editor of the *Cherokee Phoenix* noted with some pride that "not less than one thousand beeves" were to be driven to "northern markets" during that season, in addition to those destined for sale in Georgia and South Carolina. Further remarks by the editor were apparently aimed at critics of Indian backwardness:

> Those [cattle] for the north are bought by Tennesseans, not from the half breeds only, but (as the expression is) from the common Indians. This . . . may give some of our distant readers a little light as to the condition of the Cherokees, who were said to be not long since on the point of starvation, some of them subsisting on sap and roots.[8]

Clearly the Cherokee economy in the first decades of the nineteenth century was that of a nation becoming agricultural. This process was so far advanced by the 1830's that the Indian without a farm was the exception rather than the rule. Comparable progress along the "white man's road" was being made by Cherokee women, who probably grasped eagerly the white man's inventions to facilitate their manufacture of cloth and clothing. Spinning wheels and weaving paraphernalia became commonplace articles among the household possessions; when cotton became a staple crop, the distribution of thousands of cotton cards by the Indian Agent helped in the process of making cotton fibers ready for spinning and weaving.

An increase in Negro slavery accompanied agrarian progress in the Cherokee country. Always accustomed to having red, black, and sometimes white slaves around, the Cherokees in early times took slavery somewhat for granted, adding to the supply through capture of villagers, travellers, soldiers, and runaways. Growth of Negro slavery increased notably in the latter part of the eighteenth century. Some blacks were brought in by white Tories who found sanctuary in the Indian country. Many traders who settled among Cherokees had brought along a few slaves, and added to them from time to time. Undoubtedly the prime factor in the extension of slavery was the increasing success of Cherokees and half-breeds as farmers in the early nineteenth century. By 1824 more than one thousand Negro slaves were living and working among the Cherokee Indians; the census of a decade later showed that the number had increased to fifteen hundred.[9]

As in white regions, many Cherokee owners treated their slaves humanely. When missionaries began offering religious and secular education in the Indian country, numbers of slaves were permitted to attend church and school. Cyrus Kingsbury noted something of this kindness in 1818: "There are many of this class of people, in bondage to the Cherokees, & they all speak english. Their masters, so far as has come to our knowledge, are all willing to have them instructed & generally very indulgent in giving them time to attend meetings."[10]

During a visit to Major Ridge's home, Daniel S. Butrick preached to "8 or 10" slaves at Ridge's request. One Negro especially caught the preacher's attention: an old woman who seemed "particularly attentive." Butrick learned that "she raised her family with the natives, & yet as a pious mother has them all repeat their prayers morning & evening & learns them some beautiful lines of the crucifixion of our Savior [*sic*]. . . ." In spite of the fact that most slaves had little time off during the week for religious activities, the Christian workers in the Cherokee country were heartened by their zeal. Some of them came "12, 15, or 20 miles" to mission services. As the mission work progressed, many slaves found it possible to come on Saturday night and remain the following day, with good results.[11]

The crossing patterns of red, white, and black cultures in the

Cherokee country very naturally produced some strange manifestations. One example was brought out in 1808 when Principal Chief Black Fox, speaking for the Cherokee Council, ordered a white man named Evan Austill to give up

> a woman and her Children which you have in your Possession which appears to be one of our own people and you can not have any objection to Deliver up as she is free born as any White woman – as the Man who is near kin of hers had made it appear that her mother was taken prisoner during the War and the Woman Demanded was born in the Settlement – although you have paid for her as a Slave . . . [you] must have a recourse to the Man you bought her of. . . .[12]

Another curious instance was noted a decade later by men of the American Board, who learned that among the more devout Negroes attending services at Brainerd were two slaves who were teaching their Cherokee mistress "to read in the bible."[13]

A case of inter-marriage created one of the most unusual problems. The Cherokee Chief Shoe Boots married a white woman, by whom he had two children. Later his white wife deserted him, taking the children with her. Shoe Boots thereupon married his favorite Negro slave, a girl named Lucy. When two blackred children had been born from this marriage, the chief petitioned the Council to grant the children free status. This request was granted, but the Council cautioned Shoe Boots against "begetting any more such legal problems."[14]

The Cherokee law-makers concerned themselves from time to time with the problems of slavery. In 1819 they announced that "no contract or bargain entered into with any slave or slaves, without the approbation of their masters shall be binding on them." The following year the Council ruled that no person could purchase any goods from slaves without the permission of owners, and that no slave was to sell liquor unless he had obtained permission.[15] Although these laws restricted the commercial activities of slaves, the very fact of their passage indicates the existence of a liberal attitude toward the bondsmen, at least until 1819.

Later Cherokee slave codes indicate a growing prejudice against Negroes, probably arising from white contacts. In 1824 a law required free Negroes to secure a permit from the Cherokee government to remain in the nation, and a second law banned slaves from possessing livestock. In the constitution of 1827, "negroes and descendants of white and Indian men by negro women who may have been set free" were denied the right to vote. Furthermore, Negroes and their descendants "either by the father or mother side" were held ineligible to "hold any office of profit, honor or trust under this government." When the General Council resolved the following year to punish individuals who might disturb any religious services, it was announced that "if any negro slave shall be convicted . . . he shall be punished with thirty-nine stripes on the bare back."[16]

Another source for farm labor, aside from family and slaves, came from hired hands or "croppers." Two of the latter, named William Schrimshear and Richard Martin, were certified to a Cherokee named John Boggs in 1808. A definite procedure existed for issuing certificates to these farm laborers, in which several neighbors swore to the "cropper's" character. Schrimshear's certificate exemplifies this formality:

> These certify that William Schrimshear is an honest industrious Citizen a good neighbor free from Disipation & may in our opinions be safely admitted into any Society or neighborhood given under our hand this 21st of April 1808
>
> Alex Moore
AMD Cowan
Thos Nesmith
William Coquor

In 1820, however, the Cherokee Council made it illegal to hire white men as agricultural laborers or overseers.[17]

While it is certain that the primary economy of the Cherokees in this era was agrarian, there was a smattering of industry, and more important, a thriving commerce. Artisans of various sorts had drifted in and out of the Cherokee country since early in the eighteenth century. Later, when the United States government sought to civilize the Cherokees, a deliberate effort was made to bring in specialized craftsmen. Benjamin Hawkins had anticipated such a program, and Return J. Meigs took some steps to bring it about. He projected a "general manufactory" where a "Wheel Right, Hatter, Tinman, Tanner & Furrier, Carpenter, Shoemakers, Blacksmith & Armorer, Leather Dresser, & Potter" could produce articles "for the benefit of the Cherokees." The operations of the blacksmith-armorer, carpenter, and wheelwright would be free to the Cherokees for one year, after which they would work for profit. At the outset, Meigs thought that it would be practicable to use artisans from the garrison at Hiwassee, a proposal based on a previous suggestion of the Secretary of War.[18]

The Cherokees probably made immediate use of craftsmen whose work was a useful complement to their farming. A blacksmith for the nation's use was apparently hired by the Indians, judging by a communication from Meigs' deputy agent, Major William Lovely. Writing in July, 1802, Lovely revealed something of the Cherokees' method in utilizing the blacksmith:

> Mr Samuel Hall. blackSmith for the Cherokees — his time is expired some time will wait on you for a Settlement of his accts, — . he has been makeing use of his own tools, — for a considerable time . . . the usual hire in the Nation . . . would be about — One Shilling Sterling pr day . . . he has done his duty faithfully, and with the approbation of the Chiefs . . . of this Nation.[19]

After the organization of the republic, the legislature turned its attention to the problems of incoming artisans and professional men, and legalized their presence in the Cherokee country under certain stipulations. In 1819 the Council

> *Unanimously agreed,* That school masters, blacksmiths, millers, salt petre and gun powder manufacturers, ferrymen and turnpike keepers, and mechanics, are hereby privileged to reside in the Cherokee Nation under the following conditions, Viz:
>
> Their employers procuring a permit from the National Committee and Council for them, and becoming responsible for their good conduct and beheavior [*sic*]. and subject to removal for misdemeanor; and further agree, that blacksmiths, millers, ferrymen and turnpike keepers, are privileged to improve and cultivate twelve acres of ground for the support of themselves and families, should they please to do so.[20]

Later the Cherokee leaders passed a series of measures designed to produce skilled workmen among their own people. A law of 1825 announced that "good and sober mechanics" could enter the nation for four to five-year periods under the auspices of "such respectable individuals as are interested in the improvement of the youths of this country. . . ." These artisans were to set up shop and take native apprentices who would be bound out by local district courts. Upon the completion of training, the Council guaranteed that it would purchase tools and equipment to outfit the new "mechanics." On October 18, 1826, the republic appropriated

$57.25 to buy blacksmithing tools for George Candy, one of the first to avail himself of the apprenticeship opportunity. He received "one bellows, one anvil, one vice, one screw-plate, three hammers, one rasp, and half a dozen files."[21]

Other forms of industry were to be found in the busy activities of the various mills which became fairly common in the Cherokee country. Sawmills and gristmills predominated. Some were put up by the United States government through the Indian Agent. On one occasion a gristmill was given to the Cherokee Indians as part of the consideration for a land cession. Other mills were built by individual Cherokees and by missionaries. In 1819, while Brainerd men were mulling over the feasibility of putting up a sawmill in their area, they were informed that "our neighbor, Mr. John Ross, would build one immediately on the nearest mill seat to the establishment [the mission], if he could obtain workmen." The Cherokee Census of 1824 indicated that twenty gristmills and fourteen sawmills were in operation, as well as fifty-five blacksmith shops and six cotton gins. The districts registering the greatest amount of this activity were Coosawatee, Amohee, Chattooga, and Chickamauga.[22]

The economic activities of a leading Cherokee are interestingly portrayed in a letter to the Indian Agent written by Doublehead in 1802:[23]

Sir

When I saw you at the Green Corn Dance—you Desired me to come & see you and get some goods from you — My intention is to come and trade with you But I am so Engaged Hunting and Gathering my Beef Cattle that I expect it will be a moone or two before I can come—I . . . have now one Request to ask of you—that is to have me a boat Built—I want a good Keal Boat some 30 to 35 feet in length and 7 feet wide—I want her for the purpose of Descending the River to Orlians & back I want her to be lite & well calculated to stem the Streem I am Determined to by the Produce of this place & the Return back by Water. . . . I shall want two of your big guns to mount on the Boat — I am Determined for to see up the White & Red Rivers in my Route & oppen a trade with the western wild Indians—Let me here from you soon—I am Ser Your Reale

friend & Brother—DOUBLEHEAD

Wrote by
J. D. Chisholm
who presents his Compliments

A decree of the Cherokee legislature in 1819 reveals much of the merchandising activities in the Indian country, and of the republic's attitude concerning such business. This edict announced that all Cherokee citizens who had established a store to "vend merchandise" must obtain a license from the Clerk of the National Council, paying for it twenty-five dollars yearly. Cherokee citizens would be allowed to have a "permanent store within the Nation"; others must obtain a license from the United States Agency as well, and pay the Cherokee Nation eighty dollars annually. Noncitizens were further banned from selling liquor, on penalty of forfeiting the whiskey and having "the same disposed of for the benefit of the Nation." Citizens could sell it, but if any fell into the hands of outsiders, it would be forfeited and a hundred-dollar fine exacted. The Council ruled, however, that

> nothing shall be so construed in this decree, as to tax any person or persons bringing sugar, coffee, salt, iron and stleel [*sic*] into the Cherokee Nation for sale; but no permanent establishment for the disposal of such articles can be admitted to any persons not citizens of the Nation.[24]

Cherokee commerce was largely concerned with transit through the nation. The extension of better roads through Indian lands was eagerly sought by Americans, and permission to construct them was normally obtained through treaty or by the Indian Agent. The Cherokees were usually reluctant to make such grants. Their view was well expressed by Doublehead in 1801: "A great many people, of all descriptions, would pass [over] them [the roads]. . . . We mean to hold fast the peace which is subsisting between you and us; to preserve this, we hope you will not make roads through this country. . . ." Yet after arrangements were effected to construct or improve roads, influential Cherokees took advantage of the opportunity to construct public-houses (or "stands") along the roads at strategic points, and to secure toll-gate franchises from the Cherokee Council. In 1803, with the help of James Vann, Colonel Meigs obtained the Cherokee Council's approval for a road to run north and south from the Hiwassee River into Georgia. After the road was built, Vann was one of the first to profit. He put up a store and a public house by the roadside at Spring Place.[25]

Increasing pressure of their white neighbors caused the Cherokees in 1813 to acquiesce in a road connecting Tennessee and Georgia. A company was formed consisting of representatives from the Indian nation and the two states concerned. This group laid out a road which was completed in three years, on a route through northeastern Georgia from the Tugaloo River, along the Nacoochee Valley, the Unicoy Gap, the Hiwassee River, and over the mountains to Chota in Tennessee. Along this road, known as the Unicoy Pike, several "stands" soon appeared. These establishments, operated usually by mixed-bloods, offered bed and board to the travellers. The "Federal Road" was the name often given to another well-traveled highway, which ran in a northwest direction through the Cherokee country. It was the main post and stage coach road between Augusta and Nashville, and was also used by Tennessee cattlemen seeking markets in Georgia or the Carolinas.[26] (See map B.)

Transportation and communication enjoyed a brief growth during the 1820's and early 1830's. Ferries were established and roads built. National and privately owned turnpike gates existed on the main roads passing through Cherokee territory. The Indian council issued five-year franchises on these toll roads and specified maximum tolls. Furthermore, the holders of turnpike grants were to "keep the roads in good repair," under penalty of losing both franchise and bond. In November, 1822, for example, James Brown and Samuel Canda were

> permitted and authorized to open and keep in good repair, the old road from Lowry's Ferry, on Tennessee River, by way of Nickojack, through the Narrows and on by Canda's, as far as the Lookout Mountain, and to assist Hicks & Co., in working over the mountain, and to establish a turnpike gate on the same. . . .

On one occasion the Indian legislature stipulated the manner of road building and repair: "The road to be cut and opened twenty-four feet wide, clear of trees, and the causewaying to be covered with dirt, together with the digging of mountains and hills, to be fourteen feet wide, clear of rocks, roots and grubs, and the banks of all water courses to be put in complete order."[27]

Typical of the rates for Cherokee turnpikes was the schedule announced for the two national toll-gates to be leased on the Federal Road to the highest bidders:

Wagon and team,	$1 00	Black-cattle	2¢
Ditto. two horses,	75	Man and Horse	12 1-2
Do. one horse,	50	Pack-horse	12 1-2
Two-wheel carriage,	50	Loose Horse	6 1-4
	Hogs, sheep and goats	1	

Further legislation granted free passage for Cherokee citizens through all turnpikes, toll-bridges, and ferries in the nation; made it illegal to open, improve, or repair any roads, bridges, or ferries in the Cherokee country without the approval of the Council; and fixed toll-setting responsibility on the circuit court of the district concerned, except for those already under national control. In 1826 an attempt was made by Georgia and Tennessee through the Indian Agent Hugh Montgomery to secure rights for a "cannal [*sic*] connecting the Tennessee and Chattahoochee waters." The Cherokee Council refused to grant the request.[28]

A United States mail service was established through the Cherokee Nation during the second decade of the nineteenth century. The first post office was at Ross's Landing in 1817; the second was established at Spring Place two years later. By 1830, other postal stations had been placed at Carmel, Head of Coosa, High Tower, Willstown, and New Echota.[29]

The existence of a postal service was one of the favorable conditions contributing to the success of the *Cherokee Phoenix* in its early years. Not only were many of its subscribers outside the Cherokee Nation, but also much of its copy came from the exchange newspapers received from Washington, New York, Philadelphia, and other locations. Irregularity of the service, however, was a source of constant difficulty for the Cherokee newspaper, and the editor was required frequently to apologize to his readers for delayed delivery. For example, on April 28, 1828, he noted that

> Our readers may wish to know the reason why they do not receive their papers as soon as they might. All the papers that are sent by mail are regularly and punctually put into the postoffice in this place, but according to the present arrangement of the mails, they are obliged to lie at Springplace nearly a week. Application has been made to the General Post Office to remedy this inconvenience; and we hope the application will be complied with.[30]

The columns of the *Cherokee Phoenix* afford interesting glimpses of the routine business life of these Indians. Typical notices told of "FLOUR for sale low for CASH or HIDES"; the opening of a boarding-house for mission school children; a thief breaking into Elijah Hicks' store at New Echota and stealing "pocket Knives, shoes, boots, sugar, whiskey, &c."; and sale at public auction of "all the property belonging to the estate of T. B. Adair, deceased, which consisted of three negroes, JOE his wife NELLY and CHILD, from five to six hundred bushels of CORN, four stacks of FODDER, four head of HORSES, eleven head of CATTLE, fifty head of HOGS, one road WAGGON, one yoke of OXEN, one LOOM, one RIFLE GUN, together with household and kitchen FURNITURE."[31]

A fair indication of the financial peculiarities in Cherokee affairs is seen in the advertisement for a stolen pocketbook which appeared August 27, 1828. The "large Washed Leather Pocketbook" contained "one note on the State Bank of Georgia for $10, one note of hand of Elijah Hicks for $85 . . . a receipt on Henry Meygr of the State of New York, for two notes on Jolin Byers of the said State, and some other papers. . . ." Concerning the Hicks note, the owner (George Harlin) forewarned "all persons from trading for said note," and also cautioned Hicks not to pay anyone but Harlin for the note.[32] Repudiation of notes must have been a relatively common occurrence, for announcements such as the following frequently were published:

NOTICE. All persons are forewarned against trading for a Note of Hand, drawn by John Martin, in favor of John McCarver, and Munce Gore of East Tennessee, for three hundred and fifty dollars; payable on the first day of March next, dated January 1st, 1828. As the consideration for which said note was given, has proved to be unsound, I am determined not to pay unless compelled by law.

JOHN MARTIN[33]

As official organ of the Indian nation, the *Cherokee Phoenix* usually carried a number of legal advertisements. Three of these may be cited here as examples of the financial and commercial activities of the young republic. The first is an announcement by John Martin, the Treasurer of the Cherokee Nation, that he was required by law to "give notice to all such as are indebted to the Treasury, to come and redeem their bonds by paying principal and interest, on the day that they became due, as such bonds cannot be renewed after the first Monday of October next." Failure to comply, said Treasurer Martin, would result in prosecution by Cherokee officials.[34] Another notice from Martin announced the letting of bids on "the several shares of the Federal Road . . . agreeabley to a late resolution of the General Council." A third type of legal notice was that of judgment sales. On November 12, 1829, Joseph Lynch, a Cherokee marshal, announced that there would be sold to the highest bidder on the 1st day of December next, at the late residence of James Pettit near Conasauga, between sixty and seventy acres of CORN as it stands in the field, and from six to seven hundred bushels of Corn in the Crib, and twenty five stacks of FODDER. ALSO, on the 2nd of December, at the house of Edward Adair, seventeen head of CATTLE, and one likely negro man, named GABRIEL, all levied on as the property of James Pettit, to satisfy a judgment against said Pettit in favor of Elizabeth Pettit. The above property will be sold unless redeemed.[35]

The peculiarities of legal affairs in the Cherokee country comprised another strange overlay on the confused structure of the red-white culture. Indian councils, the Indian Agent, and later the Cherokee courts sought to administer justice for their people. But Indians who found themselves involved in litigations with white men often wound up in a Tennessee, Georgia, or Alabama county court, where existing white man's law had to be fitted to the red man's problem. Sometimes an adjustment could be made. Other times in the absence of applicable law, the Indian was judged by prejudice.

When Cherokees were involved with neighboring state courts, white men often gave them assistance, and usually billed the Indian Agent for services rendered. In 1803 William Overton of Nashville assisted "Stone a Cherokee Indian," whose case was tried in a Tennessee court. Overton informed Return J. Meigs that

> The U States it is presumed will of course think it reasonable to make me some compensation for the trouble I have been at as a Lawyer &c. Agreeably to charges for services somewhat similar which I have formally [*sic*] rendered the Govt. It would appear reasonable that I should have $30 for attending as a Lawyer, correspondence &c and $10 for drawing Petition &c.[36]

One of the most curious legal tangles involving Cherokee and white law was the litigation over the estate of James Vann in 1809. James Vann was the half-breed Indian whose support in the Cherokee Council at the beginning of the century helped to bring approval for the Moravian Mission. When the missionaries were established, he had been very cooperative, offering the use of his Spring Place property while buildings were being constructed, and later building a grist mill primarily for the use of the Moravians. He was a wealthy man, owning a large house, slaves, and considerable other property, including a ferry on the Chattahoochee River.

Vann was a constant source of difficulty, however, for his frequent use of the bottle brought a series of misfortunes upon himself and family. The missionaries, who described him as "a half-breed with two wives, very dissipated and drunken," worked hard to convert him to a better life. Yet Vann continued to drink, exhibiting an excessively cruel nature when intoxicated. He soon became "far-famed, little beloved, and greatly feared" in the nation. As might be expected, he finally went too far. A shooting skirmish with a son-in-law in 1808 incited a feud which resulted in Vann's murder in February of the following year, at the age of forty-one. He was survived by his second wife, Margaret ("Peggy"), and six sons and daughters. The oldest son, Joseph, was obviously his father's favorite, for James Vann's will, dated May 8, 1808, disposed of his possessions as follows:

> 1st. I hereby give & bequeath unto my beloved wife, Peggy . . . all my household furniture.
> 2—All the rest residue of my property which I shall or may die possessed of by that whatsoever it may or wheresoever it may I give and bequeath to my natural son, Joseph to have and hold forever.
> In the name of God amen.[37]

Two months after Vann's death sixteen ranking Cherokees met in Council and set aside the dead man's will to this extent:

> the will of James Vann decd having been read to the Chiefs in Council & it appearing from the face of the will that all the property was left to one child named Joseph Vann, but the Chiefs think that all the children are of one father who ought to receive some share of the property & also the widow ought to share alike with the other children & to remain in the House as long as she pleases & no doubt Joseph Vann will agree with the chiefs in opinion when he comes to years of maturity — Wherefore the Chiefs and warriors made the following provision for the Children.
> The executor shall allow the greatest share to Joseph Vann & after which you are to allow to the other children & widow such share of the property as you judge right. . . . The chiefs and warriors expect that Peggy will treat the people well as usual when they come to the house.

But the legalities were not over. Probably because Vann owned property in nearby Jackson County, Georgia, his will and the Council's amending decision were filed there.. Further, the Inferior Court of that county buttressed the ruling of the Cherokee Chiefs by ordering that Vann's property "be disposed of as is directed by the said Council as far as is possible the will being considered by this Court as illegal and of no effect."[38] A basis for the action of the Indian government in this case is found in their first written law, dated September 11, 1808. One clause of this statute authorized the newly legalized Regulating Parties

to give their protection to children as heirs to their father's property, and to the widow's share whom he may have had children by or cohabited with, as his wife, at the time of his decease, and in case a father shall leave or will any property to a child at the time of his decease, which he may have had by another wife, then his present wife shall be entitled to receive any such property as may be left by him or them, when substantiated by two or more disinterested witnesses.[39]

The Cherokees were thus by the mid-1830's progressing far, if peculiarly, along the white man's road. Their recently adopted agrarian culture had helped to foster commerce and business activity. A nationalistic and benevolent legislature seemed to be looking toward a day of great prosperity. To the progressive Cherokee leaders, that day could not arrive soon enough. Perhaps the new literacy in their own tongue would be the needed stimulus.

TEN

THE SEQUOYAN MIRACLE: TALKING LEAVES AND PRINTED PAGES

By 1820 the Cherokee Indians were well on the road toward the white man's culture. Voluntarily or under pressure Cherokees were accepting variously his agriculture, trade, money, habiliments, shelter, religion, and republicanism. Many were also using his language.

The absence of a native written language was perhaps the most serious hindrance to Cherokee development. In earlier times symbolism, such as the waving of eagles' tails at formal conferences, had served in part to convey ideas. Belts or strings of beads called wampum were similarly used as late as the 1790's.[1] But the necessity of accurately recording and permanently preserving important treaties, rulings, and events led to some use of the English language. Furthermore, Indians desiring to advance themselves in the paths of civilized progress, or to understand treaty discussions, sought to master the white man's language.[2] In the nineteenth century English-speaking Cherokees became the nation's leaders and endeavored to educate others.

Prominent Cherokee half-breeds had long been interested in bringing to their people the type of formal education that would put them on a level comparable to that of their white neighbors. At first educational advantages were necessarily reserved for a small minority. Daniel Ross's school for his children in the 1790's was probably the first one in the Cherokee Nation. Others followed, maintained by well-to-do white parents, Indian mixed-bloods, or by itinerant teachers operating on their own. Perhaps the earliest of these independent pedagogues in the Cherokee country was John Daniel Hammerer. In 1765 Governor James Habersham of Georgia reported that Hammerer spent several years "among the Cherokee Indians where he taught their youths to read, write &c, in which they made a surprising progress. . . ." Later a Daniel Sullivan was authorized to teach by the Cherokee Council about 1800. In 1806 a Kentuckian named George Helm wrote Agent Return J. Meigs that he had heard "there is School Masters wanting among the Indians." He wanted the United States to employ him; Meigs replied that it was "impracticable at present." Despite the Agent's early opinion, Cherokees looked to the United States for aid in education. The instructions given a delegation sent to Washington in 1817 reveal this interest:

> The late council of our warriors at Eto,wer [Etowah] having requested the Principle Chiefs to ask our father the president . . . his aid in Educating our Children . . . you are authorized to ask his aid in the benevolent education of our children, that they may be lead in the knowledge of our creator and in the redeeming merits of his son. And that they may be also taught in the habits of Industry to gain livelyhood while here on Earth. . . .[3]

The development which provided the Cherokees with the most effective means for learning the English language was the introduction of mission schools in the nation. Most of the missionaries realized that the most feasible way of bringing Christianity to the red heathens was to make them literate in English. The Cherokee leaders were anxious for this literacy. Consequently the mission schools had little difficulty getting under way; and a large number of young Cherokees received at least an elementary education from religious workers.

The independent teachers did not fare as well. Furthermore, they constituted a continuing problem for missionaries, who often received into their own schools the products of these short-term teachers. The clergymen were usually disgusted with the operations of itinerant instructors. On one occasion in 1819 a Cherokee transferred his boy from Brainerd to a private school. After a few months, during which the lad "became worse," he was returned to the American Board school. In some ire the missionaries remarked: "We hope the time will soon come when this people can no longer be imposed upon by these sham schoolmasters, who, by idleness or dissipation, have been driven from civilized society to be a nuisance among the Indians."[4]

Cherokee employers also found fault with "sham school-masters." In some areas where these teachers were at work, dissatisfaction often caused natives to appeal for mission schools. The father of David and Catherine Brown reported in 1820 that the chiefs in his area were very anxious for a good school; that a white teacher had been hired by them, but before his school began he "stole a drove of hogs, & run off."[5]

Such events created hostility to private instruction, and the growing success of mission-operated schools made the teaching business more and more difficult for the independents. In 1828 a white man attempted to operate a private school at the Cherokee capital. He inserted this advertisement in the *Cherokee Phoenix*:

EDUCATION!!

THE NEW ECHOTA ACADEMY has commenced and is expected to continue.

All those wishing to become students during the winter session are requested to make application previous to the 25th inst. No pains will be spared, on the part of the Instructor, for the advancement of those placed under his care.

Board, lodging, and washing may be had for $1.00 per week.

WM. HORN

After two months the New Echota Academy closed "for want of sufficient scholars." The editor of the Cherokee newspaper attended an evening session before the school suspended and heard with pleasure some students "exercised in parsing, and repeating the English Grammar."[6]

The course of Cherokee educational and literary development was sharply accelerated by a remarkable achievement early in the 1820's: the invention and acceptance of a syllabary of eighty-six characters. For the first time the Cherokees had a written language. This invention is considered the more remarkable because of the character and status of its inventor, Sequoyah, or George Guess (Guest? Gist?). Son of a Cherokee woman and a white trader (now thought to be Nathaniel Gist), Sequoyah was born about 1775 in Tuskegee on the Tennessee River. In early childhood he was afflicted with a disease which made him permanently lame. As a less active youth he became skilled at silver-working and the blacksmith's craft; he also took up his father's profession of trading, and his later home near Willstown became a gathering place for Indians desirous of his wares. Unfortunately there was a period of several years during which his trading establishment became even better known as a tavern, and Sequoyah as a drunkard. Just as his life appeared ruined, he was taken in hand by George Lowrey, who persuaded Sequoyah to sign and keep a temperance pledge. In October, 1813, Sequoyah volunteered for service in the Cherokee troops then being assembled to help Americans in the Creek War. He participated in the Battle of Horseshoe Bend, and was discharged from the army shortly after. In 1815 he married Sally Benge; and during the following year he began to participate to a limited extent in national affairs.[7]

Since about 1809 Sequoyah had been nursing an idea, one that seemed to him perfectly logical: if the white man could make marks on "leaves" (paper), and then make the marks "talk" back to him, why couldn't the Indian do the same thing? He thought it was possible; the difficulty was to find the marks which would do it. The idea was one of great import to his nation's culture, yet the chiefs and villagers laughed at him. After all, the missionaries had long labored to produce a Cherokee alphabet, and they seemed to be far more suited for this effort. During twelve long years of experimenting, of collecting and discarding Cherokee syllables, Sequoyah perfected his dream. At one time he accompanied an emigrating party westward; during the long boat trip to the Arkansas he practiced with his "talking leaves." Eventually he isolated eighty-six syllables, and gave each a symbol of his own making. Finally in 1821, after returning East, he persuaded George Lowrey that the syllabary was feasible. Lowrey asked the National Council to give Sequoyah a hearing. The Council, having heard from Alabama Cherokees that a "witch" named Sequoyah should be condemned to death, was glad to send a group of young chiefs to listen. After a seven-day hearing, the young men could read and write "Cherokee"! They proudly presented Sequoyah to the Council, where he was given great honor. More important, his invention was officially proclaimed as the national Cherokee language syllabary.[8]

The rapid spread of the Sequoyan syllabary seems remarkable. Within a few months, several thousand Cherokees had learned to read and write the symbols and were teaching others.[9] They were enthusiastic to learn the syllabary, for with it they could write to members of their families heretofore thought lost in Arkansas; and they could keep records of their farms and businesses. More important, however, was the realization on the part of leading Cherokees that here was a great opportunity to crystallize in Sequoyan print their institutions and culture. The invention made the proposed constitution a more useful project, for now the law of the land could be written down so that every Cherokee could read it. Hopes of cultural growth also quickened as the council sessions sparkled with discussions and plans for a national literature, a national library and museum, a national press, and a national academy.[10]

The idea of a Cherokee "national free school" was broached to Brainerd Superintendent Ard Hoyt in August, 1823, by Charles R. Hicks, who asked whether the American Board could procure a director "at the national expence." The academy was discussed in Council and though approval was general, opinion was divided over "whether it shall be of higher order, or to admit those who have received no education." John Ross favored the advanced instruction, while Charles Hicks preferred an elementary school. A year later Ross suggested the creation of a "national female academy." The widespread success of Sequoyah's new language encouraged this interest on the part of Cherokee leaders for the better education of their youth. On October 15, 1825, a resolution of the National Committee and Council projected a national academy as a future development. Three years later a School Inspections Act was passed, providing for committees of Cherokee statesmen who would inspect the various mission and private schools in the nation.[11]

A further interest in the Sequoyan syllabary came from missionaries, who realized the great value of this invention for their work. Men like Evan Jones and Daniel Butrick abandoned attempts to produce a Cherokee alphabet, and with their colleagues began to translate Scripture, hymns, and sermons for their church members and students. Samuel A. Worcester arrived in the nation in this period, and he lent valuable assistance and advice in the advancing literacy. He worked especially well with Elias Boudinot, and the two began planning for a development long sought by Cherokee leaders: the creation of a national press and newspaper.[12]

At New Echota the Council issued two important resolutions in October, 1827, one calling for the establishment of a "weekly newspaper at New Echota, to be entitled the CHEROKEE PHOENIX," whose editor (not named in the resolution) was to print translations in Cherokee of important news as well as official publications. The other edict named Isaac N. Harris as "Official Printer for the Cherokee Nation."[13]

Samuel Worcester went at once to Boston, where he arranged

for the casting of Cherokee characters into type and for the purchase of printing supplies. He also hired an assistant printer, John F. Wheeler. While in Boston, Worcester displayed to the public five verses of Genesis printed in Sequoyah's syllabary in the *Missionary Herald* of December, 1827. This was the first appearance of Sequoyah's great invention in the new type. Meanwhile in the Cherokee country Elias Boudinot, having been appointed editor of the proposed newspaper at an annual salary of three hundred dollars, made arrangements for the expected return of Worcester and the arrival of the printers and supplies. Anticipating its authorization of the newspaper by a year, the Council had already ordered the construction of a printing office. From this building the first copy of the *Cherokee Phoenix* was issued on February 21, 1828.[14] This was a momentous day for the Cherokees, the culmination of months of hard work and planning; more important, it probably marked the greatest expression of their nationalism.

Editor Boudinot was anxious that the intentions and purposes of the *Cherokee Phoenix* be appreciated by its reading public, which was to include not only Indians but white men as well. Furthermore, he wanted it known that this new publication represented the best interests of the Cherokees. Consequently he published in his first issue a "Prospectus," outlining an ambitious yet logical editorial policy for "the benefit of the Cherokees." Reminding readers that the paper was a national organ, and that the printing establishment belonged to the Cherokee Nation, he said it was his intention to devote the paper to national purposes:

> The laws and public documents of the Nation, and matters relating to the welfare and condition of the Cherokees as a people, will be faithfully published in English and Cherokee. . . . We will invariably state the will of the majority of our people on the subject of the present controversy with Georgia, and the present removal policy of the United States Government. . . .

The Cherokee journalist asserted that "Indians . . . are as capable of improvement in mind as any other people," especially if they remained in "their present locations." The concluding paragraph of the "Prospectus" explained the title selected for the newspaper in phrases glowing with national pride:

> We would now commit our feeble efforts to the good will and indulgence of the public, praying that God will attend them with his

blessings, and hoping for that happy period, when all the Indian tribes of America shall rise, Phoenix-like, from their ashes, and when the terms "Indian depredations," "war whoop," "scalping-knife," and the like, shall become obsolete and forever be buried deep under ground.[15]

In addition to this editorial pronouncement, the initial issue contained the first three articles of the Cherokee Constitution, printed in Cherokee and English in parallel columns. It also reproduced official correspondence between the Cherokee Nation and the United States War Department on the subject of westward emigration, with an editorial comment berating the scheme. Other features were a Cherokee translation of the Lord's Prayer, a contribution of "W" (presumably Worcester), and a letter from Thomas Jefferson, written in 1809 urging the Cherokees to organize a republican government. Like most newspapers of its day, the *Cherokee Phoenix* contained much miscellany, usually short items extracted from exchanges. This first issue contained several such pieces, including "A Good Conscience," "Flattery," "Rains," and an anecdote on the military career of George Washington. The masthead announced subscription and advertising rates, and on the last page appeared some "Remarks on the Cherokee Alphabet," also by "W," and an advertisement repudiating a "Note of Hand."[16]

Subsequent editions of the newspaper showed a faithful inclination on the part of the editor to carry out his announced intentions. He published as much material in Cherokee as the printers could manage to assemble, or as much as he could wring from his Indian correspondents with such appeals as this:

> If any of our Cherokee readers think we have slighted them, we can assure them that it has not been through neglect. . . . We have a heavy task, & unless relieved by Cherokee correspondents, a greater amount of Cherokee matter cannot reasonably be expected. We hope those of our correspondents, who take a lively interest in the diffusion of intelligence in their mother language, will lend us aid in this department . . . [which is] the most arduous part of our labors.

Whenever possible, he published correspondence from readers, sometimes in Cherokee but more often in English. Occasionally a letter would bring a rebuke of this type: "SCIPIO's Communication has been received, but it is too personal for insertion."[17]

Of primary importance to the Cherokee leaders during this era, however, was the growing clamor in Washington and the states of Georgia, Alabama, Tennessee, and North Carolina to remove the Cherokee Nation westward. In accordance with its announced intention of promoting the Cherokee cause, the *Cherokee Phoenix* devoted much of its space to upholding Cherokee progress, and in replying to demands that the Indians be removed to the western country to join the sizable community of Cherokees already located there. Individual Indians were allowed to express their feelings on the issues confronting their nation, through the medium of the paper. Often Editor Boudinot printed his own comments on removal. In 1828 a reader protested against outside criticism and cited instances of Cherokee advancement; he suggested that the future held much for the nation's greatness. Boudinot remarked:

> Provided, however, the strong arm of the United States protect us in our rights and not disorganize us by recommending projects of emigration, when it is contrary to our wish. We do not expect ever to be a great nation, in the common sense of the word, for our population is too trifling [small] to entitle us that appellation. We may, nevertheless, by our improvement in the various departments of life, gain the respect and esteem of other nations.[18]

Some advocates of westward expatriation registered favorable opinion of the Cherokees. Thomas L. McKenney, who had had over ten years' experience in Indian agency supervision with the War Department, had written the Secretary of War in 1827 concerning the Indian situation, and the *Cherokee Phoenix* reprinted this letter in its first issue. McKenney admitted in the letter that his knowledge of the Cherokees was based on reports of others, but he had "high commendation" for their progress: "They seek to be a people, and to maintain by law and good government those principles which maintain the security of property, defend the rights of persons, etc. They deserve to be respected, and to be helped. . . ." But McKenney urged the Secretary of War to take steps to prevent the writing of a Cherokee constitution. As an alternative, he suggested that the Indians would probably be quite willing to follow the Chickasaws, Choctaws, Creeks, and other Cherokees into the western country. While Editor Boudinot appreciated McKenney's compliments, he regretted the colonel's conclusion that the Cherokees would willingly leave. Instead, said Boudinot, the nation was determined to remain, and he cited historical examples of reiteration of this determination by Cherokee chieftains.[19]

On another occasion, McKenney was quoted again on Indian removal. This time, he had reported to the War Department on the probable cost of sending the Indians westward. Boudinot took these statements as an opportunity to show the high cost of a forced Cherokee migration. In the *Cherokee Phoenix* for May 5, 1828, duplicating McKenney's methods of cost estimation, the editor outlined a long list of expenses, including $520,000 for houses and farm equipment; mills, grist and saw, $25,000; sixty-two shops, $3,000; orchards, the same; fences, $200,000; "7,683 horses . . . at $40 per head, will cost $307,320"; and so forth. The total cost, including that "for the expense of the Government, the Schools, the Military," would be $2,229,662. Boudinot suggested a more appropriate use for this money:

> If this project is intended, as we are told by its advocates, for the good and civilization of the Cherokees and other Indians, cannot this sum be put to a better use? – Supposing with this money, the United States begin to establish Schools in every part of this Nation? With this money let there be a college founded, where every advantage of instruction may be enjoyed. Let books, tracts, &c be published in Cherokee and English, and distributed throughout the Nation and every possible effort be made to civilize us, let us at the same time be protected in our rights. What would be the consequence? If we fail to improve under such efforts, we will then agree to remove.[20]

Part of the platform of the Indian newspaper, announced in the second issue, was to publish "An Account of the manners and customs of the Cherokees, and their progress in Education, Religion, and the arts of civilized life," as well as "miscellaneous articles, calculated to promote Literature, Civilization, and Religion among the Cherokees." To this end, the *Cherokee Phoenix* devoted many of its columns to dissemination of the native culture, and more especially to improvement of Cherokee literacy in "the Alphabet, lately invented by a native Cherokee."[21] The printing office made up copies of Sequoyah's syllabary, which were advertised for sale.[22]

Samuel A. Worcester's interest in promoting the educational growth of the Cherokees brought a number of instructive lessons in sentence structure, spelling, conjugations, and other phases of grammar and composition. Much of this probably appeared in Cherokee, but an occasional English article reveals Worcester's method and something of the structure of the Cherokee language. The second issue of the *Cherokee Phoenix* contained, for example, a lesson on pronouns, of which the following is an excerpt: "Nouns of relationship are not used in Cherokee except in connexion with inseparable pronouns. Thus we cannot say *a* father, *the* father, *the* son, but *my* father, *thy, his, our,* father, etc. . . ." In several other issues, "W" offered systematic conjugations (in English and Cherokee) of the major verbs.[23] Of course, the bilingual nature of the newspaper itself offered many an excellent opportunity for improvement both in English and their native tongue, a situation which probably contributed considerably to the demand for copies of the paper.[24]

But even more important to Samuel Worcester was the task of spreading the Gospel. He had long recognized the significance of a printing press with Cherokee characters for this work, and early began to submit hymns, Scriptures, and sermons for the Cherokee language columns in the *Cherokee Phoenix.* On April 17, 1828, he began a translation of Matthew, completing it a year later (April 8, 1829). He offered short prayers for the use of the Indians, and occasionally gave English translations from the Cherokee idiom.[25]

Meanwhile the press itself was busy printing religious matter for use in the Christianizing program. The limitations of Boudinot's plant were such that while he was able to supply some tract material and a few hymn books from time to time, three months after the press began operations he was forced to announce that

> We are sorry not to be in a condition to meet the demands on our press. The Publication of Scripture, Tracts, and Hymn books, must depend entirely on the limited force now connected with the establishment; and as yet the paper has escaped the full attention of our printers. . . . At present our Cherokee readers will obtain Hymns, and the Gospel of Matthew, through the medium of the *Phoenix.*[26]

Despite its limitations, however, the Cherokee press by 1830 had produced 225,400 pages.[27]

Thus the *Cherokee Phoenix* in some respects served the purposes of a religious journal. Like any newspaper of today, however, it also chronicled more or less routine events in Cherokee life reflecting the religious influence. Marriages, deaths, church meetings, camp meetings, and general missionary operations were recorded. During February, 1828, for example, the paper announced the marriage "at Oochgelogy" of Alexander J. Copeland and Mary R. Gambold, daughter of John Gambold; the deaths of Richard Neely, "formerly a missionary of the Methodist Episcopal Church and late a citizen of the Cherokee Nation," and Ard Hoyt, "very suddenly"; the marriage of a Methodist missionary, James J. Trott, and a Cherokee woman named Sally Adair; and the death "at Coosewattee, [of] KEELECHULE an aged member of the National Council." Occasionally an obituary accompanied the death notice, as in the issue of June 4, 1828:

DIED – On the 27th inst [May], about 1 o'clock AM Captain JOHN SPEER, in the 48th year of his age. He was a Kind Husband, an affectionate Father, a faithful Friend, and a good neighbor.

He has left a very affectionate wife and several children to lament their irreparable loss.

He has served about ten years as Interpreter for the United States at the Cherokee Agency, which office he filled with credit to himself and with faithfulness to the government and to his own people.

He was a brave man in the field, and distinguished himself at the battle of the Horse Shoe, where he commanded a company of the Cherokee, and where he received a severe wound in the left breast, which no doubt was eventually the cause of his death. . . . His burial was numerously attended, and his neighbors, who knew full well his worth, sympathized freely in the many tears shed by his friends.

(COMMUNICATED)[28]

The publicity given by the *Cherokee Phoenix* to native participation in religious activities was a boon to the missionaries. Their own accounts of church services, and especially Cherokee conversions, gave evidence of the work they were accomplishing. Carmel (or Taloney) was one of the active missions whose preachers sent in accounts of church work. In April, 1828, for example, a Carmel report stated:

We had a very solemn and interesting meeting on the Sabbath. The congregation was large. Three full Cherokees were baptized. . . . The Cherokee members of this church, and those of the church at Hightower, have formed societies to hire a Cherokee brother to go as their missionary into those dark towns north of us [probably the mountainous country to the northeast], to carry bibles, tracts, hymn-books.[29]

Intemperance and crime, as previously noted, were serious problems. Elias Boudinot discussed the situation in his newspaper from time to time. He was especially unhappy over the "existence of a league between white and Cherokee thieves. This is the worst of all confederacies; for as soon as a stolen property passes the boundary line, the owner need not flatter himself to see it." The editor called on the nation's civil authorities to "secure these vagabonds who carry with them . . . the deep stain of the guilt of stealing." It was high time, he thought, to arrest the practice, "by inflicting an exemplary punishment on those who are now acknowledged by all to be guilty." Apparently, he continued, the native government was failing in its duty. The criminals "are permitted to go at large, running stolen horses to . . . the frontier of Georgia." The remainder of the editorial discussed a generally "poor policing" in the nation.[30]

Murder was the cause of special concern. Shortly after the *Cherokee Phoenix* was begun, Boudinot printed a short news item about the murder of an Indian named William Fallen near the village of Sumach. The item revealed that "the name of the Murderer [is] Bear's Paw." A month later, the editor editorialized at some length on the fact that "Bear's Paw, who committed Murder not long since at Sumach, is allowed to run unmolested." It seemed to the editor that the Cherokee marshals were very indifferent in the performance of their duties. Boudinot explained that Bear's Paw, acting as policeman at Sumach, tried to make a confessed thief promise to "be a good man in the future." Upon the criminal's refusal, "Bear's Paw struck him dead with an axe." The editor's closing remarks struck a significant note, in the light of increasing criticism reaching him from outside the nation:

> It is to be wished that the [Cherokee] officers . . . were more vigilant and more attentive to their duties. Unless they do speedily go to work, they will make themselves liable to public reprehension; and these frequent thefts and murders will go to confirm the world in the opinion that we are still savages.[31]

Murder often had its origin in excessive drink. Shortly after the events related above, a lead editorial in the *Cherokee Phoenix* announced two more murders in the Indian country, and commented, "We do not remember ever to have noticed so many instances of murder within so short a time. Such frequent cases speak a language, not to be misunderstood, to the dealers of ardent spirits."[32] In subsequent issues, further examples of crime produced by the "pernicious effects of intemperance" were noted and deplored.[33]

One method used by Boudinot in combating intemperance was the printing of tract and exchange material describing the evils of drinking and the joys of sobriety. Almost every issue contained at least one such item, and most editions contained several. On June 24, 1829, the newspaper began to use a special column-heading, "INTEMPERANCE," under which the anti-liquor pieces were printed.

The *Cherokee Phoenix* had tough sledding financially. Frequently the editor called on subscribers to pay their accounts. On at least one occasion he upbraided well-to-do Cherokees for not subscribing.[34] Paper, ink, and such supplies had to be shipped from Savannah or Knoxville, and this added to the expensive process of printing. The newspaper secured monetary assistance from patrons in the United States and abroad, especially those interested in reading about the missionary progress. Judging from the amount of advertising which appeared in the paper, very little income seems to have been realized from that source. Next to the legal advertisements, the most predominant type were those which promoted other publications, such as the *New York Amulet and Ladies Chronicle,* "to be published by an association of Gentlemen" for the purpose of checking the "progress of two alarming evils . . . Intemperance and Infidelity."[35]

Contrary to the practice of contemporary journals, the Cherokee newspaper published no patent medicine advertising. Medical advice, usually extracted from other papers, was occasionally given in the news columns. Medical journals were often advertised. In March, 1830, for example, there appeared in several issues an announcement describing the forthcoming *Journal of Health,* to be published by "An Association of Physicians." This periodical pledged itself to oppose all quack remedies, "whether it be . . . nursery gossip, mendacious reports of nostrum makers, and vendors, or recommendations of even scientifically compounded prescriptions without the special direction of a physician the only competent judge."[36]

Among other problems hampering smooth operation of the *Cherokee Phoenix* were supply and the communication system. Insufficient stores of paper or ink brought delays in printing which usually meant that news items were crowded out. A paper shortage in 1828 caused this editorial note in the issue of April 24: "In consequence of the difficulties of procuring paper, we shall not be able to issue our 11th no. until week after next. A few weeks hence we hope to have a large supply of *good* paper from the North."[37]

From its outset, the *Cherokee Phoenix* was troubled by difficulties with the mail system. Although Samuel Worcester was the United States postmaster at New Echota, and consequently in a position to expedite mailing the newspaper to subscribers and exchanges, travel inadequacies and interference by the forces of nature nullified much of his assistance. In the first issue, Boudinot announced that failures of two mail deliveries, "by the late freshets," had made his paper "destitute of intelligence." He further complained that "our receipt of Washington papers have been so irregular, that we are not able to present . . . what is doing in Congress in regard to affairs of Indians."[38]

The most serious threat to the proper circulation of the *Cherokee Phoenix* was the growing hostility to the Indian nation on the part of Georgia, Tennessee, North Carolina, and Alabama neighbors. Indeed, the paper itself, as an advertisement of the nationalistic and intellectual growth of the Cherokee Nation, had come into being at a time when the State of Georgia was beginning to raise a particularly loud clamor for Indian removal. In April of 1828, Elias Boudinot acknowledged the animosity existing between Georgians and Indians, but urged that Cherokees be moderate in their thinking, and recognize that "there are many [Georgians] who are real friends to the Indians; many whose friendship we greatly prize." Among the latter Boudinot mentioned one who had written to the editor expressing a hope that religious feeling would replace racial hatreds, when "all commotions and angry feelings shall be buried in oblivion, and all become the family of God . . ."[39] During succeeding months, the situation became more tense. In February, 1829, the Cherokee newspaper significantly added a new phrase to its masthead title; the paper became the *Cherokee Phoenix and Indian Advocate*.[40]

During this hectic period, the Indian newspaper was active in asserting Cherokee rights, defending the progress of the nation, printing correspondence and exchanges which condemned the states' and the federal government's policies, and denying rumors of an immediate intention on the part of the Cherokees to remove to the western country.[41] In November, 1829, Assistant Principal Chief George Lowrey recognized the seriousness of the situation when he called on "the Christian people of the nation" to set aside the first of January, 1830, as a day of fasting and prayer. Elias Boudinot directed attention to this proclamation in a leading editorial:

> The peculiar situation of the nation renders the observance of such a day necessary and highly important. The opportunity, no doubt, will be eagerly seized by those who feel that help in this interesting crisis must come from above. We have before taken occasion to lay the subject before our readers at a distance, & we would now at this time, ask, will not our Christian friends abroad meet at the time appointed & pray for the Cherokees? . . . The day will generally, if not universally, be observed by the religious people of the nation.[42]

During the early 1830's Georgia and the federal government further heightened their efforts to remove the Cherokee Indians. In 1832 President Jackson sent emissaries to arrange a removal treaty; at the same time, the State of Georgia surveyed the Indian country and distributed vast sections of it through a lottery. With thousands of Georgians rushing in to take over their newly won lands, and federal agents stirring up dissension, Principal Chief John Ross sought to unify his people behind a no-removal banner. Elias Boudinot, however, as editor of the national Cherokee organ, felt it his duty to air both sides of the problem, leaning somewhat toward acceptance of removal with the best possible terms. The result of this schism was that John Ross forced Boudinot's resignation, which was announced in the *Cherokee Phoenix* on August 11, 1832.[43]

At the same time that he publicized his intention to retire from the editorship, Boudinot stated his position by quoting his letter to John Ross, dated August 1, 1832. In his message, the editor stressed five points: (1) His "scanty salary of $300" was insufficient. (2) Four years of service to the Cherokee Nation had been "far from beneficial" to his health. (3) In view of the increasing difficulty of securing money and supplies, it would be too expensive to continue the *Cherokee Phoenix* further. (4) The Indian newspaper "had done all that it was supposed to do, in defending Cherokee Rights, and in presenting Indian grievances to United States people." (5) His own position as editor was "peculiar and delicate." He was convinced that the Cherokees should be shown the dangers before them. Furthermore, he said,

> I could not consent to be the conductor of the paper without having the privilege and right of discussing those important matters — and

from what I have seen and heard, were I to assume that privilege, my usefulness would be paralyzed, by being considered, as I have unfortunately already been, an enemy to the interest of my beloved country and people. . . . I should think it my duty to tell them the whole truth, or what I believe to be truth, I cannot tell them that we will be reinstated in our rights when I have no such hope. . . .[44]

In transmitting Boudinot's resignation to the council, Ross wrote that he could not agree that the *Cherokee Phoenix* had exhausted its usefulness. Instead, he said,

I deem it to be essentially important that the paper should be kept up. It is an incontrovertible fact, that the circulation of the paper has been greatly instrumental in the diffusion of science and general knowledge among our own citizens – the pecuniary embarrassments of the nation by no means ought to influence you to discontinue the paper, if a suitable person can be found to conduct it. . . . The views of the public authorities should continue, and ever be in accordance with the will of the people; and the views of the Editor of the national paper be the same. The toleration of diversified views to the columns of such a paper would not fail to create fermentation and confusion among our citizens. . . .[45]

John Ross had "a suitable person" in mind for the Cherokee newspaper; this was his brother-in-law, Elijah Hicks. On September 8, 1832, Hicks took over as editor.[46] Hicks apparently agreed with Ross about the evil of expressing "diversified views" in the newspaper; his editorials and exchange extracts on the Indian question condemned Georgia and the Jackson administration, and continually urged Cherokees to resist removal.

Without the experienced hand of Elias Boudinot the *Cherokee Phoenix* began to falter. Hicks, who seems to have had no journalistic experience, and far less education than Boudinot, could not continue the paper in the same tempo as had his predecessor. In the first place, the publication appeared with less regularity.[47] Secondly, it is a curious fact that although Hicks became editor with the intention of upholding a strong no-removal policy, the pages of the *Cherokee Phoenix* actually began to have less matter pertaining to that problem. Hicks' third issue, for example, contained three pages of selections in English on such subjects as "The Early Introduction of Christianity into Scotland," "Blackhawk's Invasion," "Passion," and "Late [news] from China." Aside from the masthead, the only Cherokee type in this edition totaled about three-fourths of a column on the last page, which also contained two editorials in English praising a Mobile paper for opposing removal, and despairing of the value of a proposed trip through the Cherokee country by the Governor of Tennessee.[48]

Even Elias Boudinot would probably have had great difficulty maintaining a newspaper in the face of the problems which mounted up against Hicks. The postmaster installed at New Echota after Samuel Worcester was a Georgian named William J. Tarvin, who harassed the dispatch of the *Cherokee Phoenix*. According to Hicks, Tarvin was a "dangerous incumbent of this office." The editor recited past deeds of Tarvin's which had hampered the newspaper:

> He has refused to deliver to us our exchange papers several times, for the only reason that this paper was not published regularly some time ago. He was informed that the Phoenix was not discontinued, and yet in the face of this notice he has gratuitously and officially advised editors, on this point, without authority and perfectly untrue.

Hicks quoted a notice he had found in a Nashville paper:

> Post-Office, NEW ECHOTA, GA. June 16, 1833
>
> EDITORS OF Newspapers that exchange with the CHEROKEE PHOENIX, will please stop sending their papers directed to it in exchange, as it is discontinued.
>
> WM. J. TARVIN[49]

The pressures on the little Cherokee newspaper were too great. With the appearance of the last issue of Volume V on May 31, 1834, Elijah Hicks announced that owing to a lack of funds, the *Cherokee Phoenix* was closing down "for a few weeks." During the interim, it was hoped that the outstanding subscription and advertising bills would be paid, which should provide sufficient money to continue the paper. Furthermore, stated Hicks, "the health of its editor has been in a feeble condition for a long time past," and a few weeks' vacation would be a good opportunity for "recruiting himself." The final paragraph of this announcement, however, contained a message of nationalistic defiance and encouragement to a persecuted people, which was symbolic of the entire six-year career of the *Cherokee Phoenix*:

> To our Cherokee readers, we would say, DON'T GIVE UP THE SHIP; although our enemies are numerous, we are yet in the land

of the living, and of our clearly recognized right. Improve your children, in morality and religion, and say to intemperance now growing at our doors, depart ye cursed, and the JUDGE of all the earth will impart means for the salvation of our suffering nation.[50]

The "suffering nation" of Cherokee Indians was destined to suffer even more. During the 1830's wholesale trespassing by white men and a forced expatriation of the majority of the nation decisively interrupted further progress.

ELEVEN

EBB-TIDE

IN JANUARY, 1833, the *Cherokee Phoenix* voiced this aggrieved complaint:

> The beautiful and beloved country of the Cherokees is now passing into the occupancy of the Georgians. . . . [Our land] is wedged with settlers, and droves of land hunters, to which the Indians daily cry, and it is literally, "Robery! Robery!"
>
> This crusade on our rights forms a new era in the history of the United States by which the Cherokees are denationalized, treaties destroyed, the legislation of Congress to carry them into effect annulled, and the faith of the republic fled to the western wilds. . . .[1]

The Indian country was indeed "wedged" with white intruders, and no power on earth was in sight to save the Indian nation from a forced westward expatriation.

This tragic turn of events, so devastating to the Cherokees, was expedited by the State of Georgia. Arrogant over successful expulsion of the Creek Indians,[2] and indignant at manifestations of Cherokee nationalism, the Georgians began to press northward. The discovery of gold on Cherokee-Georgia borders late in 1828 sealed the fate of the Indians. Tennessee, Alabama, and North Carolina also pressed for Cherokee removal. But Georgia was the moving force in the expulsion of the Cherokee Nation in the 1830's, and the actions of that state will be examined briefly as representative of Indian-removal efforts on the part of Southern whites.

Since 1802 Georgia had hoped for outright federal removal of the Cherokees, but had been disappointed by piecemeal cessions. The Cherokees, meanwhile, seemed intent on settling down; each evidence of such progress found Georgians the more determined to remove them. Finally in 1827, outraged at the impudence of a Cherokee constitution and a proposed newspaper, the legislature of Georgia issued a resolution to "extend her authority over the Cherokee country if the United States should further refuse to assist her." In the year that followed this expression of firm intent, sentiment for Cherokee removal grew apace.[3]

On December 20, 1828, a sweeping edict was passed by the state legislature, designed to cancel Cherokee authority and assert Georgia sovereignty over the coveted Indian territory. The act placed the entire Cherokee Nation under Georgia law, and specifically assigned various areas of the Indian country to the frontier counties of Carroll, DeKalb, Gwinnett, Hall, and Habersham. Appropriate sections of the Georgia legal code were to be applied to the new region, and all whites therein were declared subject to these laws. The act voided Indian sovereignty with these words: "All laws, usages, and customs made, established, and in force in the said territory, by the said Cherokee Indians, be, and the same are hereby, on and after the first of June, 1830, declared null and void." Further it was announced that no Indian could be considered a competent witness in Georgia courts in cases to which white men were parties.[4]

Coincident with the announcement of this legislation came startling news from northeastern Cherokee Georgia. Gold had been found! Although the first strike was probably made in 1828 by a John Witheroods along Duke's Creek in Habersham County, several other locations farther west shortly were made known. By mid-1829, a gold rush was in full swing. The center of the ore-bearing region seemed to be in the eastern part of the Cherokee Nation, a sparsely populated mountainous country. Prospectors poured in and took up claims without regard to Indian ownership. Within a year nearly ten thousand gold-fevered men were crowding this part of the nation. Many were unscrupulous characters of the worst sort, and the region soon became noted for its lawlessness. Cherokees attempting to extract gold were usually thrust out of their mines. Pillaging and fighting made mere existence in the area dangerous for Indians, and many began to shift farther west.[5]

By an earlier law of the Cherokee government, gold or other metals found within Indian borders were to be considered Cherokee national property. Consequently the Council ordered intruders out of the gold country and called upon Indian Agent

Hugh Montgomery to remove them. Although he responded by obtaining United States troops, the force sent was inadequate and had little effect upon the rapidly deteriorating condition in the mining areas. It was soon apparent that neither red nor white national governments could maintain order. Georgia capitalized on the situation by reiterating its law of 1828 in a new and more inclusive edict issued on December 19, 1829, by the terms of which sovereignty was reasserted over the Cherokee country, and the previous year's decrees restated. But the new law went even farther: no one was to prevent any Indian from enrolling for westward migration; any Indian could sell or cede Indian lands; and a term of four years in the state penitentiary was to be meted out to violators of state rulings.[6]

The presence of United States troops in the Cherokee gold country was humiliating to Georgians, who appealed to Governor Gilmer. He notified Andrew Jackson that recent state legislation made Cherokees subject to Georgia, and asked that federal troops be withdrawn so that he could send in a Georgia force. Jackson, entirely willing to go along with this suggestion, removed the American soldiers.[7]

On the Cherokee removal question President Jackson was in full sympathy with Georgia. He favored leaving the "poor deluded Cherokees to their fate, and their annihilation." Their condition, he thought, had been brought on by listening to "wicked advisers," who had probably told the Indians that the longer they held out for their rights, "and opposed the views of the government, the greater would be the offers made by the Executive." Then, "all the missionary and speculating tribe would make fortunes out of the United States."[8]

Emboldened by the President's attitude and anxious to possess the Cherokee territory, Georgia took further steps. After United States troops were withdrawn from the gold country, the legislature created a sixty-man "Georgia Guard" and assigned it to the area; eventually this unit extended its jurisdiction to the entire Indian nation. The same act, passed December 22, 1830, provided that no Cherokee governing body could meet except to cede lands, and Indian officials holding any kind of court were to receive four years of hard labor. Finally, the law declared that by March 1, 1830, all whites remaining in the Cherokee Nation must possess a license, which was to be issued only to those taking an oath to uphold the laws of Georgia.[9]

Cherokee hopes for United States interference were dampened

by the passage of a bill in Congress on May 28, 1830, "to provide for an exchange of lands with the Indians residing in any of the states or territories, and for their removal west of the Mississippi." Some consolation was found in the closeness of the vote which in the Senate was 28 to 20 and in the House, 103 to 97, and also in the hue-and-cry over the Removal Bill raised by speakers and writers throughout the country.[10]

With Georgia's deadly intentions clear, and federal antipathy to Indian distress also evident, the Cherokee situation in the early 1830's was grim. Established legal processes were voided at a stroke by Georgia law. The missionary program, with its accompanying educational and literary values, was threatened by the act requiring licenses for whites. The missionaries stoutly refused to swear the oath of allegiance to Georgia since they firmly believed that the state had no right to enforce its laws in the Cherokee Nation. Political, social, and economic progress faced a "dead end." All in all, the Cherokees of the early 1830's confronted an almost hopeless situation. The United States Supreme Court was the only remaining recourse. William Wirt of Philadelphia was retained as counsel by the Cherokee Nation, and an issue anxiously sought which would take the Indian question to the Supreme bench.[11]

In 1830 an opportunity came. A Cherokee Indian named George Tassel was convicted of murder by Hall County Superior Court and sentenced to death. Wirt and his associates appealed the case to the Supreme Court. On December 12, 1830, Georgia was cited to appear in Washington and show cause why a writ of error should not be issued in the Tassel case. Georgia not only ignored the message, but expedited Tassel's execution.[12] This abrupt action indicated a contempt for federal interference which spelled an end to Cherokee hopes for justice.

By the time the writ of error came up on the Supreme Court docket, it had been made a part of a new and stronger appeal. The new case was a request for an injunction against the State of Georgia for numerous violations of Cherokee sovereignty. William Wirt and Winthrop Sargent argued for the Cherokee Nation that it was "a foreign State, not owing allegiance to the United States, nor to any State of this Union, nor to any prince, potentate, or state other than their own." The court was asked to void Georgia's laws in the Indian territory and remove that state's officials from Cherokee lands. Georgia disregarded the Supreme

Court's summons to attend the hearing; the court's ruling, however, indirectly favored the state's position. Chief Justice John Marshall announced on March 5, 1831, that the Cherokees were a state, but not in the sense meant by the Constitution, and therefore his court had no jurisdiction in the matter.[13]

This decision set Cherokee hopes back another notch. Grimly determined to hang on if possible, the Indian leaders waited for an opportunity to meet Supreme Court jurisdictional requirements. Meanwhile they sought to help their people through the unhappy days at hand. One source of trouble was the President of the United States. Jackson had already implemented the terms of the federal Removal Act by appointing Benjamin F. Curry of Tennessee to serve as "Superintendent of Cherokee Removal from Georgia"; and Curry began to stir up Indian sentiment for emigration.[14]

Georgia's order requiring white men to secure licenses and swear allegiance to the state became effective on March 1, 1830. Shortly afterward, officers of the Georgia Guard arrested American Board missionaries Samuel A. Worcester and John Thompson and brought them before the Gwinnett County court on a writ of habeas corpus. The judge released them, however, since the two were utilizing United States funds in their work and were alleged to be agents of that government. Georgia's governor soon clarified this issue. He contacted Washington and established that the missionaries were not federal agents. It was revealed, however, that Worcester was United States Postmaster at New Echota. Gilmer thereupon requested and received Jackson's assurance that the missionary would be discharged from that office. A few weeks later, on May 16, 1831, the Governor ordered Worcester to leave Georgia.[15]

Now determined to make an example of the white clergymen who were believed by many Georgians to be advisers and instigators of Indian resistance, the state's officials moved into action. On May 28, 1831, the commander of the Georgia Guard announced a ten-day period during which all white missionaries were to leave the state, on pain of imprisonment. At the expiration of that time, eleven missionaries who refused to take oaths of allegiance to Georgia were taken into custody, treated with some brutality, and remanded for trial in the September term of Gwinnett Superior Court.[16]

Some indication of the tension existing in Cherokee Georgia

during this period may be gained from a study of the *Cherokee Phoenix* during the months of July and August, 1831. The leading editorial in the issue of July 12 discussed the second arrest of John Thompson, stating that he was confined in chains and suffered other indignities prior to being released. The affair reflected discredit on the honor of the State of Georgia, observed Elias Boudinot. Criticism of the offending state was much stronger in letters of Thompson and James I. Trott, published in the same issue. These letters described the imprisonment procedure and castigated the Georgia Guard and the officials of the state as well. Apparently the Georgia force objected to this criticism, for the following issue carried an editorial in which Boudinot maintained stoutly that as far as he knew the *Cherokee Phoenix* had published no "falsehoods." If, however, error had crept into his newspaper, he wanted to hear about it from "some reputable person," for, he continued, "it is far from our wish to injure any set of men, among whom we take the liberty to include the Georgia Guard."[17]

The following week, Boudinot recapitulated the entire affair of missionary arrests and scored Georgia's "vindictiveness." In the editor's view, Georgia's sole object in requiring the oath of allegiance was to get the missionaries out of the country. As for the Georgia Guard, the editor repeated a rumor that the unit had been ordered to "inflict corporeal punishment on such females as may be guilty of insulting them. . . . We think first, it is very undignified for a female to exercise it [an insult] under any circumstances; and second, it is equally undignified, for any gentleman to inflict a corporeal punishment on a female."[18]

The answer of the Georgia Guard to the newspaper articles was swift. Elias Boudinot was hailed before the organization's commanding officer, Colonel C. H. Nelson, who reprimanded the editor and threatened him with whipping. In an account printed in the *Cherokee Phoenix* on August 12, 1831, Boudinot stated:

> The Col. observed to us that there [had] been a great deal of lies, & abusive libelous articles published in the Phoenix. These slanders have been directed against the State of Georgia and the Georgia Guard. Heretofore they [the Guard] had exercised forbearance toward us . . . [but] we must now look out. He also observed that as they could not prosecute us for libel, the only way that we could be punished would be to deal with us in their individual capacity, to tie us to a tree and give us a sound whipping. . . .
>
> We are not aware of having slandered Georgia and the Guard, and

if we have, we think it a very poor way indeed to convince the world of it by flagellating us. . . . Truth *has* been our object and truth *shall* be our object.[19]

The Cherokee editor was receiving other threats, too, from various Georgians who objected to material he published on Cherokee removal and the state's actions. Three protesting letters were published in August, 1831, as typical of the feeling of "a certain class in Georgia," although Boudinot stated that he had no wish "to shock the feelings of the honest and worthy people of Georgia, nor to intimate in the least that the spirit exhibited in these letters will be approved generally by even those who are eager for the Indian lands." One of the letters headed "GAINSVILL, 19th July, 1831," read:

Dr Sir In looking over the last Cherokee Phoenix I noticed the remarks you made in that paper concerning the Georgia Guard &c. and about the President &c. Now you d——d little frog eater and worsp [wasp] destroyer . . . you favor a negro more than a d——d Indian. The treatment you and your countrymen are receiving is in payment of your d——d rascally treatment you have treated the whitemen when you had the power to do so . . . you d——d mountain rainger and wolf eater. . . . Your with indifference RALPH SCRUGGS[20]

Another of the letters dated July 7, 1831, was properly described by Boudinot as "significant." Under the sentence "You can answer this if you wish," there was drawn a figure hanging from a rope. On the four sides of the drawing were these sentiments: "Hang the Traitor," "Cut his Throat," "Death to the Rebbell," and "Shoot him."[21]

Colonel Nelson became so dissatisfied with Boudinot's conduct that he summoned the editor before the Georgia Guard again, and reprimanded him for allowing his sheet to be a medium of communication for disgruntled missionaries. According to Boudinot, Nelson suspected that Worcester or another missionary was the brains behind the *Cherokee Phoenix,* since the Colonel thought the editor to be "peaceable, passive, inoffensive and an ignorant sort of a man, and as not possessing sufficient talents to write the editorial articles in the Phoenix."[22]

The eleven missionaries were found guilty of violating Georgia laws on September 15, 1831, and sentenced to four years of hard labor. Nine of them promptly accepted Georgia's offer of a pardon in exchange for an oath of allegiance. Worcester and

Elizur Butler remained in the penitentiary, while Cherokee advocates petitioned the Supreme Court for justice.[23]

The case of *Worcester versus Georgia* was heard in the court at Washington in February, 1832. To the great joy of the Cherokee Indians and their supporters, the court ruled that the State of Georgia was in error. John Marshall announced that only the United States government could legislate for Indians, and that any state laws attempting to do so were null and void. Georgia was ordered to release Worcester and Butler from the penitentiary.[24]

Cherokee reaction was instantaneous and enthusiastic. At last it seemed that down-trodden Indians could overcome the humiliation of the past three years and re-assert their national sovereignty. A number of leading Cherokees, including Elias Boudinot, were in Washington during the Worcester hearing, attending court sessions and seeking additional aid. The Cherokee editor wrote his brother, Stand Watie, about the decision:

> It is glorious news. The laws of the State are declared by the highest judicial tribunal in the Country null and void. It is a great triumph on the part of the Cherokees so far as the question of their rights were concerned. The question is forever settled as to who is right and who is wrong, and the controversy is exactly where it ought to be, and where we have all along been desirous it should be. . . .
>
> Expectation has for the last few days been upon tiptoe—fears and hopes alternately took possession of our minds until two or three hours ago. . . . I will take it upon myself to say that this decision of the Court will now have a most powerful effect on public opinion. It creates a new era on the Indian question.[25]

But the court's emphatic statement of "who is right and who is wrong" failed to vouchsafe the right so defined. To the disappointment of Cherokee Indians and their supporters throughout the country, the State of Georgia defied John Marshall. Samuel Worcester and Elizur Butler were kept in custody and the state legislature continued to pass laws tyrannizing the Cherokees. On November 6, 1832, Governor Wilson Lumpkin told the General Assembly that he would resist to the utmost the Supreme Court's effort to "prostrate" Georgia sovereignty. Much encouragement for Georgia came from the nation's chief executive, who seemed willing to let Marshall enforce his own ruling. Jackson told friends that the decision was part of an effort of his enemies to embarrass him during an election year. He urged Lumpkin and other Georgians to continue with their anti-Cherokee activities, with a warning that it would be wise to avoid doing anything which might fall within the Supreme Court's jurisdiction.[26]

Although grateful for this advice, Georgia hardly needed the encouragement. Under authority of a law dated December 21, 1831, state authorities had established white government in the Indian country by creating a "Cherokee County," comprised of "all the lands lying west of the Chattahoochee River and north of the Carroll County line, within the limits of Georgia," including the Indian areas previously assigned to five counties.[27] Local officials were elected by Georgians already in the Cherokee area, and their administration sought to replace the legal structure of the Cherokee republic.

With Georgians clamoring for Indian lands and the gold rush booming, the state's next step was to announce a gigantic lottery in which Cherokee County would be raffled off in individual lots. Enabling legislation for this distribution had been passed in 1830, and surveyors were ready to issue maps. Drawings for "gold lots" and "land lots" of 40 and 160 acres were available to all white adult males in Georgia who had lived in the state for at least four years. Certain others were privileged as well, including physically handicapped persons, veterans and their widows or descendants, and soldiers. No one who had previously won land in the Creek Lottery was eligible. The Cherokee Lottery occurred in 1832, and during that year Cherokee County was subdivided into ten smaller counties: Cass, Cherokee, Cobb, Floyd, Forsyth, Gilmer, Lumpkin, Murray, Paulding, and Walker.[28]

The rush of thousands of whites into Cherokee territory to secure newly won land lots heightened the turmoil and confusion among the Indians. Some Georgians found empty cabins whose owners had already been persuaded to emigrate. Others arrived at their new lands to find them occupied, and forcibly ejected the Cherokee occupants. In most cases, however, the newcomers waited until the Indians could be removed from the region by treaty or other means. The distraught condition of the Cherokee Nation was further troubled by the inevitable clashes of red and white gangs. Embittered and disillusioned, the Indians still hoped for relief from their sufferings.[29]

The Cherokee government was of little assistance. Its small police forces were powerless to bring order. Within the National

Council and Committee the specter of factionalism loomed ominously. Federal and state agents, anxious to persuade prominent Indians that a removal treaty was the only sensible solution, encouraged the growing split in native ranks. Meanwhile discouraged missionaries saw their own establishments subject to confiscation by the "fortunate drawers," and faced the perplexing problem of continuing a Christian evangelization in the midst of terror and despair. The experiences of two are typical. Worcester and Butler (now pardoned after taking Georgia's oath, following the Supreme Court incident) were under orders to leave Cherokee Georgia as soon as practicable. The American Board told them not to surrender mission property without exercising every legal right — although the Board admitted that it was "heartily tired of this trouble with law, courts, & political men."[30]

Butler's mission establishment at Haweis was obtained by Georgians in January, 1834. In the same month Worcester was advised by his superiors to release his house at New Echota: "You had better get along as well as you can, if you are driven from your house, till next fall, & then cross the Mississippi."[31] In February Worcester received this message:

> It becomes my duty to give you notice to evacuate the lot of land No. 125, in the 14th District, of the third section, and to give the house now occupied by you up to Col. William Harden, or whoever he may put forward, to take possession of the same and that you may have ample time to prepare for the same, I will allow you until the 28th day of this month to do the same. Given under my hand this 16th day of February 1834.
>
> William E. Springer
> Agent for the Cherokees, in Georgia[32]

By 1835 some Indians came to the realization that the troubles with Georgia would end only with removal, and that a treaty under the best possible terms was necessary. Notable among leaders adopting this view were Major Ridge, John Ridge, Elias Boudinot, and Stand Watie. On March 10, 1835, John Ridge reported to his father and others from Washington that he had succeeded in getting "a treaty made to be sent home for the ratification of the people. It is very liberal in its terms — an equal measure is given to all. The poor Indian enjoys the same rights as the rich — there is no distinction. We are allowed to enjoy our lands in the West."[33] At the same time that Ridge and associates were in Washington, however, a delegation under the personal leadership of Chief John Ross was also seeking federal assistance. In successive visits to the American capital, Ross had steadfastly refused to consider any negotiations leading to a relinquishment of Cherokee territory east of the Mississippi. When he learned of the John Ridge treaty he and his delegation advanced a counter-proposal, suggesting that an allowance of $20,000,000 be paid the Cherokee Nation for the cession of its lands, and that an indefinite number of claims be paid also. Subsequently Ross pared this demand down to whatever figure might be considered reasonable by the United States Senate. On March 6, 1835, the Principal Chief was advised that the Senate's opinion was that the Cherokees should be paid not more than $5,000,000. Ross in disgust suspended treaty discussions.[34]

In the meantime John Ridge had returned to the Cherokee country with his treaty. Accompanying him was a New York clergyman named John F. Schermerhorn, appointed by President Jackson to negotiate the removal. Ridge's treaty was presented to the Cherokee Council at Red Clay (on the Tennessee-Georgia border) in October, 1835. Its most important provisions gave $3,250,000 to the Cherokees for their eastern lands; $150,000 for depredative claims (including Creek War losses); restated a guarantee to 13,000,000 acres of western territory granted in treaties of 1828 and 1833 to previously emigrated Cherokees; and gave an additional 800,000 acres in that same region to those going west. The opposition of John Ross's faction proved too formidable for the Ridge party at Red Clay, and the Cherokee Council rejected the proposed treaty. Even John Ridge and Elias Boudinot turned against Schermerhorn and voted refusal, although that agent raised his offer to the full $5,000,000 suggested by the United States Senate.[35]

During the Red Clay negotiations Schermerhorn called on the Cherokee Council to meet again at New Echota the following December, for further treaty conferences. The Red Clay Council, however, authorized John Ross to conclude the best possible treaty. Realizing that Schermerhorn had no additional terms to offer, Ross proceeded to Washington to resume negotiations there.[36]

During John Ross's absence his Cherokee republic in the South fell apart. Meeting in December with Schermerhorn, a small group of about three hundred Cherokees signed "The Treaty of New Echota." In the list of signatories were Major Ridge, John Ridge, Elias Boudinot, and Stand Watie. With several amendments, which were approved by the Cherokee signers, the treaty was ratified by the United States Senate and announced as law by the President on May 23, 1836. By the terms of this document, the Cherokee Nation ceded its eastern territories and released all claims for damages, for the sum of $5,000,000; it received in exchange guarantees to the western lands then partly occupied by Cherokees West, with the further stipulation that it should never become a part of another state or territory without Cherokee consent. The United States agreed to remove the Indians across the Mississippi, and to grant them a year's subsistence thereafter.[37]

During the next three years John Ross and his Cherokee followers, and many white friends as well, set up a mighty complaint over the "fraudulent" treaty, the signing of which by a minority had violated every previous principle of Cherokee land cessions. But these protests were futile. Federal enrolling agents began to round up Cherokees for westward emigration, and appraisers commenced valuing Indian property. General John E. Wool and a force of United States soldiers were stationed in the ceded country with instructions to maintain order in the event of a Cherokee uprising. The Cherokees themselves were for the most part disappointed and confused by the new turn of events, and under the continued leadership of John Ross made little effort to get ready for a large-scale migration. A few went west in small bands, including the Ridge-Boudinot-Watie group, where they joined with the "Old Settlers West" in a party which was to offer further opposition to John Ross after 1838.[38]

Effective removal of the majority of Cherokees to the western country did not begin until late in 1838; such was the power of John Ross's leadership, coupled with the confusion of state, federal, and Indian agencies operating simultaneously in the Cherokee Nation. For a time it appeared that favorable action might occur in Washington, so intensely was the Cherokee removal question debated. Ross and his friends were there on numerous occasions, presenting memorials and petitions to Congress and interviewing prominent people. But in the spring of 1838 the President ordered General Winfield Scott to the Cherokee Nation to supervise an enforced removal. Many Indians thereupon submitted, and by mid-summer the total number removed since 1835 exceeded six thousand. Finally John Ross gave in. By authority of a Cherokee Council resolution, he suggested to General Scott that the Cherokee Nation assume the task of rounding up and dispatching the remaining Indians, at an estimated cost of $65.88 per person. This request was granted, and final Cherokee removal began in late December, 1838.[39]

The story of the Cherokees in the 1830's is a tragic one, featuring an uneven struggle between an ineffectual red minority and a powerful and determined white majority. In the inevitable defeat, the Cherokees lost lives, property, and territory. Their enforced westward trek in 1838-39 cost them nearly one-third of the population. Small wonder that it came to be known as the "Trail of Tears."[40] Left behind, hidden in the mountains, were a thousand of their countrymen whose eventual destination was to be a small reservation in western North Carolina. Also abandoned in Georgia were the remnants of a once-promising nation — houses, cabins, farms, ferries, schoolhouses, and here and there an occasional fragment of Sequoyan print.

The relics left by departing Cherokees are forceful reminders of the curious red-white amalgam which by 1830 was their peculiar culture. After centuries of gradual progress in a primitive state, the Indian was confronted with the white man as a disturbing influence. His menace brought Cherokees into closer relations with each other, put them into a diplomatic cross-fire, and exposed them to death and destruction. The peaceful ways of the trader and the traveller were temporarily reassuring; but as the Cherokee Indian began to absorb the white man's culture, fresh warfare in the late eighteenth century suddenly restored the tomahawk and the "rifle gun" to tragic importance.

The beginning of the nineteenth century saw Cherokees and white men entering into a new relationship. With comparative peace assured for the frontier, overtures from a benevolent government in Washington and encouraging suggestions from white friends and half-breeds combined to beckon the Cherokees down the alluring road called "the white man's path." For a third of a century these Southern red men moved steadily toward the culture of the white men about them. Indians of initiative and energy improved their farms, and some became country gentlemen. A few built up thriving mercantile businesses, while others profited from ferries, toll-gates, and public-houses. Young mixed-blood progressives acquired power in the Cherokee government and became champions of a state patterned on that of the white men. Missionaries flocked in to bring Christianity and schooling.

In the midst of these developments Sequoyah introduced his syllabary, which became the most dynamic force in the social progress of his people. Within a decade thousands of Cherokees had utilized this valuable invention for their cultural improvement. A stimulated Indian government formed a constitutional republic, and, with missionary help, created a nationalistic press and newspaper. Cherokee journalists produced thousands of pages of bilingual print to hasten the enlightenment of their eager countrymen.

But by the 1830's the high tide of Eastern Cherokee social development was ebbing. At a moment of great promise for Indians moving impressively toward the white man's way of life, the white man himself obstructed that progress by thrusting the Cherokees out of their native lands. Expelled to a wild country, Cherokees faced harsh problems of reconstruction. Perhaps their best implements in this new crisis were the memories of remarkable progress in their eastern homelands.

NOTES

CHAPTER ONE

1. Based upon language similarities with Northern red men, and certain traditions of the Delaware Indians, this theory is accepted by a number of Indian experts, principally the following: James Mooney, "Myths of the Cherokee," *19th Annual Report of the Bureau of American Ethnology, 1897-98,* Part I (Washington, 1900), 17-18, 21; and John R. Swanton, *The Indians of the Southeastern United States (Bulletin 137.* Bureau of American Ethnology, Washington, 1946), 14. Recent ethnological investigations by F. G. Speck cast some doubt on this theory, suggesting that striking resemblances between the Cherokees and other Southern Indians indicate a possibility that both Cherokees and Iroquois had a common cultural origin in the South. Speck, *Decorative Art and Basketry of the Cherokee (Bulletin* of the Public Museum of the City of Milwaukee, II, July 27, 1920), 64, 68. Perhaps the most important rebuttal to this idea comes from A. L. Kroeber, in his *Cultural and Natural Areas of Native North America* (University of California *Publications* in American Archaeology and Ethnology, XXXVIII, Berkeley, 1939), 95. William H. Gilbert offers a clear statement of the two theories in *The Eastern Cherokees (Anthropological Papers,* No. 23, *Bulletin 133* of the Bureau of American Ethnology, 169-413, Washington, 1943), 313-15. Other theories of Cherokee origin include that of James Adair, a Scotch-Irish trader and historian, who thought they were the remnant of the Ten Lost Tribes of Israel, in *History of the American Indians, particularly those Nations Adjoining to the Mississippi, East & West Florida, Georgia, South and North Carolina, and Virginia* (London, 1775), 226-56. In 1832 a Cherokee named Oconosta stated that his ancestors came from Asia. Horatio B. Cushman, *History of the Choctaw, Chickasaw, and Natchez Indians* (Greenville, Texas, 1899), 19, 66. Another theory of Cherokee origin is stated in the "Legend of Kituwah Society," a tradition which persists among some Cherokees today. According to one explanation of it, Cherokees and other Indians "must have lived somewhere east of South America, on islands in the Atlantic Ocean," and later, under divine guidance, some were led to America. "Legend of Kituwah Society," from statement by Levi B. Gritts, Nov. 14, 1930, in Cherokee Files, Archives Division, Oklahoma Historical Society (OHS), Oklahoma City.
2. Gilbert, *Eastern Cherokees,* 181; Kroeber, *Cultural and Natural Areas,* 95.
3. *Final Report of the United States DeSoto Expedition Commission* (76 Cong., 1 sess., House Executive Document No. 71. Washington, 1939), 187-93. (Based on the travel accounts of the Gentleman of Elvas, Rodrigo Ranjel, and Garcilasso de la Vega.) Considerable controversy has developed over the question of the particular route followed by De Soto, especially through Georgia.

The report of the De Soto Commission, which was headed by John R. Swanton, offers telling evidence that the party travelled through Georgia (although not along the Coosa), Tennessee, and Alabama. It seems certain that these Spaniards saw Cherokee Indians while on this expedition.

4. Mooney, "Myths," 28-29; Fletcher M. Green, "Georgia's Forgotten Industry: Gold Mining," *Georgia Historical Quarterly*, XIX (June and Sept., 1935), 96-98; John G. Shea, *History of the Catholic Missions among the Indian Tribes of the United States, 1529-1854* (New York and Philadelphia, n.d.), 59. It should be noted that James Mooney states that this priest, whom he calls Father Roger, did not work among the Cherokee Indians. It seems possible, however, that Rogel (r) might have encountered Cherokees, since he refers specifically to them.
5. Gilbert, *Eastern Cherokees*, 178-79; Mooney, "Myths," 14; Albert Gallatin, "A Synopsis of the Indian Tribes within the United States east of the Rocky Mountains and in the British and Russian Possessions in North America," *Archaeologica Americana, Transactions and Collections* of the American Antiquarian Society (Cambridge, Mass., 1836), II, 90.
6. Gilbert, *Eastern Cherokees*, 178; Harry C. Ash, "Ethnology of the Indian Tribes formerly occupying the Territory of Georgia," (unpublished masters thesis, Emory University, 1932), 13.
7. John P. Brown, *Old Frontiers: The Story of the Cherokee Indians from Earliest Times to the Date of their Removal to the West, 1838* (Kingsport, Tenn., 1938), 14, 538; Samuel C. Williams, ed., *Early Travels in the Tennessee Country* (Johnson City, Tenn., 1928), 27n.
8. For an exhaustive list of the flora and fauna of the Cherokee country, see Gilbert, *Eastern Cherokees*, 184-85.
9. R. S. Cotterill, *The Old South* (Glendale, Calif., 1939), 40-42; Herbert R. Sass, *Hear Me, My Chiefs!* (New York, 1940), 110 ff; Angie Debo, *The Road to Disappearance* (Norman, Okla., 1941), 25 *et passim;* Wilbur R. Jacobs, *Diplomacy and Indian Gifts* (Stanford, Calif., 1950) 27.
10. Charles C. Jones, Jr., *Antiquities of the Southern Indians, Particularly of the Georgia Tribes* (New York, 1873), 7; Swanton, *Indians of Southeast*, 14. For Cherokee relations with the Indians of the Carolinas, consult Chapman J. Milling, *Red Carolinians* (Chapel Hill, 1940); and Douglas L. Rights, *The American Indian in North Carolina* (Durham, N. C., 1947). Samuel C. Williams, in his *Early Travels* (p. 174 n.) refers to the "almost constant" warfare between the Shawnees and the Cherokees. Consult also James H. Malone, *The Chickasaw Nation: A Short Sketch of a Noble People* (Louisville, Ky., 1922), 301-303; Cotterill, *Old South*, 42; Theodore Roosevelt, *The Winning of the West* (New York, 1900), I, 78-79.
11. Gilbert, *Eastern Cherokees*, 317. Mooney states that a persistent Cherokee tradition fixes the date of the introduction of guns as about 1700. Mooney, "Myths," 32. However, it has been asserted that the Cherokees were observed using muskets as early as 1673. Clarence W. Alvord and Lee Bidgood, *The First Explorations of the Trans-Allegheny Region by the Virginians, 1650-1674* (Cleveland, 1912), 83.
12. From transcript of "Journal of the Commissioner of Indian Affairs [Col. George Chicken] on his journey to the Cherokees and his proceedings there, 1725," from Office of Public Record, London, Colonial Office 5, vol. 12, p. 96, in London Papers File, Archives Division, OHS; John Haywood, *Natural and Aboriginal History of Tennessee, up to the First Settlements therein by the*

White People, in the Year 1768 (Nashville, 1823), 238.

13. William Bartram, *The Travels of William Bartram* (Mark van Doren, ed., New York, 1928), 381; Samuel C. Williams, *Tennessee During the Revolutionary War* (Nashville, 1944), 210; Milling, *Red Carolinians,* 276 *et passim;* Samuel C. Williams, ed., *Adair's History of the American Indians* (Johnson City, Tenn., 1930), 86 n. Biographical sketches of Attakullakulla may be found in Williams, ed., *Early Travels* 127 n.; and Frederick W. Hodge, ed., *Handbook of American Indians North of Mexico* (59 Cong., 1 sess., House Executive Document 926, Washington, 1907), I, 115.
14. Hodge, *Handbook,* II, 105-106; Dumas Malone, *et al,* eds., *Dictionary of American Biography* (New York, 1928-), XIII, 621-22; XIV, 111-12; Williams, *Tennessee During Revolution,* 210; Milling, *Red Carolinians,* 29 *et passim.*
15. Brief sketches of these Cherokee leaders may be found in Hodge, *Handbook;* Brown, *Old Frontiers;* and Samuel C. Williams, *Dawn of Tennessee Valley and Tennessee History* (Johnson City, Tenn., 1937).
16. Quoted in Debo, *Road to Disappearance,* 31.
17. See "Letter of Abraham Wood," in Williams, ed., *Early Travels,* 29, 32-33, and editor's notes, 17-23.
18. Milling, *Red Carolinians,* 267-68. Earlier contact may have occurred between Cherokees and Englishmen. James Mooney (in "Myths," p. 31) cites a statement to this effect from the *Cherokee Advocate,* Jan. 30, 1845. No further corroboration has been found.
19. Lords Proprietors to Governor Nathaniel Johnson, May 1, 1703, in A. S. Salley, Jr., ed., *Commissions and Instructions from the Lords Proprietors of Carolina to Public Officials of South Carolina, 1685-1715* (Columbia, S. C., 1916), 169. That the governors made an effort to carry out these instructions is indicated by the Indian records of the colony; see A. S. Salley, Jr., ed., *Journal of the Commissioners of the Indian Trade of South Carolina, Sept. 20, 1710-April 12, 1715* (Columbia, S. C., 1926). Consult also Mary U. Rothrock, "Carolina Traders Among the Overhill Cherokees, 1690-1760," East Tennessee Historical Society's *Publications,* I (1929), 3-18.
20. Allen D. Candler, ed., *The Colonial Records of the State of Georgia* (26 vols. Atlanta, 1904-1916), I, 31 *et seq.*
21. Statement by William Byrd, quoted in Verner W. Crane, *The Southern Frontier, 1670-1732* (Durham, N. C., 1928), 115. For a careful description of Virginia's participation in the Indian trade, see W. Neil Franklin, "Virginia and the Cherokee Indian Trade, 1673-1775," East Tennessee Historical Society's *Publications,* IV (1932), 3-21; and V (1933), 22-38.
22. Crane, *Southern Frontier,* particularly Chapter V, "The Charles Town Indian Trade."
23. Bartram, *Travels,* 286-87; Williams, *Dawn of Tennessee,* 70. For the life of James Adair, consult *D.A.B.,* I, 33-34. See also Adair's *American Indians;* introduction and notes by Samuel C. Williams in his *Adair's History;* and Mooney, "Myths," *passim.*
24. "Journal of Cuming," in Williams, ed., *Early Travels,* 138-41; Samuel G. Drake, *Early History of Georgia, Embracing the Embassy of Sir Alexander Cuming to the Country of the Cherokees in the Year 1730* (Boston, 1872); Carolyn Foreman, *Indians Abroad* (Norman, Okla., 1943), 44 ff.
25. Henry Timberlake, *The Memoirs of Lieut. Henry Timberlake* (London, 1765), *passim;* Foreman, *Indians Abroad,* 65 ff; *The London Magazine,* Feb., 1760, p. 96.
26. Crane, *Southern Frontier, passim;* Jacobs, *Diplomacy and Indian Gifts,* 124, 163-64.

27. Milling, *Red Carolinians,* 283-85; Mooney, "Myths," 40. The territory ceded included the present-day counties of Abbeville, Cherokee, Chester, Edgefield, Fairfield, Greenwood, Laurens, McCormick, Newberry, Richland, Saluda, Spartanburg, and part of York.
28. This war is well described in Milling, *Red Carolinians;* Brown, *Old Frontiers;* Corry, *Indian Affairs in Georgia;* and Mooney, "Myths." A vivid description of the Loudun massacre is to be found in Brown, *Old Frontiers,* 100-103.
29. Brown, *Old Frontiers,* 103, 123-26; John R. Alden, *John Stuart and the Southern Colonial Frontier. A study of Indian Relations, War, Trade, and Land Problems in the Southern Wilderness. 1754-1775* (Ann Arbor, Mich., 1944), *passim.*
30. Brown, *Old Frontiers,* 123-24.
31. For a detailed account of the events surrounding these treaties, and their terms, see Charles C. Royce, "Indian Land Cessions in the United States," *Eighteenth Annual Report of the Bureau of American Ethnology, 1896-97* (Washington, 1899), II, *passim.*
32. From "Abstract of a Letter from Alexr Cameron Esqr Commissary in the Cherokee Nation, 27 August 1766," and John Stuart to Board of Trade and Plantations, July 10, 1766, in London Papers File, OHS.
33. *Ibid.*
34. Archibald Henderson, *The Conquest of the Old Southwest* (New York, 1920), 221-25.
35. Charles C. Royce, "The Cherokee Nation of Indians: A Narrative of their Official Relations with the Colonial and Federal Governments," *Fifth Annual Report, Bureau of American Ethnology, 1883-84* (Washington, 1887), 149-50.
36. Royce, "Cherokee Nation of Indians," 150-51; see also Brown, *Old Frontiers;* and Williams, *Tennessee During the Revolution.*
37. See Chapter III.
38. Mooney, "Myths," 53. The pockmarks resulting from the smallpox epidemic so humiliated some of the Indians that they committed suicide. Marion L. Starkey, *The Cherokee Nation* (New York, 1946), 14-15.
39. In 1789, for example, U. S. Commissioners to the Indians recorded that there were about 600 "gunmen" in the Cherokee Nation. Report of Commissioners Benjamin Lincoln, and others, to Secretary of War, New York, Nov. 30, 1789, in *American State Papers: Class II, Indian Affairs* (Documents, Legislative and Executive, of the Congress of the United States, Dec. 4, 1815—March 3, 1827, Washington, 1834), I, 79. The botanist-traveller, William Bartram, compiled a roster of forty-three towns which he said existed in the Cherokee Nation in the 1770's, locating them by rivers. Bartram, *Travels,* 301-302. For a discussion of the Cherokee population during the years 1759-1779, consult Thomas Jefferson, *Notes on the State of Virginia* (Philadelphia, 1801), 200. See also other Cherokee vital statistics in Mooney, "Myths," 34; Adair, *American Indians,* 227; Royce, "Cherokee Nation of Indians," 142; and Drake, *Embassy of Cuming,* 4.

CHAPTER TWO

1. John Hammerer [an early teacher in the Cherokee country] to Rev. Ettwein, 1766, quoted in Williams, ed., *Early Travels,* 246; Milling, *Red Carolinians,* 12-13; Gilbert, *Eastern Cherokees,* 184.
2. Bartram, *Travels,* 296.
3. "Bro. Martin Schneider's Report of his Journey, 1783-84," in Williams, ed., *Early Travels,* 260-61.
4. *Ibid.;* Bartram, *Travels,* 296.
5. Bartram, *Travels,* 297-98.
6. Opinion of J. T. Gregory of Inola, Indian Territory, in letter to Emmet

Starr [native Cherokee historian], Aug. 20, 1900, in "Cherokee Files Miscellaneous," Archives Division, OHS.

7. *Memoirs of Timberlake,* 32; Bartram, *Travels,* 298; Swanton, *Indians of Southeast,* 379.
8. "Letter of Abraham Wood," in Williams, ed., *Early Travels,* 28; this letter with varying notes and introduction is also given in Alvord and Bidgood, *First Explorations.* For a discussion of Chota, see Williams, *Adair's History,* 166 n.
9. "Colonel George Chicken's Journal," in Williams, ed., *Early Travels,* 98-99; "Journal of Antoine Bonnefoy," in *ibid.,* 152-53.
10. "Journal of Commissioner of Indian Affairs," in London Papers File, OHS; Bartram, *Travels,* 301-302.
11. Gilbert, *Eastern Cherokees,* 193; Bartram, *Travels,* 380-81.
12. Gilbert, *Eastern Cherokees,* 193-94.
13. Bartram, *Travels,* 400; Gilbert, *Eastern Cherokees,* 199.
14. Gilbert, *Eastern Cherokees,* 316; A. S. Salley, ed., *Journal of Colonel John Herbert, Commissioner of Indian Affairs for the Province of South Carolina, October 17, 1727, to March 19, 1727/28* (Columbia, S. C., 1936), 27. Colonel Herbert stated that "Old Grater-face [a Cherokee] presents me with a parcel of skins telling me that I was in a cold place & that they were to make me gloves." *Ibid.*
15. Quoted in Williams, ed., *Early Travels,* 129 n.
16. Bartram, *Travels,* 381; Adair, *American Indians,* 17.
17. Sass, *Hear Me, My Chiefs!,* 64; Zella Armstrong, *History of Hamilton County and Chattanooga, Tennessee* (Chattanooga, 1931), I, 21; William Bartram, "Observations on the Creek and Cherokee Indians, 1789," *Transactions* of the American Ethnological Society, Vol. III, pt. I (New York, 1853), 32. For examples of women participating in warfare, see Mooney, "Myths," 395, 419, 501.
18. Ash, "Ethnology of Tribes of Georgia," 88; Adair, *American Indians,* 190; Bartram, "Observations," 28.
19. Adair, *American Indians,* 126-27, 145-46; Jones, *Antiquities,* 68; *Memoirs of Timberlake,* 65.
20. Gilbert, *Eastern Cherokees,* 316-17; "Schneider's Report," in Williams, ed., *Early Travels,* 257; *Memoirs of Timberlake,* 62.
21. Speck, *Decorative Art,* 64; Williams, *Dawn of Tennessee,* 67; *Memoirs of Timberlake,* 62. Speck asserts that the Cherokees were poor basket-makers, and poor in pottery-making and esthetic ornamentation; furthermore, he adds, "beadwork never took root as an industry, painting is supposed to have been lacking," and fabric embroidery was weak. *Decorative Art,* 64.
22. *Memoirs of Timberlake,* 28, 30, 34-35; Bartram, *Travels,* 283-85; "Report of Schneider," in Williams, ed., *Early Travels,* 257; "Letter of Abraham Wood," in *ibid.,* 28-37; Swanton, *Indians of Southeast,* 302-303.
23. Bartram, *Travels,* 285; "Report of Schneider," in Williams, ed., *Early Travels,* 257.
24. *Memoirs of Timberlake,* 34-35; Jones, *Antiquities,* 233, 495 ff; "Report of Schneider," in Williams, ed., *Early Travels,* 253. The extent of the liquor traffic in the Indian country is discussed in three chapters of H. A. Scomp, *King Alcohol in the Realm of King Cotton* (n. p., 1888), 52-58, 96-112, 148-54. See also Walter H. Mohr, *Federal Indian Relations, 1774-1788* (Philadelphia, 1933), 19. "No laws appear oftener on the colonial statute books than those against this traffic [of liquor into the Indian country]," James A. James, *English Institutions and the American Indian* (12th Series, Johns Hopkins *Studies* in Historical and Political Science, x. Baltimore, 1894), 31.
25. *Memoirs of Timberlake,* 42; Jones, *Antiquities,* 40-42; Starkey, *Cherokee Nation,* 17; "Report of Schnei-

der," in Williams, ed., *Early Travels,* 261.

26. "Report of Schneider," in Williams, ed., *Early Travels,* 261; Starkey, *Cherokee Nation,* 17; Armstrong, *Hamilton County,* 21-22; Jones, *Antiquities,* 40-42.
27. Almon W. Lauber, *Indian Slavery in Colonial Times Within the Present Limits of the U. S.* (New York, 1913), 37, 49, 63, 136, 170. Lauber declares that "in all the southern colonies Indian slaves worked in the fields side by side with the negroes up to the time of the Revolution." *Ibid.,* 244. See also Crane, *Southern Frontier,* 20, 21.
28. Ash, "Ethnology of Tribes of Georgia," 20; Mooney, "Myths," 83; Starkey, *Cherokee Nation,* 18.
29. Bartram, *Travels,* 284-287; Williams, *Tennessee During Revolution,* 57.
30. Bartram, *Travels,* 285; Crane, *Southern Frontier,* 116; Gilbert, *Eastern Cherokees,* 317; Swanton, *Indians of Southeast,* 384.
31. Adair, *American Indians,* 230; Swanton, *Indians of Southeast,* 349-51; Mooney, "Myths," 82; Crane, *Southern Frontier,* 127. Adair praised the horsemanship of the Cherokees: "They are skilful Jockies, and nice in their choice [of horseflesh]." *American Indians,* 230.
32. Adair, *American Indians,* 230; "Report of Schneider," in Williams, ed., *Early Travels,* 261; Brown, *Old Frontiers,* 154, 213. As late as 1761, according to Timberlake, the Cherokees had "neither cows nor sheep." *Memoirs of Timberlake,* 47.
33. *Memoirs of Timberlake,* 47; Milling, *Red Carolinians,* 317 n; Gilbert, *Eastern Cherokees,* 185.
34. Ash, "Ethnology of Tribes of Georgia," 106; Gilbert, *Eastern Cherokees,* 317.
35. Gilbert, *Eastern Cherokees,* 317; Swanton, *Indians of Southeast,* 335. The fish trap description is by Henry Timberlake, quoted in *ibid,* 335-36.
36. Donald Davidson, *The Tennessee* (*Rivers of America* series. New York, 1946), I, 49; Swanton, *Indians of Southeast,* 593; "Letter of Abraham Wood," in Williams, ed., *Early Travels,* 28.
37. For a list of the various trails most used by early Cherokees, and the tribes connected by each, see Gilbert, *Eastern Cherokees,* 180-81; for a delightful account of the Warrior's Path, consult Sass, *Hear Me, My Chiefs,* 106 ff.
38. Rights, *Indian in North Carolina,* 152; "Journal of Commissioner of Indian Affairs," London Papers File, OHS.
39. Bartram, *Travels,* 380; Haywood, *Natural and Aboriginal History,* 272; Gilbert, *Eastern Cherokees,* 181.
40. "Journal of Cuming," in Williams, ed., *Early Travels,* 122; Jones, *Antiquities,* 11-13.
41. Gilbert, *Eastern Cherokees,* 203-209. There has been some variance as to the exact names of the seven Cherokee clans. The author chooses to accept the list given by the anthropologist William H. Gilbert. For a list of the clan names preferred by other writers on Cherokee history, see Gilbert's comparative chart in *ibid.,* 205.
42. This description of the dual governmental organization of the early Cherokees is based on William H. Gilbert's account in *Eastern Cherokees,* 319-59.
43. *Ibid.,* 348-49.
44. *Ibid.,* 356-57; Jones states that the Great War Chief, an army leader, sat to the right of the head man at Cherokee council meetings. *Antiquities,* 13.
45. Letter from William H. Gilbert to author, Nov. 5, 1951. Milling asserts that "frequently there was a peace party nearly, if not quite, as strong as the war party. . . . The followers of Attakullakulla constituted such a party from 1756 to 1760." *Red Carolinians,* 28.
46. Samuel G. Drake, *The Aboriginal Races of North America* (New

York, 1880), 367; Drake, *Embassy of Cuming,* 9; "Journal of Cuming," in Williams, ed., *Early Travels,* 122, 136; Mooney, "Myths," 35; Starkey, *Cherokee Nation,* 12. For a biographical sketch of Moytoy, see Hodge, *Handbook,* I, 953.

47. The nature of Priber's activity has been a controversial subject. The theory that he was a Utopian planner is based primarily on the research of Verner W. Crane, reported in his "A Lost Utopia of the First American Frontier," *Sewanee Review,* XXVII (Jan., 1919), 48-61. This interpretation is interestingly elaborated upon in Sass, *Hear Me, My Chiefs!,* 67-82, and is accepted by the *Dictionary of American Biography,* XV, 210. Starkey (*Cherokee Nation,* 13, 29), favors the earlier explanation of Priber's work, terming him both a "Jesuit Missionary" and a "French Agent." This is also the view of Mooney, "Myths," 15, 36-37.
48. Crane, "A Lost Utopia," *S. R.,* 55-61; Sass, *Hear Me, My Chiefs!,* 78-82.
49. Adair, *American Indians,* 158; Swanton, *Indians of Southeast,* 654-61; Mooney, "Myths," 212-13.
50. Davidson, *The Tennessee,* I, 42; Adair, *American Indians,* 158-59; Gallatin, "Synopsis," 112; Gilbert, *Eastern Cherokees,* 324.
51. Davidson, *The Tennessee,* I, 43; Paul Radin, *The Story of the American Indian* (rev. ed., New York, 1934) 351; Adair, *American Indians,* 87; "Journal of Cuming," in Williams, ed., *Early Travels,* 122. The quote from Old Hopp is in Brown, *Old Frontiers,* 30.
52. *Memoirs of Timberlake,* 63; Swanton, *Indians of Southeast,* 767. The best collection of Cherokee legends is in James Mooney, "Myths." See also J. B. Davis, *Cherokee Fables* (Siloam Springs, Ark., 1937).
53. Gilbert, *Eastern Cherokees,* 326-48, 356-59.
54. *Ibid.,* 346; Adair, *American Indians,* 121, 144.
55. Jones, *Antiquities,* 114-15; Adair, *American Indians,* 178, 185 n.
56. Jones, *Antiquities,* 34; Adair, *American Indians,* 178.
57. "James Smith's Account," in Williams, ed., *Early Travels,* 205.
58. Mooney, "Myths," 36.
59. "Colonel George Chicken's Journal," in Williams, ed., *Early Travels,* 97; "Journal of Cuming," in *ibid.,* 126; Swanton, *Indians of Southeast,* 767-69. For a description of a ceremonial dance before an athletic contest, see Bartram, *Travels,* 297-98.
60. James Mooney, *The Cherokee Ball Play* (Washington, 1890), 105-32; Swanton, *Indians of Southeast,* 674-80.
61. Journal, *Commissioners of Indian Trade,* 69.
62. Brown, *Old Frontiers,* 21-22.

CHAPTER THREE

1. The Hopewell negotiations and treaty may be found in *ASP, IA,* I, 38-46; and Charles J. Kappler, *Indian Affairs: Laws and Treaties* (Washington, 1904), II, 6-8.
2. James D. Richardson, *A Compilation of the Messages and Papers of the Presidents, 1789-1897* (Washington, 1896), I, 80; Mohr, *Federal Indian Relations,* 148.
3. *ASP, IA,* I, 14-15; George D. Harmon, *Sixty Years of Indian Affairs* (Chapel Hill, 1941), 4.
4. Harmon, *Sixty Years,* 5-7; Mohr, *Federal Indian Relations,* 104-107, 148-49, *et passim.* Excellent accounts of the history of Cherokee relations with the "State of Franklin" may be found in Samuel C. Williams, *History of the Lost State of Franklin* (Johnson City, Tenn., 1924); and Brown, *Old Frontiers,* 239-99.
5. Mohr, *Federal Indian Relations,* 164; Thomas P. Abernethy, *From Frontier to Plantation in Tennessee:*

A Study in Frontier Democracy (Chapel Hill, 1932), 93-96.

6. Mohr, *Federal Indian Relations,* 164-65; Stephen B. Weeks, "General Joseph Martin and the War of the Revolution in the West," *Annual Report* of the American Historical Association, 1893 (Washington, 1895), 460-61.
7. *ASP, IA,* I, 53.
8. *Ibid.,* 83; Clarence E. Carter, ed., *The Territory South of the River Ohio, 1790-1796* (Vol. IV, *The Territorial Papers of the United States.* Washington, 1936), 60 n.
9. *ASP, IA,* I, 123-25; 203.
10. *Ibid.,* 125.
11. *Ibid.,* 135. Hawkins had been elected to the Senate late in 1790. Merritt B. Pound, *Benjamin Hawkins, Indian Agent* (Athens, Ga., 1951), 64.
12. *Territorial Papers, South,* 18-19, 371; H. M. Wagstaff, ed., *The Papers of John Steele* (Raleigh, N. C., 1924), I, 85-86.
13. *Territorial Papers, South,* 237.
14. *ASP, IA,* I, 245, 247; R. S. Cotterill, "Federal Indian Management in the South, 1789-1825," *Mississippi Valley Historical Review,* XX (Dec., 1935), 333-52. Blount received his soubriquet of "Dirt Captain" because of his "insatiable avidity to acquire Indian lands," according to a report in *The Letters of Benjamin Hawkins, 1796-1806* (Vol. IX, *Collections* of the Georgia Historical Society. Savannah, 1916), 250.
15. *ASP, IA,* I, 247, 436-37.
16. *Territorial Papers, South,* 368.
17. *ASP, IA,* I, 235.
18. *Territorial Papers, South,* 108 n., 226 ff.; Williams, *Tennessee During Revolution,* 61; "Report of Schneider," in Williams, ed., *Early Travels,* 257; Milling , *Red Carolinians,* 319-20.
19. *ASP, IA,* I, 264.
20. An excellent summary of Spanish activities among the Indians in the Old Southwest is found in Arthur P. Whitaker, *The Spanish-American Frontier, 1783-1795* (New York and Boston, 1927). See also Whitaker's *The Mississippi Question, 1795-1803* (New York, 1934); and his "Spain and the Cherokee Indians," *North Carolina Historical Review,* IV (July, 1927), 252-69. Further sources are Jane M. Berry, "The Indian Policy of Spain in the Southwest," *Mississippi Valley Historical Review,* III (1917), 462-77; and Mohr, *Federal Indian Relations,* 141-42.
21. Whitaker, *Spanish-American Frontier,* 37, 167-68, *et passim;* John W. Caughey, ed., *McGillivray of the Creeks* (Norman, Okla., 1938), *passim; ASP, IA,* I, 327.
22. *ASP, IA,* I, 264.
23. *Ibid.,* 265.
24. *Ibid.*
25. *Ibid.,* 276, 328; see also abstract of Leonard Shaw's Report, Sept. 20, 1792, in *Territorial Papers, South,* 177-78.
26. *ASP, IA,* I, 267; *Territorial Papers, South,* 229.
27. *Ibid.,* 177; *ASP, IA,* I, 261-62, 277-78.
28. *ASP, IA,* I, 277-78.
29. *Ibid.,* 279, 288-92, 328.
30. Milling. *Red Carolinians,* 327-28.
31. *Territorial Papers, South,* 148-49, 151; *ASP, IA,* I, 265, 355.
32. *Territorial Papers, South,* 369; Milling, *Red Carolinians,* 328-29. For a list of whites from Mero and Washington Districts in the Tennessee country killed by Cherokees or their allies, see *ASP, IA,* I, 329-31. *Territorial Papers, South* (320-23), contains a summary chart of frontier depredations between 1791 and 1794.
33. *ASP, IA,* I, 433; *Territorial Papers, South,* 234; Milling, *Red Carolinians,* 328-29. John H. DeWitt, ed., "Journal of John Sevier," *Tennessee Historical Magazine,* VI (Oct., 1919, and Jan., 1920), 164.
34. *Territorial Papers, South,* 235-36.
35. *ASP, IA,* I, 438, 465. A complete account of the Overall incident is given in Brown, *Old Frontiers,* 374-75.
36. *ASP, IA,* I, 632 ff.
37. *Ibid.,* 535, 542, 551.

CHAPTER FOUR

1. *ASP, IA,* I, *passim; Territorial Papers, South, passim.*
2. *Territorial Papers, South,* 410, 422. After his selection to the United States Senate from Tennessee in 1796, Blount's national career came crashing down in 1797 when it was learned through the discovery of a damaging letter to James Carey, that Blount and others were plotting a fantastic aggression against Spanish soil. Carey apparently was to align Cherokees and Creeks as allies in the plan. Blount was expelled from the Senate, and while under bond of $1,000 during an impeachment trial, forfeited that bond by flight. See Walter B. Posey, "The Blount Conspiracy," Birmingham-Southern College *Bulletin,* XXI (December, 1928), 11-21. Yet the ex-Senator did not lose face in his home state. Instead, he was elected to the State Senate in 1798. *D. A. B.,* II, 391.
3. From biographical sketch of Hawkins by Stephen B. Weeks, in *Letters of Benjamin Hawkins,* 9; Cotterill, "Federal Indian Management," *M. V. H. R.,* 334-35; Pound, *Benjamin Hawkins, passim.*
4. Pound, *Benjamin Hawkins, passim; Letters of Hawkins, passim.*
5. Pound, *Benjamin Hawkins,* 26, 106-107, 155-56, *et passim.* Hawkins reported, however, that the children in remoter areas seemed alarmed at seeing a white man; he attributed this to the memories which still lingered from frightening invasions during the late eighteenth century, when towns like Keowee and Tugaloo were devastated. *Letters of Hawkins,* 23-24.
6. *Letters of Hawkins,* 123, 159.
7. *Ibid.,* 135.
8. Quoted in Merrit B. Pound, "Benjamin Hawkins: Indian Agent," *Georgia Historical Quarterly,* XIII (Dec., 1929), 396-97.
9. James, *English Institutions,* 32, 35; Harmon, *Sixty Years of Indian Affairs,* 100-101; Edgar B. Wesley, "The Government Factory System Among the Indians, 1795-1822," *Journal of Economic and Business History,* IV (May, 1932), 487-511; Royal B. Way, "The United States Factory System Among the Indians, 1796-1822," *Mississippi Valley Historical Review,* VI (June, 1919), 220-35; *Territorial Papers, South,* 461. See also "Journal of Proceedings of Governor Blount, in *ibid.*
10. *ASP, IA,* I, 583-84; James, *English Institutions,* 36-41; Harmon, *Sixty Years,* 100-101, 105; Wesley, "Government Factory System," *J.E.B.H.,* 490-94.
11. Harmon, *Sixty Years,* 108 ff; James, *English Institutions,* 41; *ASP, IA,* I, 646.
12. F. A. Michaux, *Travels to the West of the Allegheny Mountains, in the States of Ohio, Kentucky, and Tennessea* [sic] (1805), reprinted in Reuben G. Thwaites, ed., *Early Western Travels* (Cleveland, 1904), III, 264; *ASP, IA,* I, 653-54.
13. *ASP, IA,* I, 205; Mohr, *Federal Indian Relations,* 171; Solomon Peck, "History of the Missions of the Baptist General Convention," *History of the American Missions to the Heathen* (Worcester, Mass., 1940), 383.
14. For a description of Cherokees who had been shifted southward by frontier fighting, see *Letters of Hawkins,* 16 ff.
15. Quoted in *House Report of the Committee to Whom Were Recommitted the Petition of Hugh Lawson White and the Report of the Secretary of War Thereon* (n. p., 1797), 8.
16. *Letters of Hawkins,* 16, 21-23.
17. *Ibid.,* 18, 20-21.
18. *Ibid.,* 22-23.
19. President John Adams notified the Cherokees that he had sent "my beloved Mr. Dinsmoor in your nation . . . charged to instruct you in the raising of stock, the cultivation

of land, the arts which procure for the whites so many comforts and conveniences." *ASP, IA,* I, 640-41.

20. *Letters of Hawkins,* 232, 240-41.
21. F. A. Michaux, *Travels to West,* 264-65.
22. Mooney, "Myths," 83; Starkey, *Cherokee Nation,* 19-20; George G. Smith, *The Story of Georgia and the Georgia People, 1732-1860* (Macon, Ga., 1900), 313-14; Milling, *Red Carolinians,* 339.
23. *ASP, IA,* I, 235. In 1792 the Secretary of War wrote the Governor of Georgia: "It is to be deeply regretted, that there are so many whites on the frontier, whose resentments are so keen against all persons bearing the name of Indians, that they have adopted an opinion that it is meritorious to kill them on all occasions. The Indians, again, conceive themselves bound to retaliate every death by an indiscriminate murder." *Ibid.,* 256.
24. Material for these paragraphs on the Ross family is largely based on Rachel C. Eaton, *John Ross and the Cherokee Indians* (Menasha, Wis., 1914), especially Chapter I, "The Youth and Early Training of John Ross." Other sources on John Ross include the sketch by Edward E. Dale in *D.A.B.,* XVI, 178-79; Thomas L. McKenney and James Hall, *The Indian Tribes of North America* (repr. ed., Edinburgh, 1933), III, 293-96; Hodge, *Handbook,* II, 396-97; and Penelope J. Allen, "John Ross' Log Mansion," Chattanooga *Sunday Times* (Magazine Section), Feb. 2, 1936, p. 7, *et seq.*
25. Allen, "Ross Mansion," *C.S.T.,* 7; Eaton, *John Ross,* 2-3; McKenney & Hall, *Indian Tribes,* 293.
26. Eaton, *John Ross,* 5-6; Dale, "John Ross," *D.A.B.,* XVI, 178.
27. *ASP, IA,* I, 443.
28. From manuscript "Journal of the Georgia Commissioners to the Cherokees, January, 1803," in Cherokee Letters Collection, Georgia Department of Archives (GDA), Atlanta.
29. From report of a Cherokee Talk delivered to John McKee, Oct. 1794, in *ASP, IA,* I, 538.
30. Milling, *Red Carolinians,* 339 n.
31. Bartram, "Observations," 20; Roosevelt, *Winning of the West,* I, 80.

CHAPTER FIVE

1. *Dictionary of American Biography,* XII, 508-509. A voluminous record of Meigs' service as Cherokee Indian Agent from 1801 to 1823 is found in the Cherokee Agency Files among the Bureau of Indian Affairs Records, Natural Resources Records Branch, National Archives, Washington, D. C. (cited as BIA, CAF). (Unless otherwise noted, all letters and manuscripts cited in this chapter are from the Cherokee Agency Files). Some of Meigs' correspondence may also be found in *ASP, IA,* I, II; and Cherokee Letters Collection, Georgia Department of Archives (GDA).
2. Meigs to Dearborn, May 18, June 15, 19, 1801; W. Hooker (U. S. Factor at Tellico) to Meigs, June 10, 1801; Penelope J. Allen, "Leaves from the Family Tree—South West Point," Chattanooga *Sunday Times* (Magazine Section), Sept. 30, 1934, p. 12-13; receipt, Sept. 15, 1801, signed by "Wm. L. Lovely, Ass. Agt. for the Cherokees"; and Meigs to Lovely, "Instructions for Assistant Agent, [1801]."
3. Dearborn to Meigs, June 25, 1801; Instructions of the Secretary of War to the Agent for the Cherokee Nation, May 15, 1801, and Journal of Georgia Commissioners to the Cherokees, January, 1803, in Cherokee Letters Collection, GDA.
4. John Boggs to Meigs, Feb. 20, 1807; Meigs to Armistead, Feb. 5, 1808.

5. Meigs to Dearborn, July 30, 1806, in Cherokee Letters Collection, GDA.
6. William Tharp to Meigs, Dec. 14, 1801; and Receipt of Attwood's, Dec. 19, 1801.
7. Meigs to Governor Roane, Jan. 19, 1802.
8. Adelaide L. Fries, ed., *Records of the Moravians in North Carolina* (Raleigh, N. C., 1943), VI, *passim;* B. Harris (of Jackson County, Georgia) to Meigs, Feb. 22, 1808; Dearborn to Meigs, May 7, 1808; Penelope J. Allen, "Leaves from the Family Tree—The Vann Family," Chattanooga *Sunday Times* (Magazine Section), July 26, 1936, p. 7.
9. Meigs to Secretary of War, Jan. 11, 1802.
10. Dearborn to Meigs, July 10, 1801.
11. Benjamin Hawkins to Meigs, Sept. 15, 1801; and Dearborn to Meigs, April 30, 1802.
12. Meigs to Dearborn, Oct. 4, 1801; Journal of Occurrences in the Cherokee Nation (a manuscript record kept by Meigs from 1801 to 1804), Manuscripts Division, Library of Congress.
13. See Chapter VI.
14. Dredful Waters to "Mr. Coneal Megs," Nov. 23, 1801; Big Half Breed to Meigs, Feb. 6, 1807; The Glass to Meigs, May 30, 1807; Nov. 11, 1804; and Feb. 8, 1808.
15. Meigs to Dearborn, May 31, 1804; and Dearborn to Meigs, June 21, 1804.
16. Receipt of Dr. Wm. McNeill, Oct. 27, 1808. See also Receipt of Dr. Thomas J. Vandyke for $23.25, paid by Meigs January 16, 1813, for "attendance on James Vance wounded by one of their people."
17. Richard Brown to Meigs, March 4, 1808. In 1803 a school teacher at Hiwassee wrote Meigs that a man in that village "has a Cancer on his Leg which appears to be dangerous and wishes you to procure Some medicine for that purpose . . ." Jonathan Black to Meigs, Dec. 22, 1803.
18. Meigs to Israel Wheeler (Purveyor of Public Supplies), Nov. 21, 1801.
19. "Memorandum of Articles requested as part of the Cherokee Annuity for the Year 1803," Feb. 3, 1803.
20. William Simmons (War Department Accountant) to Meigs, Feb. 28, 1807; Dearborn to Meigs, March 2, 1807; Levi Shiftall (U. S. Agent at Savannah) to Meigs, July 29, 1807; and Receipt for part of Cherokee Annuity, 1807, dated Aug. 25, 1807.
21. "To the Cherokees . . ." Oct. 10, 1802; Meigs to Secretary of War, Dec. 7, 1802; Meigs to Major MacRea (Commanding the garrison at South West Point), Aug. 15, 1803.
22. See Chapter VI.
23. Copy of Letter of Instructions, Chiefs & Council to Deputation for Washington, Sept. 19, 1817, in Manuscripts of American Board of Commissioners for Foreign Missions, (Houghton Library, Harvard University) 18.3.1, II, item 96.
24. The Yazoo controversy grew out of huge sales made by Georgia in the 1790's to land companies seeking to exploit the state's western lands. Bribery and fraud occurred in the purchases of some sixty million acres. Finally the legislature of Georgia tried to revoke the sales, and angry land-holders carried their claims to the courts. Charles H. Haskins, "The Yazoo Land Companies," *Papers* of the American Historical Association, V (Washington, 1891), 395-437.
25. *Message from the President of the United States, transmitting certain Papers Relating to the Compact between The U. States and the State of Georgia, of 1802, &c.* (18 Cong., 1 sess., Senate Document no. 63, April 2, 1824. Washington, 1824), 6.
26. Dearborn to Meigs, April 23, 1804; Meigs to Dearborn, June 29, 1802.
27. The various Cherokee treaties for this period may be found in Kappler, *Indian Affairs: Laws & Treaties,* II; and *ASP, IA,* I, II. A descriptive list of Cherokee land

grants is contained in Charles C. Royce, "Indian Land Cessions in the United States," *Eighteenth Annual Report of the Bureau of American Ethnology*, 1896-97 (Washington, 1899), pt. 2, 527-997.

28. Kappler, *Indian Affairs: Laws & Treaties*, II, 73-74, 82-84; Royce, "The Cherokee Nation of Indians," 183-94. The government's copy of the 1804 treaty was lost, and it was not until a Cherokee delegation presented a duplicate in 1824 that the document was ratified by the Senate. Royce, "The Cherokee Nation of Indians," 188.
29. Royce, "The Cherokee Nation of Indians," 191. This practice of Doublehead's was a violation of Cherokee tradition; his continued efforts to secure personal gain at the expense of the nation resulted in his assassination by appointed executioners. Mooney, "Myths," 85.
30. Kappler, *Indian Affairs: Laws & Treaties*, II, 90-92; Royce, "The Cherokee Nation of Indians," 191, 193-94. The specific boundary line of this cession caused some difficulty, and a special treaty on Sept. 11, 1807, was necessary before the line could be clearly marked. Furthermore, Meigs had to resort again to the use of secret grants to negotiating chiefs. Royce, "The Cherokee Nation of Indians," 194, 197; Meigs to Dearborn, Sept. 28, 1807.
31. See pp. 71-72.
32. Kappler, *Indian Affairs: Laws & Treaties*, II, 124-26, 133-34.
33. *Ibid.*, 140-44.
34. Royce, "The Cherokee Nation of Indians," 213.
35. *Ibid.*
36. Mary B. Gude, "Georgia and the Cherokees," (unpublished master's thesis, University of Chicago, 1910), 2; interview with W. W. Harnage (grandson of a member of Bowls' party), Indians & Pioneers Papers, Phillips Collection, University of Oklahoma, Vol. 39, p. 102. A few years later Bowls was joined by a group of Cherokees under Tah-chee (or "Dutch"), and the combined body moved to the Red River in Texas. Brown, *Old Frontiers*, 471.
37. Eron Rowland, *Life, Letters and Papers of William Dunbar* (Jackson, Miss., 1930), 210; Annie H. Abel, "The History of Events Resulting in Indian Consolidation West of the Mississippi River," American Historical Association *Report* for 1906 (Washington, 1906) I, 243-49.
38. Meigs to Dearborn, May 31, 1804; Dearborn to Meigs, March 25, 1808; Mooney, "Myths," 102.
39. *Chickamauga Journal*, May 25, 1818, in ABC: 18.3.1, II; Ard Hoyt, and others, to Samuel Worcester, July 25, 1818, in *ibid.*, no. 112.
40. Kappler, *Indian Affairs: Laws & Treaties*, II, 177-81.
41. This and other notices of acceptance may be found in the Cherokee Letters Collection, May-June, 1819, GDA. See also "List of Cherokees entitled to Reservations," in Report of Samuel L. Hamilton (Office of Indian Affairs, War Department) to Governor of Georgia, Nov. 22, 1830, *ibid.*
42. Penelope J. Allen, "Leaves from the Family Tree—The Lowrey Family," Chattanooga *Sunday Times* (Magazine Section), May 10, 1936, p. 6.
43. The Cherokees also used private attorneys in these cases. See Petition of Spencer Jarnagin for Legal Services Rendered Cherokee Nation, 1821-1837, in Allen Collection, in which Attorney Jarnagin asked $4,000 for having attended to "five or six hundred cases" arising from Cherokee reservations under the treaties of 1817 and 1819.
44. John Lowrey to Meigs, Feb. 1, 1813; Mooney, "Myths," 88-90; Cotterill, *Old South*, 120. Meigs himself urged the War Department to employ Cherokees against the hostile Creeks; one result, he suggested, would be a widespread Cherokee interest in the war as participants on the American side. Not only did Meigs believe that many Cherokees were anxious to fight for the United States,

but he thought it was their duty in view of the advantages and opportunities for improvement given them by the white government. Meigs to Dearborn, July 30, and Aug. 6, 1813.

45. Mooney, "Myths," 93-96; John P. Arthur, *Western North Carolina: A History* (Raleigh, 1914), 292-94; Mason Crum, *Chief Junaluska* (n. p., n. d.) [3]. Cherokees fighting in the war against the Creeks received $8.00 per day for that service, and a total of $3,362 worth of clothing, arms, and ammunition. In addition, top-ranking native leaders were given special gifts amounting to $956.25. See Meigs to Secretary of War, Dec. 1813; and Meigs to Robert Brent (Paymaster of the United States), Aug. 20, 1815.
46. Charles Hicks, "Claims Journal for Depredations Suffered During Creek War," manuscript in Allen Collection. For other Creek War Claims filed during and after Cherokee Removal of 1838-1839, see "Cherokee Claims Papers," in *ibid.*, and in BIA Records.
47. Meigs to Evarts, March 15, 1819, in *Panoplist*, XV (1819), 181.
48. *D.A.B.*, XII, 509.

CHAPTER SIX

1. Journal of the Grand Cherokee National Council, Estanaula, Tuesday, 26th of June, 1792, in *ASP, IA*, I, 271-73. Conspicuously absent from this list are the names of Eskaqua (Bloody Fellow) and John Watts. In a covering letter to the journal, Governor Blount stated that Eskaqua had pled illness in the family—but the governor thought it more likely that the absent leader feared the direction of the conference would be away from his views. As for Watts, Blount reported that this Indian was "gone to Pensacola, at the invitation of Mr. Panton, on mercantile business." *Ibid.*, 271.
2. Mooney, "Myths," 71.
3. Gaston L. Litton, "The Principal Chiefs of the Cherokee Nation," *Chronicles of Oklahoma*, XV (Sept., 1937), 258; Brown, *Old Frontiers*, 444. At a treaty conference in Tellico, November, 1794, Blount stated to the Indian delegation that "in Scolacutta [Hanging Maw] I behold the true head of your whole nation." *ASP, IA*, I, 536.
4. Brown, *Old Frontiers*, 444; Royce, "Cherokee Nation of Indians," 187, 192; "Instructions given Cherokee delegation to Washington in 1817," copied in ABC: 18.3.1, II, item 96; Litton, "Principal Chiefs," *C.O.*, 258; Path Killer to Secretary of War, June 30, 1818, copied in Brainerd Brethren to Samuel Worcester, July 25, 1818, in ABC; 18.3.1, II, item 112. After the reduction of Black Fox and two lesser chiefs, the Cherokee Council moved to send a delegation to President Jefferson "to communicate to him that the Cherokees did not wish to exchange any part of their country." *Ibid.*
5. *Laws of the Cherokee Nation* (Tahlequah, C.N., 1852), 3; *Letters of Hawkins*, 134. In 1803 a group of Georgia commissioners visited an "enfluencial Cherokee" named Paris, "who is authorized and required by the Chiefs of the nation to keep a Troop of Horse allways in readiness for the purpose of detecting and bringing to punishment all those of their nation who have been, or may be guilty of Murder, Robery, theift or other outrages. . . ." From manuscript Journal of Three Commissioners from the State of Georgia to the Cherokees, 1803, in Cherokee Letters Collection, GDA.
6. *Laws of the Cherokee Nation*, 3-4.
7. *Ibid.*, 4.
8. *Ibid.*
9. Speech of Thomas Jefferson to Deputation of Chiefs of the Cherokee Upper Towns, Jan. 9, 1809, reprinted in *Cherokee Phoenix*, Feb. 21, 1828.

10. *Laws of the Cherokee Nation,* 4-5. The native term for the legislature was "Tsaligi Tinilawigi." *Preservation and Civilization of the Indians* (19 Cong., 1 sess., House Executive Document no. 102. Washington, 1826), 19.
11. *Laws of the Cherokee Nation,* 5.
12. *Ibid.,* 11-12.
13. *Ibid.,* 15-18. Although the date for this particular measure is not shown in the Cherokee law-book, Starr gives it as November 2, 1820. *Early History of the Cherokees,* 223.
14. *Laws of the Cherokee Nation,* 14-15.
15. "List of Officers in the Cherokee Nation (c. 1822)," in ABC: 18.3.1, II, no. 174-75. By 1826 all officers in the Cherokee Nation were required to take an oath similar to the following: "You do solemnly swear, by the Holy Evangelists of Almighty God, that you as Marshal of .... District, will strictly support and observe the laws of the Cherokee Nation, and to execute the decisions of the courts, and make collections without favor or affection, to any person or persons whatsoever, to the best of your knowledge and abilities; so help you God." *Laws of Cherokee Nation,* 68, 77.
16. The speaker was Elias Boudinot, who had served as Clerk of the Council, and who was later to become the first editor of the *Cherokee Phoenix.* Elias Boudinot, *Address to the Whites* (Philadelphia, 1826), 10-11.
17. [William Chamberlin] "Our Missions Among the Cherokees," manuscript in Cherokee Papers File, Oklahoma Historical Society (OHS), Oklahoma City.
18. See for example portions of the Brainerd Journal, quoted in *Panoplist,* XV (1818-1819), 42-43, 324.
19. *Laws of Cherokee Nation,* 5; "Speech of Cherokee Women to council assembled . . . June 30, 1818," copied in ABC: 18.3.1, II, no. 113.
20. Brainerd Journal, Oct. 30, 1818, in *Panoplist,* XV (1818-1819), 42-43.
21. *Laws of Cherokee Nation,* 28.
22. Manuscript "Record Book of the Supreme Court of the Cherokee Nation, 1823-1835," in Allen Collection. In 1826 Walter S. Adair replaced Richard Walker on the Supreme Court bench for one term. *Ibid., passim.*
23. *Ibid.,* Oct. 9-25, 1823; *et passim.*
24. *Ibid.,* Oct. 16, 1823; Oct. 18, 1824; Oct. 27, and Nov. 3, 1826. The "Record Book of the Supreme Court of the Cherokee Nation" usually listed names of contesting parties and the verdict, with a short statement as to the case.
25. *Laws of Cherokee Nation,* 75-77.
26. *Cherokee Phoenix,* Mar. 6, 1828. Although three were to be elected from each district, only twenty-one Cherokees were members of the Constitutional Convention; ten of these were members of the National Committee. See "Money and Principles," an article by "A Cherokee," in *ibid.,* Feb. 28, 1828.
27. *Cherokee Phoenix,* Feb. 21, 1828.
28. *Ibid.*
29. *Ibid.,* Feb. 28, 1828.
30. *Ibid.* The first justices of the revised Supreme Court were Andrew Ross, John Huss, and Walter S. Adair. Other Cherokees serving during the following seven years were Lewis Ross, George Waters, William Coody, Daniel McCoy, and Arch Fields. "Record Book of the Supreme Court of the Cherokee Nation," Oct. 24, 1828, *et passim.*
31. *Cherokee Phoenix,* Mar. 6, 1828.
32. *Ibid.*
33. Mooney, "Myths," 113-14.
34. *Cherokee Phoenix,* April 24, 1828.
35. *Ibid.,* May 14, 1828.
36. *Ibid.,* May-August, 1828.
37. *Ibid.,* May 6, 1828.
38. *Ibid.,* July 21, 1828.

CHAPTER SEVEN

1. Elias Boudinot, *Address to the Whites,* 9; "Chickamauga Journal, Jan. 26, 1818," in Papers of the American Board of Commissioners for Foreign Missions: 18.3.1, II (see note 26 below).
2. David Brown to Baron de Campaigne, May 1, 1823, in ABC: 18.3.1, III, no. 345.
3. Quoted in John P. Brown, *Old Frontiers,* 467-68.
4. George W. Hinman, *The American Indian and Christian Missions* (New York, 1933), 40.
5. The standard reference for source material on Moravian activity in the South is Adelaide L. Fries, ed., *Records of the Moravians in North Carolina* (7 vols., Raleigh, 1943). A survey of Moravian missions to Cherokees and Creeks, with liberal use of records not found in Fries, is Edmund Schwarze, *History of the Moravian Missions among Southern Indian Tribes of the United States* (Bethlehem, Pa., 1923). For a brief account of Moravian as well as other missions in the Cherokee Nation, with emphasis on the missionaries' involvements in Cherokee political affairs, see Linton M. Collins, "The Activities of the Missionaries among the Cherokees" (unpublished masters thesis, Mercer University, 1922).
6. "Wachovia Memorabilia, 1801," *Records of Moravians,* VI, 2665; Frederic W. Marshall, "An Account of the Rise and Progress of the United Brethren's Settlement in North Carolina, 1794," *ibid.,* 2451, 2455; Schwarze, *Moravian Missions,* 62.
7. Williams, ed., *Early Travels,* 245-46; Schwarze, *Moravian Missions,* 32.
8. Muriel H. Wright, *Springplace Moravian Mission and the Ward Family of the Cherokee Nation* (Guthrie, Okla., 1940), 39; "Bro. Martin Schneider's Report of his Journey, 1783-84," in Williams, ed., *Early Travels,* 245-65.
9. Quoted in Schwarze, *Moravian Missions,* 55; see also "Wachovia Memorabilia, 1800," *Records of Moravians,* VI, 2640, 2664-66. A summary of early Moravian work in the Cherokee country is found in "Brainerd Journal, Nov. 7, 1819," in ABC: 18.3.1, II.
10. *Records of Moravians,* VI, 2665-67; Thomas Smith, *The Origin and History of Missions* (Boston, 1837), I, 110.
11. The Moravians reported that they had been given until January 1, 1804, to establish a school—otherwise they would have to leave. "Salem Board Minutes, 1803," *Records of Moravians,* VI, 2743.
12. *Ibid.,* 2759, 2799-2800; Schwarze, *Moravian Missions,* 80-82.
13. Mrs. Anna Gambold acquired an excellent reputation among the Cherokees, as evidenced by a request sent to the Indian Agent in 1814: "Sr my two Darters Cathy and Sarey has requested me to Beg the faver of you to Rite by the first oppertunity to Mr. Gambold to know if Misses Gambold will take Charge of them to Instruck them for three months they have heard Soe mutch of that old Ladey's Good morrels that they wish to be instruced by hur for a few months.
    2 April 1814 Saml Riley"
    (from BIA, CAF)
14. *Records of Moravians,* VI, 2798-99; VII, 3435.
15. Schwarze, *Moravian Missions,* 124-32.
16. *Records of Moravians,* VII, 3445, 3450, 3465, 3493-94, 3510-11; *Methodist Magazine,* III (April, 1820), 153; Smith, *History of Missions,* I, 107.
17. *Cherokee Phoenix,* Feb. 28, 1828. Gambold's Oothcaloga Mission is still standing a few miles east of Calhoun, Georgia; two hundred yards from the old building is a gravestone with this inscription: "JOHN GAMBOLD, born June 16th 1760, at Shechem, New York, departed this life Nov. 7th, 1827."
18. Samuel C. Williams, "An Account of the Presbyterian Missions to the Cherokees,. 1757-1759," *Tennessee*

Historical Magazine, ser. 2, I (Jan., 1931), 125-38.

19. The Bullen quotation is in Schwarze, *Moravian Missions*, 41; Ernest T. Thompson, *Presbyterian Missions in the Southern United States* (Richmond, 1934), 140-41; Belle M. Brain, *The Redemption of the Red Man: An Account of Presbyterian Missions to the North American Indians of the Present Day* (New York, 1904), 26.
20. E. H. Gillett, *History of the Presbyterian Church in the United States of America* (Philadelphia, 1864), I, 446; II, 203; E. Thompson, *Presbyterian Missions*, 142; Brain, *Redemption of the Red Man*, 26; William B. Morrison, *The Red Man's Trail* (Richmond, 1932), 40. See also V. M. Queener, "Gideon Blackburn," East Tennessee Historical Society's *Publications*, VI (1934), 12-28.
21. "An Account of the Origin and Progress of the Mission to the Cherokee Indians; in a series of letters from the Rev. Gideon Blackburn to the Rev. Dr. Morse," *Panoplist*, III (Boston, June, 1807-May, 1808), 39-40, 84-86.
22. *Ibid.*, 84-86, 322-23; "Wachovia Memorabilia, 1804," *Records of Moravians*, VI, 2758.
23. Armstrong, *Hamilton County*, I, 92; E. Thompson, *Presbyterian Missions*, 142.
24. "Report of 6th Annual Meeting, Sept. 20, 1815," in *First Ten Annual Reports of the American Board of Commissioners for Foreign Missions, with other Documents of the Board* (Boston, 1834), 124.
25. Thomas H. Campbell, *Studies in Cumberland Presbyterian History* (Nashville, 1944), 193; Richard Beard, *Brief Biographical Sketches of some of the Early Ministers of the Cumberland Presbyterian Church* (Nashville, 1867), 92.
26. "7th Annual Report, Sept., 1816," in *First Ten Reports of ABC*, 135-36; William E. Strong, *The Story of the American Board* (Boston, 1910), 3 ff, 35-36. A voluminous collection of letters, journals, reports, and other papers relating to the operations of the American Board of Commissioners for Foreign Missions is housed in the Houghton Library, Harvard University. (Citations to these manuscripts will include code number, as well as volume and — where applicable — item designations.) See also various editions of the published annual reports of the ABCFM; Joseph Tracy, *History of the American Board of Commissioners for Foreign Missions* (Worcester, Mass., 1940); and Robert S. Walker, *Torchlights to the Cherokees: The Brainerd Mission* (New York, 1931).
27. "7th Annual Report [of the ABC]," 134; Tracy, *History of ABCFM*, 62-63.
28. Chickamauga Journal, Mar. 9, 1817, *et passim*, in ABC: 18.3.1, II; "8th Annual Report, Sept. 1817," *First Ten Reports of ABC*, 154-55.
29. Chickamauga Journal, Sept. 28, 1817; Brainerd Journal, July 26, 1818, in ABC:18.3.1, II; *ibid.*, Jan. 24, 1819, in *Panoplist*, XV (1819), 326.
30. "Pecuniary Accounts of the Board, 1819," *First Ten Reports of ABC*, 251; Jedidiah Morse, *A Report to the Secretary of War of the United States, on Indian Affairs, Comprising the Narrative of a Tour* (New Haven, 1822), 293.
31. Brainerd Journal, May 27, June 21, 28, 1819, in ABC:18.3.1, II.
32. ABC Papers, *passim*. When numbers of Cherokees began to emigrate westward after the treaty of 1817, the American Board sent mission families to continue evangelization and education in the Arkansas country. Cephas Washburn and Alfred Finney established the first such mission (in present-day Pope County, Arkansas) in 1820, naming it in honor of Timothy Dwight, then President of Yale University. "10th Annual Report," in *First Ten Reports of ABC*, 245-46; Strong, *American Board*, 39; "Dwight Mission" highway marker, near Russelville, Arkansas.
33. Butrick to Evarts, May 10, 1822, in

ABC:18.3.1, II, no. 172. Besides Chamberlin's teaching duties, other assignments at Brainerd during the early years entrusted farm management and "direction of the mechanical business" to Abijah Conger and his assistants John Vail and John Talmage; supervision of the kitchens, Mrs. Talmage; direction of "the washing," Mrs. Conger; soap-making, Mrs. Hoyt; and ironing, Mrs. Vail. Brainerd Journal, Nov. 15, 1819, in ABC:18.3.1, II.

34. Memoranda Relating to the Cherokee Mission, May 1-2, 1822, in *ibid.*
35. *Ibid.*, May 6-7, 1822.
36. *Ibid.*, May 6-22, 1822.
37. *Ibid.*
38. Rufus Anderson, *Memoir of Catherine Brown, a Christian Indian of the Cherokee Nation* (3rd ed., Boston, 1828), *passim;* Brainerd Journal, in ABC:18.3.1, *passim;* interview with Clover Brown Barrowman (a descendant of Catherine Brown's family), I & P Papers, OHS, Vol. 33, 227-31.
39. John Arch, *Memoir of John Arch* (Boston, 1828), *passim;* ABC Papers, *passim;* "Death of John Arch," *American Missionary Register,* VI (Sept., 1825), 287.
40. Edward C. Starr, *A History of Cornwall, Connecticut* (n.p., 1926), *passim;* Strong, *American Board,* 144-45.
41. Adam Hodgson, *Letters from North America, written during a Tour in the United States and Canada* (London, 1824), II, 295; Starr, *History of Cornwall,* 147; Gabriel, *Elias Boudinot, passim.* See also Mary B. Church, "Elias Boudinot," Town History *Papers* of the Woman's Club, Washington, Connecticut, 1913. (A brief biographical sketch by one of his granddaughters.)
42. Starr, *History of Cornwall,* 147. Although very intelligent, John Ridge was an indifferent scholar at both Spring Place and Brainerd. It is probable that his father's wishes were primarily responsible for his getting into Cornwall. See Brainerd Journal, July 4, 1817; and Brainerd Brethren to Worcester, Sept. 25, 1818, in ABC:18.3.1, II.
43. Starr, *History of Cornwall,* 143-44; Gabriel, *Elias Boudinot, passim.*
44. Starr, *History of Cornwall,* 147; Brainerd Journal, Mar. 4, 9, 1820, in ABC:18.3.1, II; Barrowman interview, I & P Papers.
45. Althea Bass, *Cherokee Messenger* (Norman, Okla., 1936), 15-18.
46. See Chapter X.
47. Bass, *Cherokee Messenger,* 20; ABC Papers, *passim,* especially 18.3.1, V, nos. 225-80; VII, 234; 18.3.2, I, 176-85.
48. James W. Moffitt, "Early Baptist Missionary Work Among the Cherokees," East Tennessee Historical Society's *Publications,* XII (1940), 16; Jesse H. Campbell, *Georgia Baptists, Historical and Biographical* (Macon, Ga., 1874) 96, 138-39; Victor I. Masters, *Baptist Missions in the South* (Atlanta, Ga., 1915).
49. List of Persons Baptized by Evan Jones, 1805, in BIA, CAF; "Salem Diary, 1805," *Records of Moravians,* VI, 2809; *History of the Sarepta Baptist Association of Georgia* (Athens, Ga., 1943), II; J. Campbell, *Georgia Baptists,* 230.
50. Solomon Peck, "History of the Missions of the Baptist General Convention," in *History of American Missions to the Heathen* (Worcester, Mass., 1840), 362, 376-77; Robert Fleming, *Sketch of the Life of Elder Humphrey Posey* (n. p., 1852), *passim;* Moffitt, "Early Baptists," ETHS *Publications,* 16-17; *Christian Herald,* VI (Sept. 16, 1819), 339-40.
51. Dawson visited Brainerd in April, 1820, and discussed Baptist plans. He told them Valley Towns would open "as soon as the corn is ripe." Brainerd Journal, Apr. 27, 1820, in ABC:18.3.1, II. See also Moffitt, "Early Baptists," ETHS *Publications,* 17; and William Gammell, *History of American Baptist Missions in Asia, Africa, Europe, and North America* (Boston, 1849), 323-27.
52. Peck, "Missions of the Baptists," 390; Fleming, *Humphrey Posey, pas-*

sim; Moffitt, "Early Baptists," ETHS *Publications,* 18.

53. Memoranda Relating to the Cherokee Mission, May 6, 1822, in ABC: 18.3.1, II.

54. Peck, "Missions of the Baptists," 390; "Eleventh Annual Report of the Board of Managers of the General Convention of the Baptist Denomination in the United States," *Latter Day Luminary,* n.s., VI (June, 1825), 149-50; *Proceedings* of the Fifth Triennial Meeting [of Baptist General Convention] . . . April, 1826 (Boston, 1826), 34-35.

55. "Eighth Annual Report . . . of General Convention," *Latter Day Luminary,* n. s., III (June, 1822), 168, 172; "Ninth Annual Report . . . of General Convention," *ibid.,* n. s., IV (June, 1823), 185-86. In 1823 Valley Towns reported the following property at the station: "2 school houses, 1 log, 1 frame log, one is two-story; 1 double cabin, 1 single cabin, 1 smoke-house, 2 cribs; 2 Bed-rooms, 1 smoke-house, 1 stable, 2 corncribs, blacksmith's shop, spring-house, 6 cabins; saw-mill, and grist-mill, and cabin; school and kitchen furniture; 3 wagons, ploughs, tools; rails, iron, $28; steel, $7." Several dozen assorted livestock were also listed. "Ninth Annual Report," 184-85.

56. Peck, "Missions of the Baptist," 390; "Ninth Annual Report," *Latter Day Luminary,* n.s., IV (June, 1823), 163.

57. Quoted in Daniel Rogers, "The Beginning and Development of Baptist History Among the Cherokee Indians," "Miscellaneous Letters and Manuscripts Relating to Cherokee History" (a bound, type-script volume), Northeastern State Teachers College Library (Tahlequah, Okla., Mar. 15, 1933), 30.

58. *Report of the Baptist Board of Foreign Missions . . . April 28, 1830* (n. p., 1830), 2; Gammell, *American Baptist Missions,* 326; Moffitt, "Early Baptists," ETHS *Publications,* 25. Milling states that when John Stuart lived among the Cherokees, he was called "Bushy-head" because of his appearance; and his Cherokee descendants assumed that name. Milling, *Red Carolinians,* 339 n.

59. "Eleventh Annual Report . . . of General Convention," *Latter Day Luminary,* n.s., VI (June, 1825), 147; Moffitt, "Early Baptists," ETHS *Publications,* 21-22.

60. Gammell, *American Baptist Missions,* 327.

61. George F. Mellen, "Early Methodists and the Cherokees," *Methodist Review,* LXVI (1917), 477; "On the Necessity and Duty of Evangelizing the Aborigines of America," *Methodist Magazine,* III (Sept., 1820), 321 ff. Bishop McKendree was "considerably concerned" over the fate of the "hitherto too much neglected part of the human race," the Indian. He called on Methodist preachers to be "more actively and extensively engaged than we have been heretofore" in converting the neighboring aborigines. "Copy of an Address to some of the Conference, May, 1821," in McKendree Letters, Methodist Leaders Collection, II, Emory University Library. See also Walter B. Posey, *The Development of Methodism in the Old Southwest, 1783-1824* (Tuscaloosa, Ala., 1933), especially Chapter VI.

62. "Death of Richard Neely," in *Minutes taken at the Several Annual Conferences of the Methodist Episcopal Church, 1829* (New York, 1829), 37; Nathan Bangs, *An Authentic History of the Missions Under the Care of the Missionary Society of the Methodist Episcopal Church* (New York, 1832), 137; Anson West, *A History of Methodism in Alabama* (Nashville, 1893), 384 ff; Posey, *Methodism in Old Southwest,* 85.

63. "Report of the Tennessee Conference, 1823," in *Minutes 1823,* 37; Posey, *Methodism in Old Southwest,* 86-87; West, *Methodism in Alabama,* 385-86.

64. "Report of Tennessee Conference, 1825," in *Minutes, 1825,* 15; West, *Methodism in Alabama,* 388-89.

65. Mellen, "Early Methodists," *M.R.,*

478; West, *Methodism in Alabama,* 389-90.

66. Letter of Richard Neely, Mar. 9, 1826, in *Methodist Magazine,* IX (May, 1826), 193; letter of Nathaniel W. Rhodes, Oct. 23, 1826, in *ibid.,* X (Nov. 1826), 37-38.
67. Emmett Starr, *Early History of Cherokees,* 95; Mellen, "Early Methodists," *M.R.,* 479-80, 486-87. During Bishop McKendree's tour of the Cherokee Nation in 1828 he visited John Ross several times, and preached at his home. It was during the year after these visits that Ross joined the Methodist Church. *Ibid.,* 480.
68. Letter of Bishop Roberts, Jan. 20, 1827, in *Methodist Magazine,* X (Feb., 1827), 129-30; West, *Methodism in Alabama,* 393-94, 399.
69. William McMahon to Corresponding Secretary, Methodist Episcopal Missionary Society, Mar. 24, 1827, in *Methodist Magazine,* X (Apr., 1827), 315-16; "Report of Tennessee Conference, 1827," in *Minutes, 1827,* 21-22.
70. West, *Methodism in Alabama,* 397-98; *Cherokee Phoenix,* 1830, *passim.*
71. Butler to Evarts, Sept. 22, 1830, in ABC:18.3.1, VI, no. 74.
72. The Protestant Episcopal Church seems to have made no effort to Christianize the early nineteenth century Eastern Cherokees. William Cutter, "Missionary Efforts of the Protestant Episcopal Church in the United States," *History of Missions to the Heathen,* 563-94; and interview with Edgar Pennington (Historian of the Episcopal Church), Nov. 9, 1951.
73. *Cherokee Phoenix,* Feb. 21, 1828, *et passim.* For a contrasting re-translated Lord's Prayer as used by Moravians, see Schwarze, *Moravian Missions,* 146.
74. *Cherokee Phoenix,* July 9, 1828.
75. Memoranda Relating to the Cherokee Mission, May 6, 1822, in ABC: 18.3.1, II; Chickamauga Journal, Mar. 31, 1817, in *ibid.*
76. Journal of Daniel S. Butrick, in *ibid.,* III, no. 141; Chamberlin to Evarts, July 8, 1824, in *ibid.,* no. 24; Butrick to Evarts, Aug. 20, 1829, in *ibid.,* V, no. 391.
77. Brainerd Journal, Nov. 7, 1819, in ABC:18.3.1, II; Memoranda May 5, 1822, in *ibid;* Letter of Evan Jones, Oct., 1837, in *Baptist Missionary Magazine,* XVIII (Jan., 1838), 18; *Cherokee Phoenix,* June 4, 1828.
78. *Cherokee Phoenix,* June 4, 1828.
79. West, *Methodism in Alabama,* 398; "Census of Eastern Cherokees," BIA files, 66.
80. "Missions Among the North American Indians," *Quarterly Register* of the American Education Society, III (Boston, 1831), 60; Schwarze, *Moravian Missions,* 168, 184; and Gammell, *American Baptist Missions,* 349.

CHAPTER EIGHT

1. Elias Boudinot, *Address to the Whites,* 6; Mooney, "Myths," 81. "Census of the Eastern Cherokees, 1835," p. 66, in Bureau of Indian Affairs Records, National Archives. In 1828 Cherokee Agent Hugh Montgomery gave the following estimated census data: "Total Eastern Cherokee Area: 7,258,160 acres [approximately 20,000 square miles]; population: 13,568 Cherokees, 147 white men, 73 white women, and 1,277 slaves." Montgomery to Governor (of Georgia) Forsyth, May 19, 1828, in Cherokee Letters Collection, GDA.
2. Brainerd Journal, Dec. 29, 1818, in ABC:18.3.1, II.
3. "A List of Places in the Cherokee Nation," in *ibid.,* item 168; Brainerd Brethren to Jeremiah Evarts, Mar. 8, 1822, in *ibid.,* item 148. Charles R. Hicks reported to the mission family in 1822 that Hightower was the "largest Town" in the nation, and was some "30 miles long." *Ibid.,* item 148.
4. "A List of Places in the Cherokee Nation."

5. *Laws of the Cherokee Nation*, 62.
6. *Ibid.*, 63-66.
7. *Ibid.*, 81.
8. Quoted in the *Indian Record*, Vol. I, No. 6.
9. The career of this newspaper is discussed in detail in Chapter X.
10. *Laws of the Cherokee Nation*, 114. The act was passed Nov. 17, 1828.
11. Brief references to the Council House may be found variously in the Missionary Records (Boston), the *Cherokee Phoenix*, and other sources. The variant shape of the building is noted in Gabriel, *Elias Boudinot*, 112.
12. *Cherokee Phoenix*, Nov. 19, 1828, contains White's advertisement. Other issues of the Indian newspaper contain references to the mission, the post-office, and the various stores and taverns.
13. A number of contemporary observers have testified as to the shifting population of New Echota during and after council sessions. See, for example, various quotations from Samuel Worcester, given in Bass, *Cherokee Messenger;* Gabriel, *Boudinot;* and Starkey, *Cherokee Nation*.
14. From the "Vaill Manuscripts," quoted in Gabriel, *Boudinot*.
15. Quoted in [Church] "Elias Boudinot," 14-18.
16. *Cherokee Advocate*, Jan. 20, 1877 (clipping on file in Litton Mss., Cherokee Files, OHS).
17. See Chapter XI.
18. Drane's map and field notes are preserved in the State Surveyor-General's Records, Department of Archives, Atlanta, Georgia. Drane's notes covering the New Echota area are dated April 13, 1832, under the title "Measurement to find the Area of the 14th District of the Third Section by Stephen Drane Surveyor," p. 23.
19. *Ibid*, p. 61, and map.
20. Descriptions of early nineteenth century Cherokee houses may be found in the Claims Papers, Allen Collection; ABC Papers; and BIA Records.
21. For contrasting descriptions of Cherokee homes of varied social levels, see B. B. Edwards, ed., *Memoir of Elias Cornelius* (Boston, 1833), 76; and William J. Cotter, *My Autobiography* (Nashville, 1917), *passim*.
22. Cyrus Kingsbury, "Journal of Missions to the Cherokees, Jan. 18, 1817," in ABC:18.3.1, II; personal interview with Mrs. Penelope J. Allen, Chattanooga, Tennessee, June, 1951.
23. "Census of the Eastern Cherokees, 1835," 3; Claim of Joseph Vann, Jan. 26, 1842, in Claims Book, Phillips Collection, U.O., no. 25, p. 60. Some controversy has existed over the question of who built the Vann House. The writer believes that it is the house which was inherited by Joseph from his father James Vann in 1809, and was probably built about 1804 when James sought to capitalize on a new road. It is likely that most of the house's beautiful refinements were added by "Rich Joe" during the 1820's.
24. Memoranda No. 1, May 2, 1822, in ABC:18.3.1, II.
25. George W. Featherstonhaugh, *A Canoe Voyage up the Minnay Sotor; With an Account of the Lead and Copper Deposits in Wisconsin, of the Gold Region in the Cherokee Country. . . .* (London, 1847), II, 198-99.
26. Cherokee Claims Papers, in Allen Collection and Phillips Collection. While it is possible that these claims contain exaggerations of losses, it is more likely that they are fairly accurate. Certainly it seems plausible that any people living in houses, being exposed to white advantages through personal contacts, mixed-breed influences, missionary example, and tradesmen's wares, should have obtained some of these items. Furthermore, the Cherokees and their leaders must have known that such claims would receive close scrutiny by government agents. Finally, it must be remembered that the Cherokees had long possessed a reputation for personal honesty and integrity. If exaggerations exist in

these papers, it is far more probable that they lie in the Indian's interpretation of the value of his lost items, and not in their nature.

27. Bundle of sixty-five claims, marked "Etowah District," in Allen Collection.

28. In June, 1824, John Quincy Adams saw a delegation of Cherokees in Washington. He wrote that "the manners and deportment of these men have in no respect differed from those of well-bred country gentlemen. . . . They dress like ourselves, except that Hicks, a young and very handsome man, wore habitually a purfled scarf." Charles F. Adams, ed., *Memoirs of John Quincy Adams* (Philadelphia, 1875), VI, 373. For similar views of Cherokee upper-class dress, see E. S. Abdy, *Journal of a Residence and Tour in the United States of North America, from April, 1833, to October, 1834* (London, 1835), 63-64; "Salem Diary, 1805," in *Records of Moravians,* VI, 2806; and pictures of John Ross, Major Ridge, and others, in McKenney and Hall, *Indian Tribes, passim.*

29. Statement by Charles Rogers, Feb. 1, 1808, in BIA, CAF. On Cherokee dress, see Butrick Journal, in ABC: 18.3.1, III, no. 142; I & P Papers, Phillips Collection and OHS, *passim,* especially Reminiscences of John Falling and Charles W. Lofton. Lofton states that "I have a pair of pants, handmade, from the homewoven jeans, dyed with walnut-hull dye, that belonged to my great-grandfather, back in North Carolina." I & P Papers, OHS, Vol. 33, p. 34.

30. Quoted in Edwards, ed., *Memoir of Cornelius,* 75-77.

31. Cyrus Kingsbury, Journal of Missions to the Cherokees, Jan. 23, 1817, in ABC:18.3.1, II.

32. Brainerd Journal, Sept. 23, 1818, in *ibid.*

33. Boudinot, *Address,* 11; *Laws of the Cherokee Nation,* 53-54, 57.

34. Greene to Butrick, Aug. 29, 1835, in ABC:1.3.1, II, no. 358-59.

35. *Cherokee Phoenix,* May 21, Oct. 15, 1828, *et passim.*

36. *Ibid.,* May 21, 1828.

37. "Wachovia Memorabilia, 1810," in *Records of Moravians,* VII, 3105; "Reminiscences of Rev. Cephas Washburn," copied from *Cherokee Advocate,* May 9, 1874, in Litton Papers, OHS, 372-74.

38. "Nancy Badgers complaint of her Husband — September 14, 1805," in BIA, CAF.

39. From the Vaill Manuscripts, quoted in Gabriel, *Boudinot,* 96.

40. *Ibid.,* 97; George C. Ward, "History of Gilmer County," (unpublished manuscript at GDA), 20; Interview with Margaret Elkin, I & P Papers, Phillips Collection, Vol. 27, p. 348; Letter to the Editor from "Atticus," *Cherokee Phoenix,* Oct. 21, 1829. Numerous references to the use of corn by early nineteenth century Cherokees may be found in the I & P Papers; see especially interviews with Ida May Goodale, Jesse Adair, Jennie Bell, and Margaret Elkins.

41. *ASP, IA,* I, 655; the Liquor Act of 1822 also placed a fine of $25 on "gaming at cards," and doubled the penalty for those gamblers caught within three miles of government buildings during council sessions. *Laws of the Cherokee Nation,* 26-27.

42. The nine signatories were "ALEX. GARVICK, JOHN BEAMER, WA-LA-NE-TUH, SI-KA-WEE, CHAS. MOORE, OLD FIELD, ________ LEE, TAH-NU-WY, TE-NA-QUOO-SAW-SUH." *Cherokee Phoenix,* June 18, 1828.

43. Cotter, *My Autobiography,* 31-32. The sober sentinel idea is also given in Ward, "Gilmer County."

44. *Cherokee Phoenix,* May 28, 1828. For other examples of crimes caused by "drinking frolicks" see *ibid.,* Apr. 24, June 25, 1828; and Jan. 7, 1829. In 1829, Boudinot began a regular column headed "TEMPERANCE," which was usually filled with tract material.

45. Starkey, *Cherokee Nation,* 76; Mooney, *Ball Play,* 107.

46. Stalk Shooting is frequently men-

tioned in the I & P Papers as a sport popular among Cherokees in the Old Country. For interesting examples see the interviews with Adam Bean, Felix Barney, and Nancy Blackbird.

47. Adam Hodgson, *Letters from North America, Written during a Tour in the United States and Canada* (London, 1824), I, 275; *Cherokee Phoenix, passim.* A resolution of the Cherokee Council in 1826 announced that no one could operate billiard tables in the Cherokee country without a $200 annual license from the Treasurer of the Nation, under penalty of a $400 fine. Two years later, another enactment placed an $8 tax on "any show, or shows, such as wax figures, or such as play actors," brought to New Echota during legislative sessions. *Laws of the Cherokee Nation,* 84, 89.

48. "Reminiscences of Robert B. Ross, Sr.," (grandson of Chief John Ross), copied in "Miscellaneous Letters and Manuscripts," Northeastern (Okla.) State Teachers College Library, 114. The Stomp Dance as a carry-over from the East was described by a Western Cherokee as follows: "The full-bloods had their own native religious ceremonies, in the form of stomp-dances. At the . . . stomp ground they would meet at the time of year when green corn was ready for eating and with the barbecuing of meats and the roasting of the green corn, they would gorge themselves for three days, and on the fourth day they would take their mythical medicines which would cause them to become nauseated and they would vomit, thus cleansing their system, and soul of all impurities. They would again start eating and dancing with joy. The women folks would attach to their ankles a number of shells in which small rocks were placed and these rocks would rattle as they danced and sang, while someone beat on the . . . tom-tom." Interview with W. W. Harnage, I & P Papers, Vol. 39, p. 102-109.

49. From copy of "Diary of Richard G. Waterhouse," in Allen Collection. See also Cotter, *My Autobiography,* 31.

50. Gabriel, *Boudinot,* 70. Early nineteenth century Cherokee doctoring is recalled frequently in the I & P Papers, Phillips Collection and OHS. For a vivid description of fever-sweating, see the interview with Margaret Woodall, Phillips Collection, Vol. 27, p. 349-50. A buffalo cupping-horn which was brought from Georgia in the 1830's by her great-grandfather is described by Louise Mills, in *ibid,* OHS, Vol. 36, p. 382.

51. In the BIA Records there is this receipt: "Received of Return J. Meigs One hundred & fifty dollars it being the amount of a Note for that Sum for Services performed for the Cherokee Nation in the year 1806 The Cherokees then having the Small Pox among them & signed by the Cherokee Chiefs.

Highwassee 27th October — 1808 —
Dr Wm McNeill"

52. Moody Hall to Jeremiah Evarts, June 29, 1824, in ABC:18.3.1, III.

53. Chamberlin Journal, July 13, 1823, in *ibid.*

CHAPTER NINE

1. Return J. Meigs to Henry Dearborn, July 13, 1801, in BIA, CAF.
2. *Cherokee Phoenix,* May 14, June 11, 1828.
3. *Ibid.,* Oct. 28, Mar. 13, 1828.
4. "Census of the Eastern Cherokees, 1835," in BIA Records.
5. Manuscript Claim of Sawnee Vann, March 1, 1842, in Allen Collection.
6. "Census of Eastern Cherokees," 49.
7. *Cherokee Phoenix,* June 11, 1828; Brainerd Journal, Apr. 22, 1820, in ABC:18.3.1, II.
8. *Cherokee Phoenix,* Aug. 27, 1831.

9. *Ibid.,* June 11, 1828; "Census of Eastern Cherokees," 66.
10. Chickamauga Journal, Apr. 23, 1818, in ABC:18.3.1, II. Several months later it was noted by the American Board men that "The Cherokees in general, even the looser part of them, are very willing their slaves should receive religious instruction; for they say, it makes them better." Quoted in *Panoplist,* XV (1818-1819), 324.
11. Journal of Butrick, Aug. 1818, in ABC:18.3.1, III; Brainerd Brethren to Worcester, Sept. 25, 1818, in *ibid.,* II; and ABC Papers, *passim.*
12. Black Fox to Evan Austill, Sept. 12, 1808, in BIA, CAF.
13. Chickamauga Journal, June 7, 1818, in ABC:18.3.1, II. In August, 1818, a full-blood Cherokee youth applying for admission to Chickamauga Mission was found "able to spell correctly in words of 4 & 5 letters. He had been taught solely by black people who had received their instruction in our sunday-school." *Ibid.,* Aug. 17, 1818.
14. Starkey, *Cherokee Nation,* 18-19.
15. *Laws of the Cherokee Nation,* 8-9, 24-25.
16. *Ibid.,* 37, 39, 107; Article III, Cherokee Constitution, *Cherokee Phoenix,* Feb. 21, 1828.
17. "Croppers for Jno Boggs a Cherokee . . . ," in BIA, CAF; *Laws of Cherokee Nation,* 10-11.
18. Meigs to Secretary of War, Nov. 30, 1801, in BIA, CAF.
19. Lovely to Meigs, July 25, 1802, in *ibid.,* 1802.
20. *Laws of the Cherokee Nation,* 6.
21. *Ibid.,* 60-61, 90.
22. John M. Lea, "Indian Treaties of Tennessee," *American Historical Magazine,* VI (Oct., 1901), 375; Brainerd Journal, July 26, 1819, in ABC:18.3.1, II; *Cherokee Phoenix,* June 11, 1828.
23. Doublehead to Meigs, Nov. 20, 1802, in BIA, CAF.
24. *Laws of the Cherokee Nation,* 6-7.
25. *ASP, IA,* I, 657; Meigs to Governor (of Georgia) John Milledge, Nov. 17, 1803, in Cherokee Letters Collection, GDA.
26. Mooney, "Myths," 87; John H. Goff, "Retracing the Old Federal Road," *Emory University Quarterly,* VI (Oct., 1950), *passim.*
27. *Laws of Cherokee Nation,* 25, 35-36.
28. *Ibid.,* 94, 96, 105-106, 108; Hugh Montgomery to Governor (of Georgia) Troup, Dec. 18, 1826, in Cherokee Letters Collection, GDA.
29. Personal interview with John H. Goff, Emory University, July, 1949; Report of Post Office Department for Year ending Mar. 31, 1830, in *American State Papers: Class VII, Post Office Department* (Washington, 1834), 265-96.
30. Bass, *Cherokee Messenger,* 122; *Cherokee Phoenix,* Apr. 28, 1828.
31. *Cherokee Phoenix,* June 25, 1828; Sept. 2, 1829; May 15, 1830; and Jan. 3, 1831.
32. *Ibid.,* Aug. 27, 1828, and the following six issues.
33. *Ibid.,* Feb. 21, 28, 1828.
34. *Ibid.,* July 21, 1828. By Cherokee law, the Treasurer could lend up to $500 from the nation's surplus to any Indian borrower who could give bond and "two good and sufficient securities, citizens of the nation." *Laws of Cherokee Nation,* 50-51.
35. *Cherokee Phoenix,* Nov. 12, Dec. 3, 1829.
36. William Overton to Meigs, Feb. 12, 1803, in BIA, CAF.
37. "Wachovia Memorabilia, 1804"; "Wachovia Memorabilia, 1805"; "Salem Diary, 1809," in *Records of Moravians,* VI, 2759, 2799; VII, 3704; "Will of James Vann, 7th May, 1808," copy in Cherokee Letters Collection, GDA. One of Vann's drunken habits was to collect a pseudo-Light Horse Guard and gallop through the countryside on terrorizing expeditions. For a description of the affray which led to Vann's death, see Buckner Harris to Governor (of Georgia) Irwin, May 14, 1808, in Cherokee Letters Collection, GDA.
38. The rulings of the Cherokee Coun-

cil and the Jackson County Inferior Court, together with the contested will of James Vann, may be found in the files of the Ordinary of Jackson County, Georgia. Copies are available in the Cherokee Letters Collection, GDA.

39. *Laws of the Cherokee Nation,* 3.

CHAPTER TEN

1. At a Philadelphia conference between five Cherokees and the United States Government in January, 1792, Bloody Fellow held up a string of white wampum throughout the opening session. He told the Secretary of War: "I wish you to be made acquainted with the use and value of these beads, which, among the Cherokees, answer the same purposes as letters with you, and are held in highest estimation." *ASP, IA,* I, 203.
2. In 1765 three Cherokees in London told the Board of Trade that "they wished proper persons to teach their youth religion, and to read and write." Ella Lonn, *The Colonial Agents of the Southern Colonies* (Chapel Hill, 1945), 184.
3. *The Letters of James Habersham, 1756-1775* (vol. VI, *Collections* of the Georgia Historical Society. Savannah, 1904), 149; Eula E. Fullerton, "Some Social Institutions of the Cherokees, 1820-1906," (unpublished master's thesis, University of Oklahoma, 1931), 37; George Helm to Return J. Meigs, July 23, 1806, in BIA, CAF; Letter of Instructions to Cherokee Delegation, Sept. 19, 1817, copied in ABC:18.3.1, II, no. 96.
4. Brainerd Journal, July 20, 1819, in *ibid.* (unnumbered)
5. *Ibid.,* Mar. 4, 1820.
6. *Cherokee Phoenix,* Dec. 3, 1828; Jan. 21, 1829.
7. Standard sources on the life and work of Sequoyah are Grant Foreman, *Sequoyah* (Norman, Okla., 1938); and George E. Foster, *Se-Quo-Yah, the American Cadmus and Modern Moses* (Philadelphia, 1885). See also Samuel C. Williams, "Nathaniel Gist, Father of Sequoyah," East Tennessee Historical Society's *Publications,* V (1933), 39-54; and Albert V. Goodpasture, "The Paternity of Sequoyah, the Inventor of the Cherokee Alphabet," *Chronicles of Oklahoma,* I (1935), 121-25. A first-hand account of Sequoyah is John Howard Payne, "Story of Sequoyah," typescript copy in Allen Collection, from the Payne Manuscripts, Ayer Collection, Newberry Library, Chicago.
8. Foreman, *Sequoyah, passim;* Foster, *Se-quo-yah, passim;* Payne, "Story of Sequoyah," *passim.* For the characters in his syllabary, Sequoyah used whatever came to his mind at the moment he isolated a syllable. Much of it came from the Roman alphabet, the letters of which were reversed, up-ended, or slightly altered. (See *Cherokee Phoenix.*) A sample was reported to Washington in 1825. See Thomas L. McKenney to Secretary of War, Dec. 13, 1825, in *ASP, IA,* II, 653.
9. Foreman, *Sequoyah,* 11. It should be noted in passing, however, that the Cherokees had only to learn the symbols, since they already spoke the language.
10. Boudinot, *Address,* 12; Mooney, "Myths," 110.
11. Ard Hoyt to Evarts, Aug. 7-11, 1823, in ABC:18.3.1, III, no. 104; Moody Hall to Evarts, July 28, 1824, in *ibid.,* no. 228; *Laws of Cherokee Nation,* 47, 94.
12. ABC Papers, *passim;* see also Bass, *Cherokee Messenger;* and Gabriel, *Boudinot.*
13. *Laws of Cherokee Nation,* 84-85.
14. *Ibid.,* 81; Bass, *Cherokee Messenger,* 78-86; Mooney, "Myths," 111; George E. Foster, "Journalism Among the Cherokee Indians," *Magazine of American History,* XVIII (July, 1887), 66. The vicissitudes experienced by the staff in preparing for the first issue of the *Cherokee Phoe-*

nix were interestingly recorded by John F. Wheeler. This account is available in James C. Pilling, *Bibliography of the Iroquoian Languages* (Washington, 1888), 41-42.

15. *Cherokee Phoenix,* Feb. 21, 1828.
16. *Ibid.* Subscription rates were "$2.50 if paid in advance, $3 in six months, or $3.50 to be paid within the year." A fifty-cent reduction on the rates was available for "subscribers who can read only the Cherokee language." Subscription agents were to receive one free paper for every six sold. Advertising rates were "seventy-five cents per square for the first insertion, and 37½¢ for each continuance; larger ones in proportion." *Ibid.*
17. *Ibid.,* Feb. 21, 28, Apr. 24, May 7, 1828. In the first issue the translations were printed in parallel columns, but owing to the syllabic nature of the Sequoyan language, this method left large gaps in the column of Cherokee type. In the second issue Editor Boudinot announced that in the future translations would appear one under the other. *Ibid.,* Feb. 28, 1828.
18. *Ibid.,* June 4, 1828.
19. *Ibid.,* Feb. 21, 1828.
20. *Ibid.,* May 14, 1828.
21. *Ibid.,* Feb. 28, 1828.
22. "CHEROKEE ALPHABET. Neatly printed and for sale at this office." From May 14, 1828, on, this advertisement appeared intermittently in the *Cherokee Phoenix.*
23. *Ibid.,* Feb. 28, 1828; Worcester's interest in the Cherokee newspaper, and his frequent signed insertions, brought charges from enemies of the Cherokees that Worcester was the actual editor of the *Cherokee Phoenix,* and that Boudinot was a mere figurehead. Boudinot denied the accusation from time to time, as did Worcester. See, for example, *Cherokee Phoenix,* Nov. 12, 1828, in which both men answer such a charge by the *Holston* (Tennessee) *Messenger.*
24. On May 21, 1828, in a short message addressed to "PATRONS," Boudinot announced his inability to supply back issues.
25. *Cherokee Phoenix,* Feb. 21, 1828.
26. *Ibid.,* Apr. 10, 1828.
27. [William Chamberlin] "History of the Presbyterian Church in the Cherokee Nation." Undated manuscript in Cherokee Papers Collection, OHS.
28. *Cherokee Phoenix,* Feb. 21, 28, May 21, June 4, July 9, 1828; Sept. 10, 1830.
29. *Ibid.,* Apr. 10, 1828.
30. *Ibid.,* Apr. 3, 1828.
31. *Ibid.,* Mar. 6, Apr. 3, 1828.
32. *Ibid.,* Apr. 17, 1828.
33. See, for example, *ibid.,* Apr. 24, 28, May 21, 28, June 25, July 9, Sept. 17, 1828.
34. *Ibid.,* Aug. 9, 1828. Boudinot sometimes used a subtle approach in "dunning" subscribers whose accounts were in arrears. In one issue a small note at the bottom of a page stated: "The printer of an eastern paper says that many of his patrons would make good wheel horses, they *hold back* so well." *Ibid.,* Dec. 3, 1829.
35. *Ibid.,* Mar. 3, 1830.
36. *Ibid.,* Mar. 3, 10, 31, 1830.
37. *Ibid.,* Apr. 24, 1828. On another occasion, personnel trouble hampered proper publication: "Owing to the indisposition of one of our hands, we present to our readers this week, only half a sheet. . . . (*Half a loaf is better than none!* — Pr.)." *Ibid.,* Sept. 2, 1829.
38. *Ibid.,* Feb. 21, 1828.
39. *Ibid.,* Apr. 17, 1828.
40. *Ibid.,* Feb. 11, 1829. For the sake of brevity, the short title *Cherokee Phoenix* will be used as before.
41. See, for example, an editorial refuting "persistent claims of the Georgia prints" that Cherokees are "making extensive preparations to remove" (*Cherokee Phoenix,* July 25, 1829); letter from "a gentleman in Pennsylvania," stating that that northern state viewed with "decided disapprobation" the government's conduct in the Indian situation (*ibid.,* Aug. 19, 1829); Samuel Worcester's

letter to the editor of the Charleston *Observer* in which he hotly denied statements that the majority of the Cherokees were deteriorating as a people (*ibid.*, Oct. 28, 1829); and an extract from the New York *Journal of Commerce* praising the Cherokees for their progress in political science (*ibid.*, Dec. 3, 1829).

42. *Ibid.*, Dec. 3, 1829. Lowrey's proclamation was first printed in Cherokee on Nov. 11, 1829. ***Ibid.***
43. *Ibid.*, Aug. 11, 1832.
44. *Ibid.*
45. *Ibid.*
46. In the issues of August 25, and September 1, 1832, no editor was listed in the masthead; judging by the tenor of editorial matter, however, Elias Boudinot was apparently doing the work until his successor could take over.
47. For example, only two issues appeared between December 1, 1832, and January 10, 1833; only three more during the next three months; and one in April, two in May, none in June, and two in July, 1833.
48. *Cherokee Phoenix*, Sept. 22, 1832.
49. *Ibid.*, Aug. 24, 1833.
50. *Ibid.*, May 31, 1834. Attempts to revive the *Cherokee Phoenix* came to naught in 1835 when the Georgia Guard confiscated much of the press and equipment. Starkey, *Cherokee Nation*, 331.

CHAPTER ELEVEN

1. *Cherokee Phoenix*, Jan. 19, 1833.
2. For the removal of the Creek Indians from Georgia, see Ulrich B. Phillips, *Georgia and State Rights* (Washington, 1902), 38-65; Grant Foreman, *Indian Removal* (Norman, Okla., 1932), Book II, 107-76; and James Z. Rabun, "Georgia and the Creek Indians" (unpublished master's thesis, University of North Carolina, 1937).
3. The bibliography on the Cherokee Removal to the western country is voluminous. Excellent general accounts are available in Foreman, *Indian Removal;* Abel, "Indian Consolidation"; and Phillips, *Georgia and State Rights.* Two works which seek to justify Georgia's stand on Cherokee removal are George R. Gilmer, *Sketches of Some of the First Settlers of Georgia, of the Cherokees, and of the Author* (New York, 1855); and Wilson Lumpkin, *Removal of the Cherokee Indians from Georgia* (New York, 1908). A number of works have been very sympathetic to the Cherokee cause; among them are Starkey, *Cherokee Nation;* Sass, *Hear Me, My Chiefs!;* and Helen Hunt Jackson, *A Century of Dishonor* (Boston, 1912).
4. William C. Dawson, ed., *A Compilation of the Laws of the State of Georgia, Passed by the General Assembly since the year 1819 to the year 1829, inclusive* (Milledgeville, Ga., 1831), 198.
5. Fletcher M. Green, "Georgia's Forgotten Industry: Gold Mining," *Georgia Historical Quarterly*, XIX (June and Sept., 1935), 99-102. For eye-witness accounts of the disorder in the gold regions during 1830, see Cherokee Letters Collection, GDA, especially letters to Governor Gilmer from Allen G. Fambrough (July 12), A. R. T. Hunter (July 17), and Y. P. King (Sept. 18).
6. *Laws of Cherokee Nation*, 50; Dawson, ed., *Compilation of Laws of Georgia*, 198-99.
7. Foreman, *Indian Removal*, 230; Phillips, *Georgia and State Rights*, 73.
8. Jackson to Major William B. Lewis, Aug. 25, 1830, in John S. Bassett, ed., *Correspondence of Andrew Jackson* (Washington, 1926-1935), IV, 177.
9. Phillips, *Georgia and State Rights*, 73; Oliver H. Prince, ed., *A Digest of the Laws of Georgia . . . Previous to . . . December, 1837* (Athens, Ga., 1837), 279-80.
10. Richard Peters, ed., *The Public Statutes* at Large of the United States (Boston, 1854), IV, 411; "Present State of the Southwestern Tribes,"

Quarterly Register of the American Education Society, III (Aug., 1830), 61. Many of the speeches and writings in favor of the Indians during the consideration of the Removal Act were published in the *Cherokee Phoenix,* notably a long series of polemics signed "William Penn" which were reprinted by many papers.

11. Phillips, *Georgia and State Rights,* 74-75. Late in December, 1829, a group of missionaries from American Board, Moravian, and Baptist missions met at New Echota; their determination and agreement to uphold Cherokee rights was announced in a *Cherokee Phoenix* "EXTRA!" Jan. 1, 1830.
12. Phillips, *Georgia and State Rights,* 75-77; *Niles' Weekly Register,* XXXIX (1830-1831), 338-39; 353.
13. *Cherokee Nation vs. Georgia,* in Richard Peters, ed., *Reports of the Decisions in the Supreme Court of the United States* (Washington, 1857), V, 1.
14. Foreman, *Indian Removal,* 236.
15. Phillips, *Georgia and State Rights,* 79.
16. *Ibid.,* 79-80; ABC Manuscripts, *passim.*
17. *Cherokee Phoenix,* July 2, 9, 1831.
18. *Ibid.,* July 16, 1831.
19. *Ibid.,* Aug. 12, 1831.
20. *Ibid.*
21. *Ibid.*
22. *Ibid.,* Aug. 19, 1831.
23. Letters and Journals of Samuel A. Worcester, ABC Manuscripts, *passim.*
24. *Worcester vs. Georgia,* Peters, ed., *Reports of Supreme Court,* VI, 515.
25. Elias Boudinot to Stand Watie, Mar. 7, 1832, in Edward E. Dale and Gaston Litton, eds., *Cherokee Cavaliers: Forty Years of Cherokee History as told in the Correspondence of the Ridge-Watie-Boudinot Family* (Norman, Okla., 1939), 4-6.
26. Phillips, *Georgia and State Rights,* 82; Basset, ed., *Correspondence of Jackson,* IV, 415, 451.
27. *Acts of the General Assembly of the State of Georgia . . . Passed in November and December, 1831* (Milledgeville, Ga., 1832), 74-76.
28. Smith, *Story of Georgia,* 416, 422. The act providing for the lottery-disposal of Cherokee lands was passed December 21, 1830. *Acts of Georgia, 1830,* 127-43.
29. Excellent contemporary eye-witness accounts of this troublous era are in *Cherokee Phoenix* and ABC Manuscripts, *passim.*
30. David Greene to Elizur Butler, Aug. 17, 1833, and other letters in ABC: 1.3.1, I.
31. Chamberlin to Greene, Jan. 29, 1834, in *ibid.,* 18.3.1, VII; and Greene to Worcester,) Jan. 7, 1834, in *ibid.,* 1.3.1, I.
32. Reproduced in interview with Herbert Worcester Hicks, (grandson of Samuel A. Worcester), I & P Papers, Phillips Collection, Vol. 42, p. 143-44.
33. John Ridge to Major Ridge, and others, Mar. 10, 1835, in Dale and Litton, eds., *Cherokee Cavaliers,* 12-13.
34. Eaton, *John Ross,* 77 ff; Royce, "Cherokee Nation of Indians," 278-79.
35. Eaton, *John Ross,* 83 ff; Royce, "Cherokee Nation of Indians," 280. Under threat of Georgia laws the Cherokee government moved the site of its capital successively to Chattooga, in Alabama, and to Red Clay. Eaton, *John Ross,* 72.
36. Royce, "Cherokee Nation of Indians," 280-81.
37. Kappler, *Indian Affairs: Laws & Treaties,* II, 439-49.
38. W. M. Thompson to Elias Boudinot, Nov. 5, 1838, in Dale and Litton, eds., *Cherokee Cavaliers,* 14-16; Foreman, *Indian Removal,* 286 ff; Eaton, *John Ross,* 102 ff. In 1839 the two Ridges and Boudinot were assassinated for their part in the Treaty of New Echota.
39. Royce, "Cherokee Nation of Indians," 283-93; Foreman, *Indian Removal,* 299-300.
40. For a graphic description of the various Cherokee emigrations during the 1830's, see Foreman, *Indian Removal, passim.*

BIBLIOGRAPHICAL NOTE

THIS DISCUSSION is limited to the more important sources in Cherokee history. No attempt is made to list every item found in the footnotes.

MANUSCRIPT COLLECTIONS

The two most important manuscript collections used in this study are the Cherokee Agency Files and the Papers of the American Board of Commissioners for Foreign Missions. The Cherokee Agency Files are part of the Bureau of Indian Affairs Records Unit, Natural Resources Records Branch, National Archives. These valuable records cover the entire period of Return Jonathan Meigs' service as Indian Agent (from 1801 to 1823), and include "Letters Received," copies of "Letters Sent," and numerous miscellaneous documents such as yearly summary journals, financial statements, proclamations, notes, and personal observations of the Agent. Many of the "Letters Received" are from Cherokees, including communications from the Indian councils and from individuals. Indian Agent Return J. Meigs maintained an active interest in Cherokee welfare and progress, and his correspondence on that subject with Indians, missionaries, teachers, government officials, and others constitutes a valuable source for study of Cherokee political, social, economic, and religious development. Other documents in the Bureau of Indian Affairs Records used in this research include the manuscript "Census of the Eastern Cherokees, 1835" and "Miscellaneous Claims, Cherokee."

In 1817 the American Board of Commissioners for Foreign Missions began missionary operations in the Eastern Cherokee country and continued its work in that area until 1838. During that period the American Board's headquarters in Boston maintained an extensive correspondence with the scores of mission workers in the Cherokee Nation, some of whom included native Cherokee preachers. These letters are preserved in the archives of the American Board, now housed in the Houghton Library, Harvard University. Of particular value to this study were "Documents Pertaining to Indian Missions," "Letters to Missionaries to the Indians," and "Letters Received, Domestic."

The collection of materials on Cherokee history in the personal possession of Mrs. Penelope J. Allen, of Chattanooga, Tennessee, contains many valuable items. Chief among these are the "Claims Papers" and the "Record Book of the Supreme Court of the Cherokee Nation, 1823-1835," which Mrs. Allen obtained from Robert Ross, a grandson of John Ross.

Two collections in Oklahoma contain important material on Eastern Cherokee history, although the major emphasis of each is on Cherokee developments after 1838. Among the documents in the Archives Division of the Oklahoma Historical Society, in Oklahoma City, are several volumes of typewritten transcripts from the Public Record Office, London, pertaining to English relations with Cherokees in the eighteenth century; a "Cherokee File" of valuable miscellany; and "Cherokee Papers, 1815-1874," a set of typescript volumes containing copies of items in Cherokee history from a variety of sources. Of greatest importance to the social historian, however, are the "Indians and Pioneers Papers," a huge collection of interviews with some 25,000 aged inhabitants of Oklahoma, conducted as a WPA project under the supervision of Grant Foreman. The persons interviewed recalled experiences and customs of their parents and grandparents, many of whom were Eastern Cherokees. One set of the "Indians and Pioneers Papers" is in the Oklahoma Historical Society and another in the Frank Phillips Collection of Southwestern History in the Library of the University of Oklahoma. The Phillips Collection also contains a group of papers of noted Cherokee leaders, as well as a large assortment of scarce printed items on Indian history.

Of especial interest at the Department of Archives of the State of Georgia, in Atlanta, is a valuable collection of incoming and outgoing (copies) correspondence between Georgians and inhabitants of the Cherokee country.

Printed Diaries, Journals, Travel Accounts, and Correspondence

The printed records of white visitors and residents in the Cherokee country furnished the bulk of eighteenth century social history materials used in this study. By far the most important single collection of such accounts is Samuel C. Williams, ed., *Early Travels in the Tennessee Country, 1540-1800* (Johnson City, Tennessee: The Watauga Press, 1928), which includes the records of explorers, traders, soldiers, government agents, captives, scientists, and missionaries. Three white men of the mid-eighteenth century left valuable records of Cherokee history and institutions. The first of these was the trader James Adair, whose *History of the American Indians, Particularly those Nations Adjoining to the Mississippi, East & West Florida, Georgia, South and North Carolina, and Virginia* (London: Edward and Charles Dilly, 1775), is based on forty years of residence among Southern Indians. Adair's account of the "Cheerakes," while rich in social lore, is unfortunately colored by his theory that these Indians were descendants of the Ten Lost Tribes of Israel. A more balanced description of life in the Cherokee country is Henry Timberlake, *The Memoirs of Lieut. Henry Timberlake* (London: The Author, 1765). Timberlake took a delegation of Cherokees to London in 1761. The scientist-naturalist William Bartram has left interesting accounts of his visits to the Cherokee country in the mid-1770's, in his *The Travels of William Bartram* (Mark Van Doren, ed., New York: Macy-Masius, 1928), and "Observations on the Creek and Cherokee Indians, 1789," *Transactions* of the American Ethnological Society, III (New York, 1853), Part I, 1-81. The United States Indian Agent Benjamin Hawkins visited the Cherokees late in the eighteenth century. His penetrating observations on Cherokee progress in civilized pursuits are available in *Letters of Benjamin Hawkins* (Volume IX, *Collections* of the Georgia Historical Society. Savannah, Georgia: The Morning News, 1916). The only printed collection of letters by Cherokee Indians available for this research is Edward E. Dale and Gaston Litton, *Cherokee Cavaliers: Forty Years of Cherokee History as told in the Correspondence of the Ridge-Watie-Boudinot Family* (Norman, Oklahoma: University of Oklahoma Press, 1939). A smaller item of greater significance for this particular study is Elias Boudinot, *An Address to the Whites* (Philadelphia: W. F. Geddes, 1826), in which a well-educated Cherokee summarizes his nation's progress along the white man's pattern.

Printed Memoir and Autobiographical Material

A few items in this category were especially helpful sources for social history. *Memoir of Elias Cornelius* (B. B. Edwards, ed. Boston: Perkins & Marvin, 1833), makes liberal use of letters from an observant representative of the American Board (Cornelius) during a visit to the Cherokee Nation in 1817. The letters and diaries of two prominent Christian Indians are the bases of *Memoir of John Arch* (Boston: Massachusetts Sabbath School Union, 1828), and *Memoir of Catherine Brown* (Rufus Anderson, ed., 3rd ed., Boston: Crocker & Brewster, 1828). Among the first Georgians to enter the Cherokee country during the hectic 1830's was William J. Cotter, whose *My Autobiography* (Nashville, Tennessee: Publishing House of the Methodist Episcopal Church, South, 1917) includes reminiscences of youthful impressions of the native life and culture. Cotter's work in part attempts to justify Georgia's Indian policy, and reflects a strong bias against all Cherokee Indians except those individuals in the nation who favored removal.

Government Documents

Certain publications of the United States government are rich in source materials for Cherokee history. Of especial help are two works which reprint the correspondence and other papers of government officials whose duties included supervision of the Cherokee Indians. Among the numerous documents printed in *American State Papers: Class II, Indian Affairs* (2 volumes. Documents, Legislative and Executive, of the Congress of the United States, December 4, 1815-March 3, 1827. Washington: Gales & Seaton, 1834), are many letters and "talks" from Cherokee councils and chiefs, treaties and treaty-discussions, and descriptive comments and reports from various officials and visitors. Clarence E. Carter, ed., *The Territory South of the River Ohio, 1790-1796* (Volume IV, *The Territorial Papers of the United States*. Washington: United States Government Printing Office, 1936), is especially valuable for Cherokee history during the limited period during which the Cherokees came under territorial administration. The most useful collection of Indian treaties is Charles J. Kappler, *Indian Treaties* (Volume II, *Indian Affairs: Laws and Treaties*. 58 Cong., 2 sess., Senate Document no. 319. Washington: United States Government Printing Office, 1904).

Laws, rulings, proclamations, and decisions of the Cherokee national government during the era from 1808 to 1830 are available in English in *Laws of the Cherokee Nation* (Tahlequah, Cherokee Nation: Cherokee Advocate Office, 1852). It is difficult to overestimate the value of this work as a source in Cherokee social history. The council proceedings printed therein offer definite evidence of the Cherokee progress toward the white man's pattern of existence.

The writings of several anthropologists and ethnologists have thrown considerable light upon the history and culture of the Cherokee Indians. The pioneer in this field was the indefatigable James Mooney, whose "Myths of the Cherokee," *Nineteenth Annual Report of the Bureau of American Ethnology, 1897-98* (Washington: Government Printing Office, 1900), Part I, 11-586, is based upon extensive research as well as several years' residence among the Cherokees of Qualla Reservation in North Carolina. Mooney's very readable collection of myths and legends is especially valuable, as is his glossary of Cherokee terms. Charles C. Royce has contributed two important works: "The Cherokee Nation of Indians: A Narrative of their Official Relations with the Colonial and Federal Governments," *Fifth Annual Report, Bureau of Ethnology, 1883-84* (Washington: Government Printing Office, 1887), 121-378; and "Indian Land Cessions in the United States," *Eighteenth Annual Report of the Bureau of American Ethnology, 1896-97* (Washington: Government Printing Office, 1899), Part II, 527-997. These studies offer convenient summaries of treaties and the events which contributed to their writing and promulgation. Two recent works by eminent ethnologists are William H. Gilbert, *The Eastern Cherokees (Anthropological Papers*

No. 23, reprinted from Bureau of American Ethnology *Bulletin 133*, 169-413. Washington: Government Printing Office, 1943); and John R. Swanton, *The Indians of the Southeastern United States* (Bureau of American Ethnology *Bulletin 137*. Washington: Government Printing Office, 1946). A useful work of encyclopedic nature is Frederick W. Hodge, *Handbook of American Indians North of Mexico* (Bureau of American Ethnology *Bulletin 30*. 2 parts. Washington: Government Printing Office, 1905).

Newspapers and Magazines

Microphotography has made available to the writer a file of the *Cherokee Phoenix* (New Echota, Cherokee Nation, 1828-1834). Published bi-lingually in Sequoyan Cherokee and English, the six-year series of this little newspaper constitutes one of the most valuable of all sources in Eastern Cherokee history. Current events in Indian development were chronicled each week, along with editorial comment reflecting contemporary Cherokee opinion. The actions of Cherokee councils since the beginning of the nineteenth century were reviewed. The Cherokee Constitution of 1827 was printed, along with news and information of a civic nature. Other useful data offered in the paper's columns included lessons in Cherokee grammar, reports of religious activity, sermons and tract material, and legal advertisements of the Cherokee government. The files of the *Cherokee Phoenix* microfilmed for this study are in the archives of the American Antiquarian Society, Worcester, Massachusetts, and the Henry E. Huntington Library, San Marino, California.

Of the numerous religious periodicals consulted, the following were of greatest help: *The Latter Day Luminary* (Philadelphia), published by the Baptist General Convention; *The Methodist Magazine* (New York); and *The Panoplist,* or *The Christian's Armory* (Boston).

Printed Church Records

The printed church documents which offer the most revealing data concerning Cherokee developments are those of the Society of United Brethren (Moravian Church) in Adelaide L. Fries, ed., *Records of the Moravians in North Carolina* (7 volumes. Raleigh, North Carolina: The North Carolina Historical Commission, 1943), especially Volumes VI and VII. The *First Ten Annual Reports of the American Board of Commissioners for Foreign Missions with other Documents of the Board* (Boston: Crocker and Brewster, 1834), offers summary data of American Board missions during their early years in the Cherokee country. More statistical in nature, and less revealing in Indian social history, are the published *Minutes taken at the Several*

Annual Conferences of the Methodist Episcopal Church (New York: N. Bangs and T. Mason, 1821–). Baptist missionary work is summarized in a series of annual reports of the Baptist General Convention, and the Baptist Board of Foreign Missions.

SECONDARY AUTHORITIES

Most general histories of the Cherokee Indians have a political emphasis. The best and most recent of these is Marion L. Starkey, *The Cherokee Nation* (New York: Alfred A. Knopf, 1946), which also contains considerable treatment of the American Board missionaries. The major portion of John P. Brown, *Old Frontiers: The Story of the Cherokee Indians from Earliest Times to the Date of their Removal to the West, 1838* (Kingsport, Tennessee: Southern Publishers, Inc., 1938), is devoted to the frontier aspects of eighteenth century Cherokee affairs. Two works by a native Cherokee historian, Emmet Starr, are *Early History of the Cherokees, Embracing Aboriginal Customs, Religion, Laws, Folklore, and Civilization* (n. p., 1917); and *History of the Cherokee Indians, and their Legends and Folklore* (Oklahoma City: The Warden Company, 1921). Starr's histories are particularly valuable for tribal and genealogical data.

Biographies of leading Cherokees are limited. The only work on John Ross known to the writer is Rachel C. Eaton, *John Ross and the Cherokee Indians* (Menasha, Wisconsin: George Banta Publishing Company, 1914), which is based almost entirely on printed sources. Ralph H. Gabriel's *Elias Boudinot, Cherokee, and his America* (Norman, Oklahoma: University of Oklahoma Press, 1941), draws heavily on the Vaill Manuscripts, a private collection which includes letters of Elias Boudinot, his wife, and other members of her family. Of several works on Sequoyah, inventor of the Cherokee syllabary, the best is Grant Foreman, *Sequoyah* (Norman, Oklahoma: University of Oklahoma Press, 1938). Dr. Foreman quotes liberally from numerous contemporaries of this great Cherokee, and illuminates remarkably well a career which long remained in comparative mystery. Short biographical sketches of various Cherokees are available in Dumas Malone, *et al*, eds., *Dictionary of American Biography* (30 volumes. New York: Charles Scribner's Sons, 1928 –); Hodge, *Handbook of North American Indians* (mentioned above); and Thomas L. McKenney and James Hall, *The Indian Tribes of North America* (Frederick W. Hodge, ed. 3 vols. Reprint edition. Edinburgh, Scotland: John Grant, 1933). The last is a collection of short biographies of various prominent Indians throughout the area of the present-day United States, drawn from the personal observations and research of McKenney and Hall during the 1830's. The volumes contain color portraits, including those of seven well-known Cherokees.

Samuel C. Williams' extensive research in eighteenth century frontier history casts considerable light on Cherokee developments. Among Williams' numerous works the following were especially helpful in this study: *Dawn of Tennessee Valley and Tennessee History* (Johnson City, Tennessee: The Watauga Press, 1937); *Tennessee During the Revolutionary War* (Nashville: Tennessee Historical Commission, 1944); and *History of the Lost State of Franklin* (Johnson City, Tennessee: The Watauga Press, 1924). Williams has also issued editions of Adair's *History of the American Indians* and *Memoirs of Lieut. Henry Timberlake* with valuable annotations. Important for their emphasis on political and diplomatic developments involving early Cherokees are Verner W. Crane, *The Southern Frontier, 1670-1732* (Durham, North Carolina: Duke University Press, 1928); Arthur P. Whitaker, *The Spanish-American Frontier: 1783-1795* (Boston and New York: Houghton Mifflin Company, 1927); and Thomas P. Abernethy, *From Frontier to Plantation in Tennessee: a Study in Frontier Democracy* (Chapel Hill, North Carolina: University of North Carolina Press, 1932). Three other works of value in this period are John Haywood, *The Natural and Aboriginal History of Tennessee, up to the First Settlements Therein by the White People, in the Year 1768* (Nashville: George Wilson, 1823), whose discussion of Cherokee culture unfortunately follows Adair's theory of Hebraic origin; Carolyn T. Foreman, *Indians Abroad* (Norman, Oklahoma: University of Oklahoma Press, 1943); and Charles C. Jones, Jr., *Antiquities of the Southern Indians, Particularly of the Georgia Tribes* (New York: D. Appleton and Company, 1873).

American supervision of the Indians has been examined from several viewpoints. Of works on governmental Indian policy which help to illuminate Cherokee developments the following were useful: George D. Harmon, *Sixty Years of Indian Affairs* (Chapel Hill, North Carolina: University of North Carolina Press, 1941), which covers the period 1790-1850; R. S. Cotterill, "Federal Indian Management in the South, 1789-1825," *Mississippi Valley Historical Review*, XX (December, 1935), 333-52; and Walter H. Mohr, *Federal Indian Relations, 1774-1788* (Philadelphia: University of Pennsylvania Press, 1933). Merritt B. Pound, *Benjamin Hawkins – Indian Agent* (Athens, Georgia: University of Georgia Press, 1951) is a careful account of an Indian Agent who had a considerable interest in Cherokee progress down the "white man's road."

Outstanding among early books treating of religious efforts in the Cherokee country is *History of American Missions to the Heathen* (Worcester, Massachusetts: Spooner and Howland, 1840), a collection of six works on American Board, Baptist, Methodist, Episcopal, and Presbyterian missions. Of recent writings on religious history which include accounts of Cherokee missions, the following are of chief importance: (Moravian) Edmund Schwarze, *History of the Moravian*

Missions among Southern Indian Tribes of the United States (Volume I, *Transactions* of the Moravian Historical Society. Bethlehem, Pennsylvania: Times Publishing Company, 1923); (Presbyterian) Ernest T. Thompson, *Presbyterian Missions in the Southern United States* (Richmond: Presbyterian Committee of Publication, 1934); (Methodist) George F. Mellen, "Early Methodists and the Cherokees," *Methodist Review,* LXVI (Nashville, 1917), 476-89; Walter B. Posey, *The Development of Methodism in the Old Southwest, 1783-1824* (Tuscaloosa, Alabama: Weatherford Printing Company, 1933), especially Chapter VI; and Anson West, *A History of Methodism in Alabama* (Nashville: Publishing House of the Methodist Episcopal Church, South, 1893); (Baptist) James W. Moffitt, "Early Baptist Missionary Work Among the Cherokees," East Tennessee Historical Society's *Publications,* XII (1940), 16-27. Althea Bass, *Cherokee Messenger* (Norman, Oklahoma: University of Oklahoma Press, 1936) is an excellent biography of one of the most important of all missionaries in the Cherokee country, Samuel A. Worcester, a representative of the American Board.

In the late 1820's, at the height of Cherokee progress along the "white man's path," state and federal governments joined forces to expel the Cherokee Indians from the South. The State of Georgia led in this effort, and that state's activities are representative of such local action. The best available account of the steps by which Georgia effected the removal of the Cherokees is that found in Ulrich B. Phillips, *Georgia and State Rights* (Washington: Government Printing Office, 1902). Grant Foreman, *Indian Removal* (Norman, Oklahoma: University of Oklahoma Press, 1932) is a detailed study of the actual means by which removal to the West was accomplished; Book IV deals with the Cherokee movements.

Two state studies of the American Indian which were especially useful for this research are Chapman J. Milling, *Red Carolinians* (Chapel Hill, North Carolina: University of North Carolina Press, 1940), who deals with the Indians of South Carolina principally in the eighteenth century; and Douglas L. Rights, *The American Indian in North Carolina* (Durham, North Carolina: Duke University Press, 1947).

Physical Remains

No review of sources used in a study of Eastern Cherokee social history would be complete without mention of certain items of a non-documentary nature. Several buildings dating to Cherokee times offer mute evidence of an Indian culture far removed from tepee and tomahawk. Among those seen by the author are the two-story brick "Vann House" near Chatsworth, Georgia; the "Ross Mansion" at Rossville, Georgia; the "Oothcaloga Mission House," near Calhoun, Georgia; and the Sequoyah cabin now enshrined near Sallisaw, Oklahoma.

INDEX

CPSIA information can be obtained
at www.ICGtesting.com
Printed in the USA
LVOW12s2108300617
539955LV00002B/122/P

9 780820 335421